Safe And Effective, For Profit:

A Paramedic's Story Exposing An American Genocide

By Harry Fisher and Stephanie Pierucci

Safe And Effective, For Profit:

A Paramedic's Story Exposing An American Genocide

By Harry Fisher and Stephanie Pierucci

PIERUCCI PUBLISHING
ELEVATING WORLD CONSCIOUSNESS THROUGH STORIES.

Authored by Harry Fisher and Stephanie Pierucci

Published by Pierucci Publishing, P.O. Box 2074, Carbondale, Colorado 81623, USA
www.pieruccipublishing.com

Cover design by Stephanie Pierucci

Ebook ISBN: 978-1-962578-89-9
Paperback ISBN: 978-1-962578-55-4
Hardcover ISBN: 978-1-962578-56-1

Library of Congress Control Number: 2024941966

Pierucci Publishing books may be purchased in bulk at special discounts for sales promotion, corporate gifts, fund-raising, or educational purposes. Special editions can be created to specifications. For details, contact the Special Sales Department, Pierucci Publishing, PO Box 2074, Carbondale, CO 81623, or Publishing@pieruccipublishing.com, or toll-free telephone at 1-855-720-1111.

If you have tips, videos, images, or interest in contributing to the upcoming documentary "Sound The Alarm," please personally email Stephanie at Stephanie@pieruccipublishing.com.

Publisher's Note

PLEASE READ:
This book details the author's personal experiences and opinions about general health, prevention of disease, nutritional supplements, and/or exercise. The author is not your healthcare provider. The author provides this book and its contents as a story on an "as is" basis with no representations or warranties of any kind concerning this book or its contents. The authors and publisher disclaim all such representations and warranties including, for example, warranties of merchantability and healthcare for a particular purpose. In addition, the author and the publisher do not represent or warrant that the information accessible via this book is accurate, complete, or current.

The U.S. Food and Drug Administration has not evaluated the statements about products and services. They are not intended to diagnose, treat, cure, or prevent any condition or disease. Please consult your physician or healthcare specialist regarding the suggestions and recommendations made in this book. Except as explicitly stated in this book, neither the authors nor the publisher, nor any contributors or other representatives will be liable for damages arising out of or in connection with the use of this book. This is a comprehensive limitation of liability that applies to all damages of any kind, including (without limitation) compensatory, direct, indirect, or consequential damages; loss of data, income, or profit; loss of or damage to property and claims of third parties.

Understand that this book is not intended as a substitute for consultation with a licensed healthcare practitioner, such as your physician. Before you begin any healthcare program or change your lifestyle, consult your physician or another licensed healthcare practitioner to ensure that you are in good health and that the examples in this book will not harm you. This book provides content related to physical and/or health issues. As such, using this book implies your acceptance of this disclaimer.

In this book, we choose generally not to use the term vaccine when referring to the COVID-19 injection. This investigative injection does not work in the same way as conventional vaccines in that it does not prevent the illness; it intends to reduce the symptoms. In addition, it has not undergone the rigorous testing of traditional and effective vaccines. For these and other reasons, we have changed the term to Investigational Gene-Based Treatments in certain applicable instances or simply "vaccine."

Due to our responsibility to keep all patient information in these stories, we are neither indicating the gender nor the names, or other personal details about the patients Harry saw. He has often chosen to blur specific information to protect patients and their families. While the events are all accurate to the best of Harry's recollection, periodically, the city, town, or other details are changed to respect the anonymity of the patient and the organizations for whom Harry has worked.

Finally, it's important to note that as our understanding of the data and stories we present in this book constantly evolves, so will the scientific research. We have done our best to source all theories with footnotes. However, footnotes are also tedious to write and to read. If we are mistaken in assumptions and stories or our theories prove inaccurate, please write to the publisher at publishing@pieruccipublishing.com or hit Harry up on X.com, where he'll be happy to hear from you. We'll be the first to call ourselves out if there are any empirical errors in our theories, assumptions, stories, musings, or hypotheses. But we might need your help. Don't be shy to share your thoughts on this manuscript, whether good or bad, as we all strive to elevate world consciousness with wisdom and truth.

Harry Fisher & Stephanie Pierucci

https://x.com/harryfisherEMTP
https://x.com/S_Pierucci

On My Title

Coming up with a title for this book didn't take long. Within moments, I knew "Safe and Effective, for Profit" was the perfect choice. Society had been manipulatively force-fed those words for so long that they were always at the forefront of my mind. Of course, nothing about the mRNA injection campaign was either "safe" or "effective" for the victims of the shots, some of whom were injected under duress or out of a desire to protect their loved ones by acquiring a perceived superpower to prevent the spread of the virus through their inoculation. Later in this manuscript, we'll address that fallacy. The only thing safe about the COVID "vaccines" was the immunity they offered their manufacturers.

The "safe and effective" narrative sold by mainstream news outlets tricked people into associating the shots with protection and health, yet the reality was different. These experimental products, peddled as "life-saving," were anything but. They often harm countless individuals, sometimes irreparably and fatally. The irony is obvious.

To add insult to "vaccine" injury, the entities supposed to safeguard public health benefited handsomely from the suffering they inflicted. Behind the scenes, the machinery of profit churned relentlessly. Pharmaceutical companies, shielded by legal protections, continued to push their experimental jabs with little regard for the consequences. The casualties I couldn't save were mere statistics in a ledger to those in power, unimportant in light of the immense profits that were amassed during this genocide; the lockdown and "vaccine-injured" were human sacrifices to the god of money & greed. The lack of accountability was staggering, allowing these corporations to operate with impunity to this day. Thankfully, as you'll read in the book, some strides are being made to hold these corporate greed monsters accountable. This book will fuel your passion to stay in that fight.

This book aims to uncover the truth and shed light on the dark underbelly of an industry that prioritizes profit over people by weaponizing terms like "safe and effective," leading us into an incomprehensible genocide we've only just begun to realize.

Harry Fisher ✔
@harryfisherEMTP

I'm a paramedic that has witnessed pharmaceutical companies destroy humanity.

My name is Harry. My son's name is Harry. He is vaccine injured.

Trust me. I want blood. But I'm trying to find legal justice.

God bless

Dedication

To my mother, who calls me every day, even though I don't always answer. Who serves and loves the Lord wholeheartedly, even when no one's watching. Who loves and accepts me unconditionally. Who will be proud of me no matter what.

Chels, a beautiful soul and best friend.

Book Trailer

We were honored to capture the attention of many courageous men and women of truth, including Alex Jones. This book trailer features portions of my interview with Jones, with me performing the voiceover. Please take a watch, hit the "thumbs up," and share this trailer with friends who need to read this book.

https://youtu.be/3S1bjvjQTec

Table of Contents

Prologue
A Child's Prayer

I remember one of the first times I ever asked God for anything. I was about fourteen, lying in my bed. I stared up at the ceiling, focusing on a motionless ceiling fan. In the quiet, dark room, I focused on the slivers of light on the ceiling fan blades, tracing them with my eyes and lulling myself to sleep with sounds from my memory of my grandmother singing to me. I recall her holding me, although she'd passed on at that time several years earlier.

In the darkness, while listening to her song in my mind, I felt a wave of emotion come over me. As a father myself, I know now that empathy doesn't come readily or naturally to young children. But at that moment, I felt empathy for the world and longing for my grandmother all welling up. Sadness and compassion mingled with feelings of strength. Something was urging me to make a commitment. Instead, I said this prayer: *"Please, lord, help me be like your angel Michael. Help me protect people. So they don't hurt anymore."*

My little prayer was so earnest and authentic that I was emotionally overcome. I even tried speaking in tongues, like Grandma used to do. I'm sure it was gibberish, but God heard my heart. And then, my ceiling fan moved just a little. To me, it seemed like it started spinning rapidly. But it was just a nudge. That nudge moved my world. It moved me. And I will never forget that prayer.

Most people don't master empathy in youth, and as we grow older, we struggle even more to feel the needs, desires, or desperations of others beyond superficiality or sympathy. Throughout this book, you'll see how

I stayed true to my commitment to God and how I strive to be like that instrument Michael every day, even though I fall vastly short.

I pray this book inspires you to accelerate your purpose and fight powerfully, like Michael, for the people God loves so much.

Introduction
Medical Rape, A True Story

I always thought an invasion would come by air or sea, never from within my own country—a snake within my own home. Though I knew when taking my oath against enemies foreign and domestic preceding my own military service that it was possible for domestic enemies, I never thought much about psychological warfare tactics and how those in charge would implement them on the masses.

Forcing people to stay in their homes then allowing them access to drugs, alcohol, and junk food. Taking their businesses away. Keeping them from seeing their parents and grandparents. Canceling their church services and prohibiting people from attending funerals or censoring the outcries of broken individuals when they spoke online. They purposefully decimated people physically, mentally, and spiritually.

This is how you break minds into submission. This was the first wave of the invasion.

It took a while for many to finally realize that we weren't at war with a virus, as the TV claimed. We were at war with a ruling class that wanted us to submit, or die.

Supply & Demand

The principle of supply and demand is simple: the masses demand a product, a manufacturer supplies it, and it is consumed. During the pandemic, we witnessed an inversion of this concept. The product was created and enforced by decree, not desire.

This was not the usual clamor for a coveted commodity: it was a mandate, a decree that promised liberation from confinement, created to produce demand. Nobody desired the jabs. Their confinement was mandated and enforced, not voluntary. The shots promised freedom for a world that was locked up and "gagged" with masks if they wanted to leave the house.

Demand for the product was high under the linguistic brainwashing from television and media and the physical restraint from lockdowns. Manipulation of livelihood by prohibiting un-"vaccinated" people from participating in society or providing for their families created demand at a fever pitch. A touted miracle was sold to taxpayers as the key to reclaiming their sovereignty, returning to work, embracing loved ones, and returning to their lives. However, they needn't have been confined, jobless, or isolated in the first place. The demand was a farce. The public was drowning through mandates and media manipulation, causing them fear. The drowning public panicked. To begin with, they bought the product produced by the very scoundrels holding their heads underwater.

The problem is that people didn't need to drown. Had they composed themselves, even for a moment, they'd have seen that the ocean floor was just a few inches beneath their kicking, thrashing feet. All you needed to do was stand up and walk away.

Some of us stood up and refused to let our captors drown us. We saw the game for what it was; it was absurd. *Why would you play?*

Those of us who were awake quickly saw that the world was acting insane; that anybody who didn't merely swim away from the abuse was downright foolish to continue thrashing in that shallow water. It was evident at this time that the abuse wasn't simply against the body but against the human spirit. The entire world was, alas, bamboozled.

During this time, several notable philosophers and whistleblowers, notably Dr. Geert Vanden Bossche,[1] Dr. Robert Malone, and Mattias Desmet identified "mass formation psychosis" rampant throughout society. Professor Desmet explains:

---

1. www.drgeert.com

S,o all this free-floating anxiety, is attached to, connected to, the object of anxiety indicated in the narrative. There is a huge willingness to participate in the strategy to deal with this object of anxiety because, in this way, people feel that they can control their anxiety and their psychological discontent better. So all this anxiety connects to the subject of anxiety, and there is a huge willingness to participate in the strategy, and that leads up to something very specific. People suddenly feel connected again in a heroic struggle with the object of anxiety. So, a new kind of solidarity, a new kind of social bond, and a new kind of meaning emerges in society. And that's the reason why people follow the narrative, why people buy into the narrative, and why they are willing to participate in this strategy.[2]

Two more widely accepted schools of psychological thought explain this mass psychosis that may be more familiar to audiences reading this book. The first is cognitive dissonance. According to authors Shane Buell, Traci Derwin, and Stephanie Pierucci in their book "Sound The Alarm:"

'Cognitive dissonance' is the mental discomfort that results from holding two conflicting beliefs, values, or attitudes. People tend to seek consistency in their beliefs and actions, and this conflict causes unpleasant feelings of unease or discomfort, ultimately encouraging some change in their beliefs or actions to align better and reduce this dissonance.[3] The inconsistency between what people believe and how they behave motivates them to take actions that will help minimize feelings of discomfort. People often try to relieve this tension in various ways, such as by rejecting, explaining away, or avoiding new information altogether instead of adopting a new perspective that takes the latest information into account and adjusting their actions and behaviors to align with that new information.[4]

No matter how many tweets or videos I shared on X.com, there were and still are trolls who experience distress at the very thought of accepting the fact that their actions don't measure up with the truth: that they were tricked,

---

2. https://COVIDvaccinesideeffects.com/mattias-desmet-on-mass-formation-psychosis/

3. https://www.verywellmind.com/what-is-cognitive-dissonance-2795012

4. www.themauibook.com

scammed, and manipulated. Three booster shots, a lifelong diagnosis of myocarditis, and a bout of turbo cancer don't hurt as much as admitting to one under the spell of cognitive dissonance that they were plain wrong.[5]

Another psychological phenomenon we witnessed during the scamdemic is Stockholm Syndrome. Also, from Buell, Derwin, and Pierucci is the following description:

> *"Stockholm Syndrome" is a descriptive term for a pattern of behaviors that are used to cope with a traumatic situation.[6] This may explain why hostages sometimes develop a psychological bond with their captors, a phenomenon that is generally studied in Psychology 101 across America, ironically. Stockholm Syndrome is supposed to result from a rather specific set of circumstances, namely the power imbalances contained in hostage-taking, kidnapping, and abusive relationships, including the abusive relationship with the government, when victims live in enforced dependence and interpret rare or small acts of kindness amid horrible conditions as good treatment.[7] [8]*

Collective hypnosis gripped society, whether through cognitive dissonance, Stockholm Syndrome, or mass formation psychosis, all conspired by an insidious architect- fear. A fear so meticulously cultivated that it demanded absolute obedience. The ultimatum was stark: either one conforms or faces isolation. I chose isolation, and judging by the fact that you're reading this book, I suspect you did, too.

We're the folks who lost jobs and wages, lost respect from our families and communities, lost the ability to socialize or participate in society without compliance to mask and/or "vaccine" mandates, and may have even lost a friendship or spouse.

---

5. www.fishersbook.com

6. https://www.verywellmind.com/stockholm-syndrome-5074944

7. https://en.wikipedia.org/wiki/Stockholm_syndrome

8. www.themauibook.com

Hospitals became arbiters of life, denying essential care to those who questioned the remedy: the product nobody demanded but everybody "bought" into through manipulation.

To label these actions as malevolent would be an understatement.

In this moment, from the man who was once a little boy staring up at a ceiling fan talking gibberish into the night, serenaded by the memory of my grandmother's song and embrace, I want to tell you that I feel deeply, deeply sorry that you experienced that pain. In this book, I embrace you. Let the vibration of our kindred spirits be the melody that rocks you to sleep at night and braces you with courage when you wake up because the fight is far from over.

From my vantage point, the coup was devastating beyond the tragedy of lost wages or isolation. I bore witness to the aftermath of the mandated shots forced upon an innocent, deceived public. I saw the suffering first-hand, in my own ambulance and, sometimes, in my arms or lap, of those who suffered at the hands of the solution they were told would protect them, the miracle cure for the anguish they never had to feel, but which was forced upon them. And my own despair and helplessness made me feel at once brokenhearted… but also enraged.

I'll try another analogy that, while lurid, is the best I can come up with. Envision yourself tied to a chair, forced to observe people being victimized or raped and then murdered. That's the closest I can come to describing the impotence I've felt watching the horrors of the past few years. Now imagine it happens daily, sometimes multiple times per day. This is why I'm writing this book.

This is why I refer to the mass vaccination campaign as medical rape and murder. Victims were forced to inject a foreign, untested, and genetically altering substance inside their bodies, one that can kill a person. The only other option, for most, was death by banishment. My co-author Stephanie lived in a bit of a cowboy town out in the mountains on the Western Slope of Colorado but fought the legal system to protect her son from the jab, and, at one point, she lost everything and was homeless with a six-year-old child.

I heard stories of folks with fake vaccine cards who claim they "got around the mandates," but what abuse did their souls sustain through lying to survive?

Like the citizens who survived the deadliest fire in a hundred years on American soil in Lahaina, the only way to survive was non-compliance. But non-compliance had its costs, too.

As a medical professional caring for the abused, then trying to scream about it, I was censored; I was silenced. That was eye-opening. It all allowed me insight into the corrupt world we live in. A world I never thought could sink so low. An actual hell on earth. A Babylon that was so arrogant and defiant that they created the Tower of Babel in Genesis; so depraved that they destroyed the First Temple in Jerusalem and exiled the Jewish people, and so wicked that the Book of Revelation refers to "her" (Babylon) as a harlot; a symbol of ultimate evil.

I found myself blowing my trumpet idly as the tower of lies advanced higher and higher into the sky, an inept sentinel forced to sit down, shut up, and stand by as the public was coerced… and then killed.

Staring out over the plains of Oklahoma with sunsets so magically composed that you could be moved to fall on your face in worship or the staggering heights of Alaska's breathtaking mountains, I knew that this beautiful world had been co-opted not just by today's clear and present evil but by an evil as old as our world—our new, dystopian world.

This is the world my grandma told me to be in but not of. This is the synagogue of Satan, a perversion of those sunsets and mountains, a departure from the garden.

Everything Grandma warned me about now made perfect sense.

Part One

The Making of A Whistleblower

Chapter One
I Came To The Garden Alone

Take my yoke upon you and learn from me, for I am gentle and lowly in heart, and you will find rest for your souls. For My yoke is easy, and My burden is light.

Matthew 11:29-30, NKJV

After all I've seen, I want to have hope. But I've witnessed so many bad things that a wall often stands between me and hope; it's called reality. There is so much evil in the world. I've seen chiefly wartime in my life: men and women beaten by one another and the most horrific things.

Harry Fisher

The first death I ever saw was my grandma's. She died at home. At the time, our entire family lived in one house in Texas, Wichita Falls in North Texas, near Oklahoma. This included my cousin Joel, my grandma Josie Eileen Fisher, my grandpa Harry Edwin Fisher, my father, Harry Edwin Fisher the Second, and, of course, me, the third Harry Edwin Fisher. My mother, Debra, my paternal aunt Vickie- the oldest in my dad's family- and Bobbi, her and my father's youngest sister, lived there, too. And then there was my uncle David, who was mentally disabled. He was the second child in my dad's family of five, which included Vicky, Kathy, David, Dad, and then Bobbi—in total, nine people lived in that house. The inhabitants were all from my paternal side; my mom's family wasn't a significant part of my younger years.

25

The house was large, though. It was an old Victorian-style house with lines on each side of the steps. It was pretty. My dad didn't make much money as a salesman working 60+ hour weeks, but he supported the entire household of nine souls.

My dad and Grandma Josie were best friends. Dad was raised well. Grandma Josie and Grandpa Harry were traveling ministers, evangelizing all over the country, typically not accepting income for their work.

Although he had mental handicaps, my Uncle David was functional; he had the mindset of a fifteen-year-old with a severe stuttering problem. I suspect this gave me compassion for others later in life. My father would tell me about kids picking on Uncle David in school because of his stuttering. Those stories served as a warning to me about how I was expected to treat my peers. That, combined with my evangelical grandparents, made me believe I was destined to help others.

I was mainly homeschooled until third grade, which allowed me to travel with Grandpa and Grandma periodically. Sometimes, I would even watch Grandpa and Grandma preach. Grandma would stand on stage until her feet would bleed. She had cancer, which I didn't know at the time. She wore shoes that were so uncomfortable that she'd periodically take her shoes off on stage. I'd then see that her feet were cracked and swollen from Diabetes. But when she was ministering, Grandma Josie would stand from sun up to sun down. No amount of lotion would help. She would keep standing if people were in church, even if her feet were bleeding.

One time, when I was around five years old, Grandma and Grandpa took me to Maine, which felt like another country from Texas. My grandparents took me fishing on the side of a miniature fishing pond. I'll never forget when I caught my first fish with a Snoopy fishing pole Grandpa had given me, probably one that had been donated to him charitably from one of his congregants. My catch was a little guppy, the size of a goldfish, but it was the biggest fish in the world to me.

We left the tiny pond (and the fish we decided to release rather than gut), and they took me to Niagara Falls. We had a few ponds here and there in Texas, but mostly, I lived squarely in the middle of hundreds of miles of flat, dry land. The Hill Country of Texas was a half-day trip from where we lived in Wichita Falls. But when I saw Niagara Falls, I knew my town had been misnamed; there wasn't even one acre that qualified to be named "Falls" near me. Nothing I'd seen to that day came close to the heart-stopping power of the Falls cascading with a roar over the cliffs and cooling our faces with a steady, invigorating mist.

I remember seeing Grandma standing over the rail looking at the falls; it's the image I still see of her today. She was wearing a wig, as she'd already begun cancer treatments at that time. It was a curly, fluffy brown wig, the kind you get in neighborhoods with pawn shops and convenience stores lining the streets, not the type of wig you'd buy if you're really earnest, invested, and privileged enough to pull off a realistic-looking one. I doubt she'd paid more than $15.00 for hers. Nobody paid attention to the wig, not our family or community. The cascading layers of synthetic brown curls from Grandma's wig complimented her vibrant dresses that resembled mumuses. Although Grandma was nurturing and gentle, her presence was vibrant and magnetic.

Whenever my parents were away, Grandma was my caretaker. I loved sitting in her lap as she sang, "Blessed assurance, Jesus is mine. Oh what a foretaste of glory divine," or another favorite, "I Come To The Garden Alone:"

I come to the garden alone while the dew is still on the roses.
And the voice I hear, falling on my ear, the son of God discloses;
And He walks with me, and He talks with me,
And He tells me I am His own,
And the joy we share as we tarry there,
None other has ever known.
He speaks, and the sound of His voice
Is so sweet the birds hush their singing;
And the melody that He gave to me
Within my heart is ringing.
I'd stay in the garden with Him
Tho' the night around me be falling,
But He bids me go; thro' the voice of woe,
His voice to me is calling.

Mom took care of Grandma when she became ill at home in hospice. Even at seven or eight years old, I assisted my mother in caring for Grandma, who enjoyed it when I "painted her face" because she loved how her makeup brushes felt on her cheeks or forehead.

These were her last days, and although I knew she was dying, it didn't register on a profound level. I don't think children process emotions like death the way that adults do. I've wondered if that's due to the underdeveloped state of a child's brain. I also wonder if it's because they're more wise than adults. Perhaps kids are less scared of adults returning to a place they just left. Perhaps children are less frightened of adults going home because children have been "there" recently, in heaven.

I don't think kids fear hell, and for good reason. They aren't going there. Kids aren't scared of returning to the place we came from, where our souls were birthed. I even wonder if kids remember heaven before they can speak, sometimes, like when a baby stares at a wall. What is he seeing? Who is he laughing at? Does he remember heaven? Adults, however, acclimate to this dark world; it is then that death no longer appears to be a transition but an end. Adults begin to think this is the final stop or the only experience in the soul's long, eternal journey.

Dad lost it when Grandma died. He lost not just his best friend but also his anchor to proper behavior. He began to sow wild oats he wouldn't have planted in her presence, exploring his carnal being and becoming more accepting of the world, which Grandma disapproved of.

The family home in Wichita began to unravel and then disperse immediately after Grandma's death. Grandma had wanted the full house, and Dad provided for it. But in 1988, when she died, the relatives all went their separate ways. Without an additional six mouths to feed, my parents moved into a fancy neighborhood. Mom became the PTA president. I was part of Cotillions.

However, the silver spoon was ripped away when, at fifteen, my parents separated and moved quickly into divorce. They each went through a midlife crisis; suddenly, both of them were gone, living the lives they didn't have the chance to live as caregivers for the past fifteen years.

I dropped out of school and got a GED. Once I acquired my GED, I did odd jobs to make enough money for food and gasoline. I did anything people would hire me to do under the table, such as bailing hay or roofing. I was essentially penniless but not hopeless. I was moving from couch to couch for a while.

When I was sixteen, my best friend, who was older than me, wanted to work in the fire department. I applied alongside him, but I was too young. Therefore, I decided to enroll in EMT school.

EMT training was only four months long. I learned how to perform basic lifesaving skills, drive ambulances, stop bleeding, stabilize patients, and serve others. I did my first clinicals at seventeen with AMR, a significant service in Wichita Falls.

The first time I performed CPR on somebody, a little kid answered the door and said, "My daddy needs help." The child was half my size, perhaps seven years old. The other medics I was with taught me how to do the job. The father was in the bathroom next to the toilet, a bathroom so small that we had to pull the man out into the hallway to work on him.

As I administered CPR, the child watched in shock. He looked paralyzed; it had to feel like a tsunami was heading towards him, but he was frozen in place. I can only imagine the weight of losing his dad. The loss in my mind was akin to the loss of my Grandma at that age.

I'll never forget that I was going really fast while administering the CPR. The old paramedic said, "Hey, Fish, slow down. Remember: fast is slow. Slow is fast." I didn't know what he meant then, but I do now.

Dad and I reconnected when I was about eighteen. I was staying with my mom's parents, Grandma and Grandpa Duffy. Grandad was a military man from WW2 and every bit the stereotype. For instance, I was thirty minutes late one night when I said I'd be home. Grandpa told me I couldn't live there anymore, saying, "You're a piece of shit. You didn't follow my rules. Have you ever thought about the military?"

He was stern and direct. Although it was sometimes hard to take, I liked always knowing where I stood in his eyes. Tough love is often the best kind of love, I guess.

At eighteen, I enlisted in the Army. My Grandpa Duffy, even though he called me a piece of shit, attended every single one of my graduations, from basic training to airborne school. He even insisted on wearing my military insignia on his favorite hat. He was buried with that hat. I miss him to this day.

I was honorably discharged from the Army and took some time off from military life. I rejoined the airforce where I was honorably discharged in 2015. By that time, I was thirty-three years old. I'd been running 911 calls, jumping out of airplanes, or working in hospitals for my entire adult life. I could write a book about all of my experiences alone. Top that off with my role as a medic. There were good and bad times, but I don't need to write that book today.

So, at thirty-three, I was already a veteran not only of the military but in the art of professional life-saving. I began civilian life working as a paramedic on an ambulance in Oklahoma City, Oklahoma. I also started dating, already divorced from my first marriage, and trying not to screw up my first two children by sowing too many wild oats.

At the time of this writing, I have spent the past twenty-six years as either an EMT or paramedic. In these past twenty-six years, I've learned that the world includes pockets of corruption and carnage mixed with moments of beauty only realized through faith.

After all I've seen, I want to have hope. But I've witnessed so many bad things that a wall often stands between me and hope; it's called reality. There is so much evil in the world. I've seen chiefly wartime in my life: men and women beaten by one another, and the most horrific things you can imagine.

For instance, I was called to a situation shortly after my honorable discharge from the military where somebody had a possible miscarriage or childbirth. The fireman inside the home was beside her as she sat on the toilet. She had dead eyes, like a predator looking right through me, like she was preparing to eat me.

"Look in the toilet," said the fireman.

"What's going on?" I asked.

The woman stood up from the toilet, and inside, still attached to the umbilical cord, was a once viable baby drowned in the bathroom toilet.

I cut the cord after clamping it and asked the woman what happened.

"Ma'am, why is this baby in the toilet?"

"I don't care." She responded flatly.

Four or five kids were also in the home, lying on the floor without beds.

I felt at that moment like I'd walked into a den of demons.

I had nothing to put the baby in, so I had to put the baby in a red bio bag. I drove the woman and the baby to the hospital. She didn't speak a word the whole way.

We don't often check up on patients. I don't know if she went to jail or if the other kids were spared from whatever had possessed this woman. I did write it all in my report, but that little baby in a red bio bag was more horrifying than any death I'd ever seen.

Therefore, sometimes, I struggle to have hope. Images like that woman's deathly stare or the baby in the bag sometimes ground me into the truth of the world we live in more than I'd like. Grandma Fisher wanted me to be separate from the world, and now I know why.

However, I still cling to hope, if for nothing else, to sleep at night.

I didn't sign up for easy. I didn't sign up for a paycheck; I've never liked money that much. I signed up to help people while driving fast. I signed up for the risk and to help others in their time of need, but also because I feel like I'm needed every time my pager goes off.

When you're young, you play with G.I. Joes and dream of being the "real American hero." You realize quickly that it isn't all comic book stories and Saturday morning cartoons. Now, I know why the Lord retreated so often into solitude. The weight of suffering is heavy, though eventually, I realized the yoke is light.

That just took some time.

Poem: We're One Call Away

What's the worst thing you've ever seen?"
A prominent question that's asked me.
They see the badge and questions proceed,
"I bet you see a lot; what all do you see?"

A sigh usually follows, sometimes a forced grin,
Never knowing exactly what to say then.
So here's the answer: it might not be the best,
but hopefully, it can lay this question to rest.

My day starts slow, getting out of bed,
I don't sleep much due to the death in my head.
I go for a run, and after a smoke,
Most of the time, my debit cards broke.

I see traffic stopped often while heading to work.
I wonder what's in store, what monsters may lurk.
I check out my gear, see my partner's still here,
Check our essentials, narcs, and utensils.
I chat with some friends, place our numbers in,
and then it's time for the shift to begin.

I see screams and cries, bodies and flies.
I see tears, blood, death, and destruction.
I see countless corpses, some airways to suction.
I see abuse, neglect, bodies without function.

Rape molestation, a large homeless population.
I see the end of mothers, fathers, sons and daughters.
I see all you may think, life gone in a blink,
However, these aren't the craziest things; please let this sink.

I see life born, loved ones together at their end.
I see strangers holding hands like they've always been friends.
I see underpaid servants willing to risk all, people assisting when somebody falls.

I see bravery and love amid the despair.
I see honor and courage, many who care.
I see prayers lifted up for those in pain,
And people giving their all with nothing to gain.

YES, to the question,
We see crazy things, I must say,
so hold tight to your loved ones this Christmas Day.
And know if you need us, we're one call away.

Chapter Two
There's So Much Evil To Wade Through

"When did you first know the system is evil?" A friend recently asked me.

I sighed.

I was an online moderator for four years at "The Daily Show with Jon Stewart." Alongside three other admins, I helped move Stewart to the platform "Facebook." Jon's show sparked a lot of conversation in forums from both fans and trolls of the show. I moderated the vitriol and observed the chasm between people that they perceived as genuine differences. In truth, many of these people blamed one another or even Stewart for the ills of the world; they didn't see their hate blinded them.

It's well known that critical thinking skills are impaired when people are in fear. When I saw hatred spewed in those forums, I initially thought it was because of political or social beliefs. It wasn't. It was all rooted in fear. The more profane a person was, the more assured I was that they were scared; they were in fight or flight mode. These folks, let's say they didn't flee; they fought. Flight and fight are simply two sides of the same coin. The humans who run away and those who stay are the same: they're scared.

As you read in the book Introduction, I had an upbringing of faith. I also had a military mindset. However, at that time, I attacked right-wingers for sport. I believed the mainstream news and bought into the propaganda *hook, line,* and *sinker.* The destructive energy and ideals blasted over the airwaves didn't look nefarious. I thought it was, indeed, "the news." I'm neither Republican nor Democrat, unsure if I'll even vote in the upcoming elections. But I'm now a Patriot; I certainly don't believe what I hear or see on the news anymore.

During these four years on "The Daily Show with Jon Stewart," a man in the forum would regularly grace us with his presence, preaching about holistic health and natural medicine. I deleted his accounts repeatedly and banned him from our forums. But he kept coming back. *What a nutcase*, I thought.

However, the closer we got to COVID-19 lockdowns and the veritable upturning of our world, the closer I came to faith. I rededicated my life to God and woke up. And then, I realized I had karma to reckon with. Every time I censored the holistic health practitioner because I thought he would hurt people, I was censored a hundred times as much. It hit me that I was the enemy of my youth, now fancying myself as some sort of truth-telling member of the resistance to evil. During my time with "The Daily Show," I was part of that evil. I had drunk the Kool-Aid. And I was the one censoring people like the man I am today.

Sometime in late 2023, I sat on a quiet shift waiting for the phone to ring and for my unit to get a call and hop in our ambulances. Around me, there was nothing but snow: I was in the middle of BFE, Alaska. If you've ever walked in the snow at night, you'll have noticed that it muffles everything, including your own footsteps or the sound of your own breath. For miles, mountains of snow were around me. You've never known quiet and darkness, like in Alaska, working as an EMT waiting for your pager to buzz. During the winter, we only had a few hours a day of light, which perpetuated the silence and made it nothing less than deafening.

But between the chaos and calamity, there were many quiet hours to reflect. I didn't spend all that time reading my Bible and praying, but I used it wisely. My brain was on fire. At once, I felt the weight of my former ignorance and the simultaneous burden of righting the wrongs of who I'd once been. During those quiet hours in the dark tent in which I was stationed in the middle of nowhere Alaska, it occurred to me one typically dark mid-morning in the early winter that I had been part of what people now refer to as the "mass formation psychosis." (Head over a few pages back to the

Introduction if you need a refresher.) We'll refer to those terms a lot in this book. During my own psychosis, the system owned my thoughts. In some Orwellian dystopia, I was listening to the voice over the loudspeaker telling me that up was down and left was right; black was white, and white was black. And what made my stomach the worst was that I willingly turned that intercom up and delighted in the propaganda. I didn't see it for what it was.

There was a time long before my children started school and towards the end of my high school years when children actually read "1984" by George Orwell in schools. Imagine that. I don't suspect it was in every school or every state. Still, a cursory poll of my friends reveals that many, if not most, people in their forties and fifties learned about Orwell's work, had read 1984, and might even have had a glimpse of the true story of the Holocaust during their formative years. It was a short time later when CRT (critical race theory) entered the curriculum, and even some of my friends in their forties spent more time learning about their white privilege than about actual historical events. Sandra Cisernos and Maya Angelou, although both talented writers and poets, replaced "The Diary of A Young Girl" by Anne Frank or "Man's Search For Meaning" by Viktor Frankl. I'm not saying there's anything wrong with reading about more local issues or race issues. Still, somehow, it seems like we removed the real lousy guy from the classroom: the insidious globalist monsters who were corralling entire nations into Pfizer lines while dreaming of one-world governments and grossly depopulated communities.

I'm not here to say diversity-type literature doesn't have value. But we need to keep our eye on the enemy. Keep your friends close, but remain even more keenly aware of your enemies. The entire story of humanity is a struggle of the little guy (those of us reading this book) against Goliath: the modern-day Gates, WEF'ers, and other globalists. They want to depopulate and enslave us. Keep reading if you're still unsure of this claim, and in time, you will have more clarity, too.

By God's grace, I made my exodus from mental slavery. Waiting for my pager to beep so that I could get my blood moving, get off my ass, and go save a life. You'd think that I'd have woken up long before then, seeing as how my entire life dealt with death regularly for over ten years by that time.

When I reflected on the abuse in the Jon Stewart "Daily Show" chat rooms and recognized and repented for my bullying, I considered the first glimpse I'd had of absolute evil. The way my parents treated each other was evil. The way I felt abandoned by my parents' behavior after their divorce, forcing me to move from a lovely home to searching for couches to sleep on at night, seemed evil. But that was child's play compared to what unfolded in the next decade or so.

I used to be unable to fathom that God flooded the entire world except for Noah and his family a few thousand years ago. Millions of humans and animals drowned; so many fossils exist today of living beings that had breath in their lungs but suddenly drowned mid-flight. More fossils evidence the great flood of Noah's day than museums could ever display. All that life was gone in an instant.

Today I saw a video of a handful of Indian women being kidnapped and tied to a pole by alleged Jihadi terrorists, about to become slaves, being ripped from their mothers and children by other evil humans. And to think one human was so cruel that he or she recorded the video instead of trying to help the women escape and posted it, to boot!

I think of the horrific deaths you'll read about in this book and the actors at all levels of pharmaceutical administration and government appointments, and I think, "Yeah, we deserved that flood and the millions of balls of sulfur that might have fallen from the sky that accompanied it, too."

But even seeing all the evil in the world isn't enough to wake somebody up. It can make you angry. But it isn't possible to process this evil until you are shrouded in the light of God's love. Until then, seeing evil is scary. Like the above reference, it puts a person in "fight or flight." You might see it on TikTok or Twitter and have bad dreams or a sick feeling in your stomach. But that isn't processing evil. Until you have empathy, you can't comprehend how evil what you're seeing is. Once you understand God's radical love for His children, you simply can't comprehend just how awful it is to harm one of them. Moreover, once you know how miraculous each life is, even the ones that turn into evil adults, once you see that every human was created in God's image and, yet succumbs to wickedness, you can't comprehend the unfathomable crimes we commit against each other.

Red and yellow, black and white (as the song goes); *all are precious in His sight.* So how can you fully process one human committing an evil act on another until you understand the beauty of both sides, even the side committing the crime? As much as my heart breaks for the victims, my heart breaks for how far the perpetrator has fallen from his or her Divine Nature. Stephanie often says, "We can only judge people's consciousness to the extent that they have healed their trauma."

While writing this book, Stephanie and I had many conversations that started like this: "How could people be so stupid not to see what's happening?!"

And they ended like this, "I wish nobody had to live with so much trauma that they are unwilling or unable to wake up. God help them. God help us help them."

I don't believe anybody can understand evil until they fully understand the miraculous nature of God's love and the miraculous nature that is part of every human. As shocking as it is to see the victim, even more astonishing is to comprehend that a person created in the image of an all-loving, beautiful Creator could commit evil. That is why you can't understand evil without understanding God. You can just get angry, scared, or turn away (flee).

When you give your life to Christ, which necessarily involves not just faith but repentance for sin, you have genuine empathy. Here's the next layer. The same depravity of the criminal is the same depravity that lives in my own heart: me, Harry Fisher, a depraved sinner who needs the forgiveness of a perfect Savior. The next layer isn't sadness for the perpetrator but identification with him. I am capable of evil. I am cleansed with Christ's blood. A perfect sacrifice was made to atone for my sins. A man, Yeshua, the Messiah, suffered for me.

When a person sees his depravity and need for a Savior, that's the real flex. That's when the blinders come off. That's when the empathy kicks in. That's when the compassion is on fire. That's when you pray for your enemies. That's when you mourn for the victims as well as the perpetrators.

That's when the love abounds. That's when the tears pour down your cheeks. That's what God feels when he looks down at us.

And that's why you simply can't comprehend evil until you understand God's love. It's impossible to process fully.

As heart-wrenching as it is, seeing is gratifying. Being gutted by evil is gratifying. You don't know your capacity to be human until you feel the pain of genuine sadness. Scratch that; you don't know your capacity to be Godly until you feel the gut-wrenching sting of sin.

In the remainder of this book, I'll pull the cloak off of evil and show you a system I uncovered from the inside that is truly purely evil. A system that profits off of sickness. A system that markets itself as healthcare but is based on health havoc-wreaking and death. A system that pleases shareholders not only by helping the human being heal holistically, cheaply, and completely but also perpetuates misery, prolonged pain, and even the death of innocent people. A system that is crippled by indebtedness to shareholders who turn a blind eye to the horrors of that system's function so long as they have upticks in their stock portfolios.

When I first became an EMT in 1997, I already understood that the world had bad eggs and nefarious actors. However, I also naively trusted that those in power primarily fought for good, truth, justice, and the American way. I trusted the system. I trusted those in authority. But it all came down, brick by brick, truth by truth.

I have now removed the wall of lies erected by vast propaganda perpetrated by those at the top who use good people to place each brick.

"We don't do this for money," I remember my EMT instructor saying on the first day of class. "If you're trying to be an EMT to get paid, you're choosing the wrong profession," he said. Everyone in class remained seated. We were there to help others. To drive fast, risk all, and save lives.

That's what we believed. That's what I still believe.

But our hands are tied. We're fighting an uphill battle. We EMTs, like many of your doctors, nurses, and pharmacists, are weighed down by the constant pressure to produce corporate profits. The Hippocratic Oath is laughable; there is no commitment to "Do No Harm." There is only, rather, an explicit mandate to fall in line with corporate interests. Rushed, experimental gene-based therapies called life-saving vaccines? They're death shots with great branding and PR.

I toil with the idea that money is the root of all evil. It's not the money but the power it gives people. The love of the power that money provides is a cancer in our society. The only way to starve out that cancer is to wield the scalpel of truth and cut it out.

If you're nodding your head agreeing with me, what will you do about it?

Probably nothing. You're probably scared. Scared to lose your job. Scared of your upcoming bills. Scared to lose your insurance or retirement benefits or pension. I believed I would become an EMT to drive fast, risk it all, and save lives. But for the first two-thirds of my career, I, too, was scared.

After years of working as a civilian and a medic in the military, I moved from an EMT to a paramedic. I didn't enjoy sitting through a couple more years of school, but the tedious class hours were worth it. I gained more skills, made more money, and had more opportunities to help others.

I didn't become a paramedic for the money, but I'm proud to get paid more for more skilled work. That said, in 2020, I concluded that by sitting down and shutting up, I would cause pain for profits. And so you have the book in your hands.

The pharmaceutical industry works like a medic who causes trauma to allegedly minister to that trauma and get paid more than for having kept the individual healthy. You don't get paid unless there's a problem, so the pharmaceutical industry creates problems. And thereby, happy shareholders. Their plan isn't to heal you; it's to generate chronic sickness and, thereby, a subscription model based on your pain. You will always be at least a little sick. Therefore, they will have steady income streams from millions upon millions of people who might otherwise thrive from natural medicine. But big pharma doesn't profit from your health; they profit by keeping you sick.

The business plan is wise but wicked.

Forgive the additional analogy in case it's "overkill" (pun intended). Still, it's like causing car accidents just so you can make money in your car repair business or shattering all the car windows in your neighborhood where you have an auto glass business—a wise business plan, but wicked.

After many years of service, I was already tired in 2020 after working in the densely populated Oklahoma City for several years. I had already seen the horrors of what this world and its inhabitants have to offer.

During 2020-2023, I worked in Oklahoma City and its outskirts, Western Oklahoma, Eastern Oklahoma, New York City, and North Dakota, generally on one- to three-month contracts. My youngest children were just one and three years old, and my second marriage to their mother was becoming strained. The weight of my traveling for one to three months at a time away from my wife and the toddlers was the straw that broke the camel's back in my marriage, and we separated in 2022.

I don't think you care about my romantic life, but I bring this up to illustrate not only the stress my family and I have been under, but I want to bring up another point. My son is vaccine-injured. His mom and I don't know which shot caused it, but he's autistic and non-verbal. It happened suddenly after a "well check," before which my son developed perfectly normally.

It's not fun publicly admitting that I allowed my son to become injured. I carried him into the doctor's office and set him on the table with the white paper covering it. He was just one year old. I distracted him and smiled as the doctor probed, prodded, and eventually poked him. I told him it was okay. I tried to make it seem like a celebration that he was getting his shots.

Almost immediately, Harry's personality changed. You might not have noticed it if you weren't his mother or father. His mother was in denial of these changes until he was two years old, at which time they were severe, stark, and undeniable.

I'm not an anti-vaxxer, per se. I'm a father who has held my child and watched him deteriorate from some neurological side effects from one of the numerous vaccines he received at his one-year well-check. I'm a paramedic who has held women in my arms after still birthing babies or new widows as they wailed with sounds resembling not humans but animals after their young husbands or fathers died. I'm a sinner, a man who drank the Kool-Aid and sent my child like a sheep to be slaughtered. I even held him down so that he could receive his own irrevocable, poisonous blow. My son Harry may never live an everyday, independent life. In this way, I feel like a murderer sometimes in my dark moments. For that reason, I cannot be silent about what I've seen and what I've done.

Since the summer of 2023, I've spent much time in Alaska, working three weeks on and off. When I'm in smaller communities, such as a small camp just eighty miles from the Siberian border, I might serve a community for a whole month as their paramedic. In Alaska, I can be contracted anywhere from Anchorage, a highly-populated city, to a reservation with a blend of people resembling indigenous Native peoples to miners, geologists, archeologists, mineral miners, or folks in water purification; many of those people coming from places like Illinois, Missouri, or even my home state of Oklahoma.

When on leave from my Alaskan contracts, I'm either with my children or working as a PRN or "as needed" paramedic on an ambulance. It pays the bills and keeps me busy after the long, lonely hours in Alaska, where I have time to think, write poetry, and muster up the courage to right some of my wrongs by speaking out.

Counterintuitively, racing around the streets in ambulances also helps me recalibrate my nervous system after being in Alaska. While home, I embrace my children, and my heart skips at their little voices coming from those little lungs. I commiserate with like-minded friends, some of whom are heroes in healthcare who wish to remain anonymous; they would be severely punished if they were outed for their bravery and courage. And above all, I don't fly in any helicopters. I fly in helicopters multiple times a day in Alaska. I've lost many friends in helicopters. The only thing keeping me sane in those things is looking into the eyes or holding my patients still, keeping them calm so that I, too, can stay relaxed.

In the following pages, you'll read about what horrors I've seen before and after COVID-19. What you're about to read will provoke you to decide between evil. Does it make you angry? Or does it break your heart?

Song: In The Year 2525

"In The Year 2525"
Zager and Evans, 1969

In the year 2525
If man is still alive
If woman can survive
They may find

In the year 3535
Ain't gonna need to tell the truth, tell no lies
Everything
you think, do, and say
Is in the pill you took today

In the year 4545
Ain't gonna need your teeth, won't need your eyes
You won't find a thing to chew
Nobody's gonna look at you

In the year 5555
Your arms are hanging limp at your sides
Your legs got nothing to do
Some machine doin' that for you

In the year 6565
Ain't gonna need no husband, won't need no wife
You'll pick your son, pick your daughter, too
From the bottom of a long glass tube
Whoa-oh

In the year 7510
If God's a-comin', He ought to make it by then
Maybe He'll look around Himself and say
"Guess it's time for the Judgement Day."

In the year 8510
God is gonna shake His mighty head
He'll either say, "I'm pleased where man has been"
Or tear it down and start again
Whoa-oh

In the year 9595
I'm kinda wonderin' if man is gonna be alive
He's taken everything this old earth can give
And he ain't put back nothing
Whoa-oh

Now, it's been ten thousand years.
Man has cried a billion tears.
For what he never knew
Now, man's reign is through
But through the eternal night
The twinkling of starlight
So very far away
Maybe it's only yesterday

In the year 2525
If man is still alive
If woman can survive
They may find

In the year 3535
Ain't gonna need to tell the truth, tell no lies...[9]

---

9. https://genius.com/Zager-and-evans-in-the-year-2525-lyrics

Chapter Three

"Happy Hypoxia" and The First Wave

You only realize how predictable your life was pre-COVID once all your routines are disrupted. You got up at 6:15 and prepared coffee. You fought to get the kids dressed, the dog walked, and something resembling breakfast on the table. Maybe you'd regularly check to ensure the kids had their homework done before leaving the house. Commuting. More coffee. Lunch was usually a quinoa salad or turkey sub. You'd sneak in a 20-minute nap before heading back into the office. More dog walking. Dinner consisted of one of five meals on your heavy rotation that required neither too much prep nor too many processed ingredients. Your favorite show or podcast before bed.

Our routines aren't always sexy, but they keep us feeling grounded. When the routine is shaken up, it shakes up the very neural connections in our brains. This can be a positive thing; it can make us unstuck. However, it can also cause trauma when the shakeup is too sudden and too drastic.

My typical paramedic's shift pre-COVID consisted of arriving at the office, making black coffee from a generic brand without any frills or fluff, waiting for my partner to arrive, or else tracking him down, checking equipment—which is something you should never slack off on as a paramedic—talking to dispatch, and then hitting the road, hoping we make it to our first post for breakfast.

In large cities, ambulances typically play zone coverage. We'd move from post to post, basically from gas station to gas station. We'd cover large areas for better call times. Much of our performance depends on how quickly we arrive at an emergency. Easy calls included flu, ABD pain (abdominal pain), and cardiac arrest. Difficult ones included shootings, stabbings, childbirth and domestic violence. Both the easy and challenging calls were common on a typical day.

As paramedics, we can provide immediate care and transport to the nearest appropriate facility. If a patient is in cardiac arrest, we attempt to revive the patient by CPR, IV cardiac medications, and defibrillation. We intubate the airway and administer electricity if the patient is in what we call a "shockable heart rhythm." Not all heart rhythms require defibrillation. We are known to give the same care that an ER can provide on the scene during cardiac arrest. Shy of extensive blood diagnostics and chest tubes, we provide treatment and care comparable to most emergency rooms in such situations. At the medic's discretion, we work the patient for 20 minutes or longer. If we conclude that the patient isn't viable, we can and often do leave the patient in their homes without transporting them, calling the patient's *time of death* on the scene. My service required a call to a physician requesting termination of efforts after providing the physician with all information regarding resuscitative efforts.

Most people aren't aware of the level of care their Emergency Medical Services provide to the general public. In comparison with nurses and physicians, paramedics are relatively new. The profession hasn't been established long enough for people to understand the extent of a paramedic's expertise and the skills required to obtain our position. Needless to say, we were already busy before COVID.

But nothing could've prepared us for what was to come.

In January 2020, I received an email from a friend in Wuhan, China. He lived there at the time. I had just gotten over being sick; my entire house developed a sort of flu. We had coughs that wouldn't go away. At one point I even coughed up blood. After what seemed like weeks of coughing, I remember laying down on the bathroom floor, completely worn out, and falling asleep right there on the tile. The next morning, when I woke up, my cough was gone, but I felt sour all over, specifically in my chest. This was different than feeling achy or depleted; a toxic energy coursed through me. Weighed down by the full-body fog, it took another week before I was able to walk very far without feeling short of breath.

Thankfully, neither my wife nor my kids had this bizarre flu as bad as I had. I was startled when I received a message about a respiratory virus that had locked down Wuhan, China. I wondered if I had already caught whatever it was.

My friend in Wuhan said, "Wuhan is locked down. Something terrible is happening. Imagine a city like New York locking down overnight. They are offering us Americans an airplane ride home. They say it will be military in hazmat suits."

This friend took the offer to return home and sent pictures of the military guys and girls in hazmat suits transporting people back to the States. I kept thinking, "Why would we just transport people from a hot zone and let them spread out through our country?" Yet that's what the powers that be chose to do. Months later, after the sickness spread, America decided to go on lockdown. I still find it suspicious that we took people from the affected regions and dispersed them to their countries and communities of origin rather than containing the virus. What was even more concerning was the notion that whatever this devastating respiratory virus was, I'd already contracted it all the way in Oklahoma months before it hit the airwaves in the USA.

During lockdown, ambulance services actually had fewer calls than normal because fewer people were calling 911. Many medics quit during this time, which bit the system in the ass as soon as lockdown mandates were lifted. With fewer medics available and the sudden influx of people calling 911, the system became stressed to the brink. Out of fear, many people resisted going to hospitals. As a result, there was a tidal wave of patients on a newly crippled system once lockdowns subsided.

During the height of COVID, still several months before the "vaccine" was available, people began calling for help in the normal patterns. An average day included abd pain, flu, cardiac events, strokes, trauma, and something new we were calling "happy hypoxia." During this event, people looked normal but had oxygen saturation that was extremely low, about 50% O2 readings, or sometimes lower. Normally, this would cause the patient to turn blue, but that wasn't the case with "happy hypoxia."

These oxygen saturations and patients presenting relatively normal while complaining of "anxiety" went against everything we'd been taught. The anomalies went against basic biology, in fact. "Happy hypoxia" was an indication that the patient had "COVID." We didn't even need to test the patient. Doctors in the emergency rooms would chalk the symptoms up to COVID and place the patient on a ventilator. Sadly, the vent was typically the final step before the patient would die.

To summarize, patients complained of anxiety. Doctors would blame the low O2 saturation and anxiety on "resorting failure" and prescribe intubation. However, most patients did not present as typical respiratory failure patients. As I said, they weren't turning blue. They didn't have word dyspnea or difficulty speaking. In fact, they seemed happy, thus the term "happy hypoxia."

"Happy hypoxia" threw a wrench in our routines. We proceeded with our protocols, hoping that adhering to what we knew would help us manage what we didn't understand.

I have often wondered if the symptoms were engineered with our protocols in mind. The intubation protocol proved to be the death knell for these patients, who would, in most cases, recover from the virus had they not been placed on ventilators. It seemed like whoever engineered the Wuhan flu was intent on doing as much harm as possible. The more COVID deaths, after all, the more adoption of the gene therapy injection called a "vaccine" later on. The more willing would be the population to adhere to more mandates. The more terrified the public, the more easily they could be controlled. The more readily they would turn on one another—the more permanent the damage done via family rifts. The more willing people would be to roll up their sleeves for an experimental shot.

Even writing these words today: I can't believe we fell for this.

The mainstream news never talked about "happy hypoxia," or at least not that I saw. My fellow medics and I would discuss it on Facebook in our private groups, but I never saw it addressed outside this niche community. This presented as a red flag.

Why wouldn't this be a big story? The news loved to scare people at the time, after all.

Death statistics were blasted over the airwaves, and I won't be surprised if somebody comes out with a study or statistic that indicates that people who avoided the news also avoided the shot. Without the incessant fear porn blasted at them, those "anti-vaxxers" were able to approach the decision to surrender their arms from a place of critical thinking and reasoning.

When the shot was produced at "warp speed," deemed "safe and effective," and touted as a "miracle cure," I knew why the news wasn't discussing "happy hypoxia." The goal wasn't medical advancement or knowledge. The media wasn't curious. They were bought by pharma.

After months of abuse, the victim was finally being offered a glimmer of hope.

John and Sally would soon return to their lives: they could return to the predictable tepidness of their second cup of coffee, the predictable interruptions as they tried to work, the predictable sounds of their kids fighting to get to school, the predictable taste of the hummus at their favorite lunch spot, the predictable path they'd walked with their dogs and the voices on their favorite podcasts talking about predictably remarkable things such as a new song, a new artist, a sporting event, or something other than the virus. And nothing sounded sweeter than that.

"Safe and effective" was all they wanted to hear.

Poem: Doomed, The Pair

Love so brief, was full of life,
Now mixed with sorrow cut by strife.
Double-edged the heart which held the knife.
Mortal husband, same for wife.
"Risk" abounds while dancing on air.
Star-crossed lovers, doomed the pair.
Yet, in the moment, doubt was "rare,"
Come the end, none will fare.
Some may ask, what's to blame?
They die suddenly, all the same.

Chapter Four

A Dystopian Nightmare

Make no mistake, the world was empty during COVID. One afternoon, a group of paramedic friends I'd met joined me on a day trip to Times Square. We were alone in the middle of one of the busiest blocks on planet Earth. It felt apocalyptic; nobody was brave enough to step outside in all of Manhattan. This put into perspective the fear people felt during the plandemic.

During COVID, we healthcare workers were getting what I consider downtime. Before COVID, we were getting calls and keeping busy with some slower days and others where I rushed from patient to patient nonstop for twelve or more hours a shift. But during COVID, people were scared to call 911. The televisions (tell-lie-visions) were pushing fear and showing images we now understand were manipulated to indicate that hospitals were overwhelmed.

One day, I got a call for chest pain and shortness of breath. The patient was having a heart attack. I put my monitor on and sat with the patient for around an hour, trying to convince him to go to the hospital. "You're going to die," I stated calmly but assertively, "please come with me to the hospital."

"I'm terrified to go to the hospital," the patient replied over and over from his seated position in a comfortable spot in his home.

"But you don't have a DNR. You're going to pass out soon," I told the patient, "under certain consent laws, if you pass out on me and you don't have a DNR, I have to treat you. You're not allowed to die on me."

I don't like it when people die on me. I was determined to save this patient's life. "I'm going to take care of you," I coaxed the patient. "But if I have to sit here and wait, taking care of you until you're not coherent, I will. But then I'll take you to the hospital anyway, and you'll have less of a chance at living. If you're afraid to die, you'll come with me to the hospital and have a chance to live."

"But I'm afraid to go there and catch COVID," the patient protested, becoming increasingly weak as we sat together."

I eventually got this patient to the hospital, where he was saved by surgery… in an empty hospital. In fact, due to the number of doctors and nurses sitting in the hospital without much to do, the patients were even *safer* in the hospitals than before COVID: our largest hospitals became boutique services because of the lack of patients.

Time and again, this fear of hospitals due to malicious and false reporting on the news caused people to die. Children's hospitals were utterly empty. Brave men and women willing to speak up reinforced this evidence repeatedly, not only in the United States but also in other countries. It is said that the United States had the highest number of deaths from COVID, not due to the virus but due to tertiary issues and procedures. One of those procedures is the ventilator, which I'll refer to several times in stories throughout this book.

Maria Zeee shared with me on a podcast that multiple whistleblower nurses told her they were standing around without much to do. And who can forget the vast number of TikTok videos portraying nurses so bored that they had time to choreograph dances in the hallways? Didn't that sound the alarm for my patients?

In one propaganda piece out of Australia on Channel 11, one nurse stated:

Throughout the whole of COVID, I was the nurse unit manager at Royal Melbourne Intensive Care. We started to really see what was happening overseas and what was happening: morgues out the front of hospitals and things like that. It became a really, really scary time. There's no doubt pre-vaccination staff were terrified, and I as a leader was terrified. I would say, 'okay, we're gonna do this,' and they'd say 'okay,' and then I would go home and I'd think, 'what if that's the wrong thing? What if that process that we're doing, someone gets COVID and someone, you know, dies from COVID or takes it home to their family?'

Over the last eighteen months, we've had people die in the ICU by themselves. (Cries) Sorry, it's making me emotional. I was there from four o'clock in the morning til ten o'clock at night some days. I started living on three or four hours of sleep a night, and that definitely affected my mental and physical health. I had headaches for about four months. I started having abdominal pain and got to the point where I started having chest pain and panic attacks, and I just unraveled from there. I was diagnosed with a bit of post-traumatic stress, just sort of from COVID and the decisions that were made as a leader. If I didn't take that time, I would really worry about where I am now.[10]

There were a few red flags Zeee and I took away from this clip. Number one: people were terrified of "pre-vaccination." I don't see that to be the case. People were terrified so much that they took an experimental gene therapy marketed as a vaccine, indeed. But once the shot was rolled out, people were bullied and badgered to continue taking more jabs in the form of boosters. The fear campaign didn't stop at one shot; people took several boosters until the take rate slowed down to a crawl at the time of this writing.

The most recent booster shot at the time of this writing was unleashed in September of 2023 and marketed as preparation for the upcoming cold season. The CDC indicates that approximately 17% of Americans succumbed to this jab, which ostensibly targeted the XBB.1.5 variant, a subvariant of Omicron and, allegedly, other closely related variants that were circulating. [11] [12]

For the record, I don't see variants as a threat; those who claim to have "long COVID" or other attacks on their immune system appear not to have

---

10. https://rumble.com/v57686t-harry-fisher-paramedic-reveals-COVID-injection-carnage.html

11. https://www.cdc.gov/mmwr/volumes/73/wr/mm7304a2.htm

12. https://asm.org/Articles/2023/October/Updated-COVID-19-Booster-XBB15-What-to-Know

COVID complications but complications from the shot. We'll learn more in the upcoming years and decades… if they last that long.

Another concern from this nurse's highly dramatized interview was that she clearly stated that she was lacking sleep. A lack of sleep is like being drunk; it impairs your critical functions and decision-making capabilities. Thinking critically is paramount to being in healthcare, especially in emergency response. Terror and PTSD are not the mental states you want the person who's got your life in your hands to make decisions from. I believe that the fear clouding these healthcare workers' judgment killed a lot of people. Nurses were, indeed, afraid… to do their jobs. They were scared to perform CPR. They were worried that the stats were too low, which caused them to begin intubation protocols that might not have been necessary immediately.

How could, for instance, those healthcare providers connect the dots in such a mental state of distress to realize that Remdesivir might be killing their patients? I'll discuss Remdesivir and its history in a later chapter.

Overseas, my peers, such as Maria Zeee in Australia, saw morgues in front of hospitals in the news. However, in the United States, I never once saw a morgue out front of a hospital in New York, Oklahoma, North Dakota, or Alaska. Even during my time in Lower Manhattan, where alleged death tolls were highest, I never saw a single morgue outside of a hospital.

A running joke, which is perverse to say, among my fellow dark-humored paramedics, was to state that we saw morgues in New York… and then we'd laugh and say, "They must need an electrician; they're having a problem with their freezers!"

No morgues were set up outside hospitals, at least none that my colleagues and I saw. Instead, there were empty hallways. The news media's fear porn compared with what we saw on the ground was laughable to us at that time. That's before, of course, we saw the death counts start to skyrocket. But it wasn't from COVID… it was from the vaccine.

Later in this book, we'll talk more about when the deaths, horrifying and gruesome side effects, and the body bags began actually to pile up. In this chapter, we'll look, however, at who really suffered during COVID.

First, the patients were afraid to go to the hospitals. They let conditions worsen that went untreated because they were fearful of catching a virus that was allegedly much more severe. However, unless they were put on ventilators, they were most likely not going to die of COVID. That said, I wonder if Holy Spirit moved people to avoid hospitals to save their lives. But not from COVID. To save their lives from doctors and nurses who'd put them on the ventilators or administer Remdesivir (which many now call "run-death-is-near, for good reason).

In New York City, residents spent up to a year inside their tiny apartments without human contact. Other healthcare providers were so "scared" to enter the hospitals that, at one point, I was being paid $1,000 a shift and had my hotel room covered for that day. That's $6,000 a week plus hotel expenses I was getting paid to be available during COVID. The people who were supposed to show up to work weren't showing up because of fear. Paramedics weren't generally assigned to the ICU, although we'd certainly bring patients to the ER. However, during COVID, the scope of what paramedics could perform expanded.

The role of a paramedic is relatively new; we've only been around since about the 1970s. During COVID, our profession had a bit of a rebrand. Our role broadened to include activity in the ICU and getting paid ungodly amounts of money. Before COVID it was common for a paramedic only to receive as low as $19.00 an hour. The appeal of getting paid $1,000 for a twelve-hour shift wasn't just compelling; it was shocking. If there was a surge in deaths during COVID, let's not forget the fact that there was such a dire shortage of medical personnel that paramedics not only had their scope expanded to include ICUs, but we were paid remarkable sums of money to do it. Ironically, the paramedics I worked with were mainly from Oklahoma, Texas, and Florida, assigned to places like New York City. Why was that? I think it's because we Southern boys weren't scared of the virus! Giddy Up. These Southern boys were the same ones who joined me in Times Square on that fateful day when I saw the apocalyptic emptiness on the streets.

However, long before the "vaccine" rollout, some deaths weren't occurring yet, but were being premeditated by the messages on the news, the mandates, and by absurd recommendations for isolation and quarantine by Death Doctor Anthony Fauci.

The second group to be affected by COVID horrifically were kids. Education suffered in schools across the country. Elementary aged students lagged in reading and speech. Middle school students developed anxiety disorders. High school aged students began spending more time online where they were bullied and developed mental disorders, eating disorders, and gender dysphoria. Lockdowns were brutal on kids.

Working single adults felt desperately lonely. They stopped dating. They suffered professionally and were forced to neglect their careers or participate in advancement opportunities or continued learning. Some working in seasonal or tourism jobs never went back to work because either their jobs were no longer available or they got fat on government handouts. An already entitled generation got more lazy, more entitled, and more depressed. Lockdowns were brutal on twenty and thirty-somethings.

Families ripped their hair out trying to keep children off their Zoom screens or quiet so that they could crunch numbers on spreadsheets. Partners who once prayed for just one date night a week were suddenly thrust into situations where they couldn't get away from their partners, nor the issues they weren't ready to confront. Domestic violence rose. Children in homes with abusive family members, including parents or siblings, had no reprieve or way to escape the abuse, even if just for an eight-hour school day. Finding it impossible to work at home, some parents decided to stop working, primarily women. Lockdowns were brutal on families.

But you know who really suffered the worst during lockdowns? The elderly. Most were already fairly imobile. Some had worked their entire lives to spend time with families they were now unable to see. To spend time walking their poodles or terriers in parks they were no longer able to access. Heck, some didn't know that they were saying goodbye to public parks, trees, grass and flowers for the rest of their lives.

What's more, the elderly were often already sick. Many who were the sickest were transported from ICUs or hospitals to elderly care facilities. Families were encouraged to do precisely the worst possible thing they could do: don't touch, let alone visit Grandma. Those who were transported to elderly care facilities sometimes brought flu or other viruses to otherwise healthy elderly folks. What's more, during the unconstitutional, immoral, heinous lockdowns, there were few people more isolated than the elderly. They were isolated and stuck in cold rooms with tile floors and yellowed walls. They didn't know how to log into Zoom, and most didn't have access to a library of books, much less the technical wherewithal to download books on their phones.

What the elderly endured in their isolation was nothing short of human torture. An experiment to see just how irreparably we can break a human spirit. Lockdowns were brutal on the elderly.

Many nursing homes, especially the ones that house lower income people, were disgusting beyond imagination; and I'm telling you from experience as I walked into hundreds of them. Stepping into these facilities was like entering a dystopian nightmare. There were plastic drapes on every hall. Elderly were left lying in their own feces for excessive, indefinite periods of time. You could hear people screaming out for help, or their loved ones.

The smells, the sounds, the sight of it all. It will never go away. Every inch of it wreaked of hell. I remember one afternoon entering a nursing home; the doors creaked open, revealing a dimly lit hallway. The smell of antiseptic was overpowering; the stringent measures in place were right out of a dystopian nightmare. My eyes scanned the peeling paint and worn-out furniture; signs of a facility struggling to make ends meet were evident to anyone with eyes. The rooms within this crumbling cage were occupied by souls who once hoped their loved ones would come to see them. Now they sat, silent and frail, all hope removed.

Though clearly overworked and exhausted, the staff greeted me with a nod, their eyes reflecting a mixture of sadness and resignation. It was immediately apparent that this nursing home was under immense strain. I knew that low-income facilities often lacked funds, but the extensive COVID-19 protocols were destructive even with federal money being thrown at such facilities. The reality was bleak at best—lack of PPE, understaffed shifts, and residents isolated from the world outside. The isolation itself was torture. They kept these lonely people from those who used to hold their hands occasionally. I remember thinking this had to be straight from Satan himself.

I couldn't shake the feeling that these measures were more about control and profit than actual safety. As I moved through the corridors my skepticism grew. Many residents were confined to their rooms, their only interaction with the outside world being the fleeting visits from the overburdened staff. Or paramedics like me. Most just strangers hiding under cloth masks in uniform. I could see the immense loneliness etched into their faces, the longing for human connection that those in charge of the "pandemic" had cruelly snatched away.

In my mind, this nursing home, with its peeling walls and weary residents, was a microcosm of a larger issue—a cruel reminder of what will happen to us all if we continue to bow to tyrannical mandates and live in fear. Propagandized fear ushered in a new era of tyranny, and I knew then that our future, our souls, truly hung in the balance.

They Were Told To Let Anyone Over 70 Die…

In other countries there are reports that during this time paramedics were told to let people die.

On April 30, 2024 Christopher Stephen questioned Robert Pollock from the GMB Union, who provided testimony for the Scottish COVID-19 Inquiry.[13]

Christopher asks Pollock about "toe tagging," which means that somebody is marked for death and let to die. According to the Pollock testimony, the government in Scotland told paramedics to mark anyone over seventy as not worthy of treatment that could save their lives. Discussions then, according to Pollock, took place about reducing this age limit to anybody over fifty.

A written statement by Pollock indicates that he was a front-line operational paramedic and, at one point, was given the task of monitoring PPE (personal protective equipment) and quality for Scottish Ambulance Service workers. Pollock admits in written testimony that Scottish Ambulance Services employees received a letter from the Health and Care Professions

---

13. https://www.COVID19inquiry.scot/evidence/witness-statement-provided-robert-pollock-behalf-gmb-scottish-ambulance-service-branch

Council that there would be difficult decisions made and typical protocols abandoned, and that taking a "DNR" or "do not resuscitate" position on individuals over seventy would be permitted and "fully supported" by Health and Care Professions Council. Pollock's testimony includes:

There was reporting in the media of the "toe tagging" of patients by age group which is wording for "do not try too hard to resuscitate them" over a certain age.

Scottish Ambulance Service employees received a letter by email on Thursday 26 March 2020 from the Health and Care Professions Council which stipulated to every registrant that they realised there would be difficult decisions to be made by healthcare professionals, but they would be given full support to make decisions out with normal protocols.

The reference to normal protocols within the letter refers to the fact that ordinarily, efforts were made to try and resuscitate every single person that has a feasible chance of success. However, the Health and Care Professional Council basically indicated that if employees did not do that on these occasions to coincide with the government statement, then they would fully support employees for any challenges employees may face as healthcare professionals.

This was very frightening for workers who have family members in that age group and it caused a lot of concern and anxiety for people who were used to doing their best to preserve life. The process of resuscitation has evolved, and we have a high success rate. This did not go down well with members.

In addition, there were discussions about rumours within meetings with the Scottish Ambulance Service that the government had a plan to reduce the age group to those over 50s if COVID levels reached their expected peak and the plan for over 70s did not result in a significant enough drop in medical demand, with ages dropping depending on numbers coming through hospital. This with the backdrop of the crisis COVID caused in Italy.[14]

---

14. https://www.COVID19inquiry.scot/evidence/witness-statement-provided-robert-pollock-behalf-gmb-scottish-ambulance-service-branch

Later in this book, we'll approach the problematic topics of depopulation or the pressure from government mandates, lockdowns, and, in the case of Scotland, adherence to PPE equipment that might have fueled even more deaths during the plandemic. If it looks like the world went mad during 2020, it's because we did. And it was well-planned.

Exodus 20:12 in the New King James Version states, "Honor your father and your mother, that your days may be long upon the land which the Lord your God is giving you."

Honoring your father and mother is a commandment from God, and as many scholars point out, it's the first with a promise. Follow this command and your days may be long. Believers learn that obedience is a sign of respect and honor (Ephesians 6:1-3) and that obedience will lead to a long and prosperous life. Conversely, disobedience will shorten one's life.

America is a radically individualistic country. If you spend time abroad, you'll quickly note that Italians, Chinese, and almost any other culture invests into their elderly. They are honored. It's inconceivable to many global citizens that their parents would be "put into a home" that isn't their home. To me, it is a sign of disobedience that we discard our elderly when they can't move fast enough to keep up with the Joneses.

As I watched the dystopian hell in which we placed our elderly during the lockdowns, and still today when I take a call to assist an isolated, elderly person, I can't help but wonder if America is due for wrath from God for our disobedience.

We are a culture that does not honor our parents. On television the father has been intentionally portrayed as a fool, such as Al Bundy or Homer Simpson. How often on American television do you see a couple revered for taking care of an elderly parent or a child being blessed by the songs and stories of an aging grandmother or grandfather?

As somebody who spent my childhood in the arms of a wonderful, wise grandmother, even a sick one, I can tell you that I wouldn't be the man I am today without honoring my grandmother and my father's obedience to take care of his own parents.

This nation is about to have a do-over of the COVID-19 lockdowns. It may begin before this book is published.

Above all else, I implore you to honor your father and mother, that your days may be long. Don't ditch grandma. Hug her. Take her under your roof. Allow your children to sit in her lap. Care for her in the old age that she has earned. Honor her with your care.

And if you don't believe in God nor the Bible, take an old person under your wing. If nothing else, be motivated to be a good human. And for your obedience, I pray for you to have a more prosperous and long life, too.

Poem: Fourth of July

From Boston party to bend the knee,
Bleeding a nation that yearned to be free.
Leaders sit, say, "Follow me,"
The blind lead all who cannot see.
Taxes and death, we pay with glee,
Compliant those hanging on Liberty's tree.
Voices silenced, dissenters flee,
In shadows, whispers of what used to be.
Chains unseen, bound are we,
land of the brave, a costly fee.
Promises broken, trust last decree,
shackled the world without a key.
Dreams of dawn, a far-distant plea,
Echoes of justice now drowned with the tea.

Chapter Five

Sheep To The Slaughter

"Our modern healthcare system doesn't incentivize performance; we incentivize obedience."

Harry Fisher

The day had finally come. The experimental gene therapy referred to as "COVID-19 vaccines" had been rolled out. In the Facebook chat rooms I saw healthcare workers sharing positively ridiculous posts praising the modern advancement in medicine, the veritable miracle that were these death shots.

It was a typical day, or the "new normal" type of day for me—typical calls. My ambulance was on the north side of Oklahoma City. A call dropped, which meant it came in, and I sprung into action.

"Full arrest."

I jumped into the ambulance and raced to code the call, meaning we hauled ass to the patient's location. The event occurred in what I call a "shot line." A Pfizer "vaccine" clinic was set up in a building connected to a leading hospital. A patient who had already received their first vaccine was lying supine on the floor, CPR already in progress. I began working the code, fire department on scene, with clinic nursing staff present.

As we were working trying to revive the patient, a nurse walked over to me and said "this is the second one in two weeks." I will never forget that statement. It's haunted me. Those words were not only startling, but acted as a wrecking ball that brought down many bricks in the wall of lies built around my mind.

"Safe," I remember thinking, "This shot isn't safe."

While working the code, I looked over my shoulder and saw no one leaving the line. A patient was lying there in Corpse Pose after receiving the jab with healthcare, paramedics, and the fire department scrambling to save a life. And people just stared. Maybe they thought he had a bad burrito. A person was being defibrillated, CPR in progress. To most people, that was the closest they'd ever come to death. Most had not even seen a dead body aside from in a casket. And yet, they stood there dutifully waiting for their own death shots.

The scene was horrific. It literally looked like cattle standing in line to be slaughtered.

Like the shit-stained elderly care facilities, this image has haunted my nightmares ever since. I can't seem to wash it out of my mind. In the back of my mind, it's an image of humanity's worst. A dangerous experimental gene therapy treatment nefariously marketed to a frightened population who are standing, watching a person die in front of them, and they don't have the courage, conviction, nor common sense to get up and walk away.

I didn't take the jab. Three of my four children didn't take it. Most of my close friends aren't "vaccinated." You had a choice. Standing in that line like sheep to the slaughter: you made the wrong decision.

In a moment of clarity, I swallowed and spit out the words, directed at the nurse who muttered earlier, "second one in two weeks."

"Second one in two weeks?" I repeated, wanting it not to be true.

As we placed the patient on the backboard for transport she answered me. "Yes." And then she solemnly walked away. I knew that she had been first in line for the shot, too. That her superior had made sure every nurse on staff was already double jabbed. She may even have still had the bandaid under her blue polyester scrubs. In that moment, I felt compassion for her, an ignorant criminal administering a death shot she had been bullied, berated, and manipulated into taking and then giving to others. I wondered how she slept that night. I knew that I would be certainly tossing and turning.

My colleagues and I in the ambulance left the scene, taking the patient to the hospital that was most appropriate. The patient was pronounced dead by the ER physician. I told the ER doctor what the nurse had said. Her words still pounded in my brain. He didn't gaslight me or accuse the nurse of hyperbolic language or drama. He simply said, "there's been quite a few."

The doctor solemnly gathered a clipboard and prepared to leave the room. It wasn't business as usual for him. However, death was undoubtedly nothing unique in his position. But this one seemed to upset him. At the time, I didn't yet understand why.

Not long after this I took a contract job in New York City, in an ER and ICU. The pay was unimaginable for a paramedic. I'd earn a thousand dollars a shift. On top of that my room was paid for. This was more money than I ever thought possible for a paramedic, indeed more money than I thought I'd ever earn in my life. What I didn't know is that there was a catch...

"Don't tell the nursing staff what you're making," my superior instructed me before I had even suited up on my first day.

We paramedics were instructed to keep the core staff at the hospital from knowing what we were being compensated to be there. I later learned that federal money was being used to pay for contract workers while core staff nurses were paid much less. We were also told how people had been let go from the contract for speaking out of line. Initially, I didn't understand what speaking out of line meant. But I was beginning to realize that this was the catch.

Each day we would switch from the ICU to the ER. I assumed that this was ordered to prevent paramedics from burning out. People in the ICU were predominantly intubated, such as the "happy hypoxia" patients I'd seen in Chapter Three. Once on a ventilator, these patients wouldn't live long. We've learned due to the brave work of dissident doctors who had the courage to speak out that this is because those patients would almost immediately suffer kidney failure. The ventilators were death traps.

Intubated COVID-19 patients placed on this breathing device designed to assist with ventilation were medicated, turned, and cleaned by the contract worker paramedics, myself included. And then, we would watch them inevitably die. We'd proceed to place tags on them and put them into body bags. One after another, the patients would get intubated, medicated, turned over once or twice, and then die.

As I tossed and turned each night, images from this experience made my brain throb. I'd see the faces of people who'd just died so suddenly as I zipped them up into white body bags. However, I couldn't seem to close the zipper over my own eyes or thoughts. The zipper is stuck and the dead bodies and innocent faces are within inches of my nose. They won't go away.

We shouldn't want them to.

COVID Death Protocols

I briefly touched upon the dystopian nightmare and the ridiculous amount of money I was being offered to let people die. It wasn't for a long time thereafter that I became aware of some of the hospital shenanigans and the use of ventilators and Remdesivir to essentially murder people who could have quickly recovered from COVID-19.

One brave medical coder who left her job in an Arizona hospital was interviewed by "The Defender In-Depth," one of many news outlets distributed by "Children's Health Defense®," a 501(c)(3) non-profit organization with the mission of ending childhood health epidemics by eliminating toxic exposure. They are famous for having Robert F. Kennedy Jr. on their board alongside their astute CEO Mary Holland, Esq. As the Defender In-Depth writer Dr. Michael Nevradakis reports, the former medical coder, Zowe Smith, resigned and began speaking out about suffering she saw recorded on patient medical records, which she documented in her book "The COVID Code: My Life in the Thrill Kill Medical Cult."

Smith was tasked with exposing "the patterns of disease going on," which illuminated abnormalities when the hospitals began implementing COVID-19 protocols." From Smith:

> *I started noticing … patients trying to escape the hospital, like unplugging things, pulling out vent tubes and escaping … then I started to hear rumors about the ventilators and I knew that there was a bonus for [giving] Remdesivir.*
>
> *…Before COVID, a cold, flu or pneumonia case, you would normally be home within three days, maybe a week, unless you had other major conditions.*[15]

---

15. https://childrenshealthdefense.org/defender/zowe-smith-medical-coder-defender-podcast/

As I shared in an earlier story, I wasn't used to placing people on ventilators. In fact, it was unheard of. It surprised me and raised suspicion that I was being paid to work in an ER in New York for patients I was tasked with merely making comfortable so that they could die. But why were COVID patients placed so quickly on ventilators? Typically, this was not the protocol unless every other conceivable method was tried, and during those times, people would get off that ventilator right away. During COVID-19, patients could be on the vents for thirty days or even more. The longer you're on the ventilators, the less likely you are to come out alive.

During COVID-19, doctors immediately administered the ventilators, unless they paid me to do it. What's more, patients who were given Remdesivir would develop kidney failure within a few days. Smith stated, "I could see the lab values… they were getting worse almost immediately after the administration of Remdesivir."

Smith reported that hospitals were strong-armed into accepting these wild and abnormal protocols at the beginning of the pandemic.

> *When the world was asked to lock down … hospitals were also issued mandates … that they needed to shut down their OR [operating rooms], which is their bread and butter. That's where most of their money is made."*

She reported that hospitals were pressured to increase their ICU bed capacity and reduce the number of patients taking up those beds. Removing people who needed intensive care to make room for a wave of sick COVID-19 patients was financially penalizing for hospitals, but even more detrimental for the patients who needed the ICU but didn't have COVID-19. Smith reveals that the COVID-19 protocols "came down to us from the NIH" and that the use of Remdesivir and ventilators was incentivized for now-struggling hospitals, who got 20% of the revenue for every dose of Remdesivir they administered to a patient. If the ventilator was used, they got the maximum payment.[16]

16. https://childrenshealthdefense.org/wp-content/uploads/Follow-the-Money_Blood-Money-in-US-Hospitals_BRIEF_9-Jul_2022.pdf

"'I began seeing some incredibly crazy cases,' Smith said. 'I began to notice more cases … of near-instant death, like within an hour of multi-organ failure. Massive inflammation, brain death, things that we had never, ever seen before.[17] In my 11 years of medical coding, I had never seen a case like that,'" reported Dr. Nevradakis.[18]

In another interview, Smith reported on video some of the horrors I've been witnessing throughout this book so far, particularly about the rapidity of death among patients while hospitals were following the NIH-conceived COVID-19 protocols as well as after they rolled out the mRNA jabs.

> *I didn't know it was possible for a human to die so horrifically, so quickly, before they rolled out the mRNA injections…It was insane, I've never seen anything like that. The worst of them, they called it sepsis, but it was like instant multi-organ failure… Like, within hours patients would die of liver, lung, kidney… failure [all at once]… Some of the records…[from the] emergency crew that found them [the injection victims], it's like their body tried to reject everything. [In] some of these cases, their family would be there 30 minutes before, and then within an hour they're dead.[19]*

In the succeeding chapters, I'll work to reveal to you *why* this corruption was allowed to happen. Although I could write an entire book on every sentence you'll read, I'll work to provide references for books and studies that Stephanie and I read in order to give you a brief but directed distillation of the genocide and its nefarious but undeniable foundations.

---

17. https://childrenshealthdefense.org/defender/link-heart-inflammation-pfizer-moderna-COVID-vaccines-cdc-advisory/

18. https://live.childrenshealthdefense.org/chd-tv/shows/good-morning-chd/life-in-the-thrill-kill-medical-cult/

19. https://lionessofjudah.substack.com/p/hospital-whistleblower-doctors-are

Chapter Six

Run: Death Is Near

On the topic of hospital protocols and corruption, this chapter will provide a quick history lesson about Remdesivir, which many awakened people now refer to as "run-death-is-near."

Enter Dr. David E. Martin: an American entrepreneur, financier, public speaker, and author known for his work in innovation finance and global economic development. He is the founder and chairman of M·CAM Inc., a firm specializing in intangible asset finance and innovation. Not officially on his resume but in our firm opinion, David is also a damn genius and a divine gift to humanity.

Dr. Martin has been involved in various initiatives aimed at transforming business practices and promoting ethical economic development.[20] Over the years that she has been a publisher for high profile whistleblowers in medicine or government, Steph has gotten to know Dr. David and his wife Kim. She has shared that they are never, ever too busy to provide her and her authors support. They're the real deal.

Dr. David is one of the original COVID-19 whistleblowers, and probably the most important one on the subject of financial crimes and the paper trail of corruption that goes back decades up to the 2020 bioweapon attack. This was possible in part because in his professional career Dr. Martin has analyzed trends in the economy and patents for a living, among many other things. He was one of the first reputable superheroes to come out and suggest that the virus was lab-generated,

20. https://www.davidmartin.world/about/

tracking down patents to prove it long before mainstream media gave up hiding that fact.

The movie Plandemic 2: Indoctrination, directed by Mikki Willis, was primarily based on Dr. David's work. Plandemic 2 alleged that influential individuals and organizations orchestrated and/or exploited the pandemic for profit and control. The documentary exposed government agencies, pharmaceutical companies, and influential figures who manipulated data to increase vaccine sales, control populations, and centralize global power. The primary bad guys Plandemic 2 exposes are the World Health Organization and Dr. Anthony Fauci.

One of the most critical bad guys Martin exposed was Ralph Baric, PhD, whom he calls the inventor and weaponizer of Coronavirus. Baric is a virologist and epidemiologist who studied coronaviruses extensively.

Dr. Vladimir Zelenko was among the other first whistleblowers about Baric's corrupt ties in his book "How To Decapitate The Serpent," wherein he calls COVID-19 a "weapon of mass destruction, a biological bomb if you will," and states, "My research and observations have led me to conclude that Dr. Baric was involved in the engineering and design of both components."[21]

Dr. Baric was involved in the original research relating to the cross-species transmissibility of viruses, what later became known as "gain of function;" they were working on a delivery system to have a virus cross species. Baric and a team through the UNC-Chapel Hill applied and were granted a patent (US7279327B2)[22] that reveals funding for their technology from the NIH. This patent was secured in 2017 for up to twenty years, and secured by a company called "Gilead Sciences."

Baric received a $6 million grant in 2017 from the National Institute of Allergy and Infectious Diseases (NIAID), then headed by none other than Dr. Anthony Fauci.[23] Despite the monumental failure of the drug in

---

21. https://amzn.to/48yAYA8

22. https://web.archive.org/web/20200324191627/http:/patft.uspto.gov/netacgi/nph-Parser?d=PALL&p=1&u=/netahtml/PTO/srchnum.htm&r=1&f=G&l=50&s1=9724360.PN.&OS=PN/9724360&RS=PN/9724360

23. https://sph.unc.edu/sph-news/gillings-researchers-receive-6m-grant-to-fight-infectious-disease/

ebola trials, Gilead acquired FDA approval to initiate two Phase 3 clinical trials to see if COVID-19 could be treated with the deadly drug. [24] The Department of Defense identified a "cooperative research and development agreement with an industry partner [Gilead] to gain access to an antiviral drug for treatment use in our medical centers."[25]

The FDA fully approved Emergency Use Authorization of the drug in October 2020.[26] [27]

Just how deadly was this chain of events? How deep does the rabbit hole go? And for how many years were these bad actors installed and planning their deadly massacre?

In the book "Zelenko," co-author Brent Hamachek writes,

Going back to the 1990s, Dr. Ralph Baric started researching coronavirus and looking at cross-species transference. He eventually progressed to the point where he obtained patented technology that could do precisely that. Along the way, he discovered a method for treating coronavirus in its early stage. While he published that research, he did not demand to be heard early in the coronavirus outbreak so he could share his knowledge with the world. Before that, halfway between his finding of a treatment and the outbreak, he conducted research to produce a chimeric version of a virus, which was performed in conjunction with Chinese researchers.... To put two and two together, the research work that Baric helped oversee that took place in the Wuhan lab was, according to him, not responsible for the pandemic, but it was responsible for the "vaccine."[28]

---

24. https://www.gilead.com/news/news-details/2020/gilead-sciences-initiates-two-phase-3-studies-of-investigational-antiviral-Remdesivir-for-the-treatment-of-COVID-19

25. https://www.militarytimes.com/news/your-military/2020/03/10/army-signs-agreement-with-drug-giant-gilead-on-experimental-COVID-19-treatment/

26. https://www.fda.gov/drugs/news-events-human-drugs/fdas-approval-veklury-Remdesivir-treatment-COVID-19-science-safety-and-effectiveness?os=vb__&ref=app

27. https://www.gilead.com/news/news-details/2020/gileads-investigational-antiviral-veklury-Remdesivir-receives-us-food-and-drug-administration-emergency-use-authorization-for-the-treatment-of-patients-with-moderate-COVID-19

28. Excerpt from "Zelenko: How To Decapitate The Serpent" by Vladimir Zelenko, MD and Brent Hamachek. Copyright 2022 by Brent Hamachek.

So Baric had his hands in the Wuhan virus. But, in addition, he had his hands in the drug that, according to Dr. David Martin:

> *…Allegedly used to treat patients with COVID, except for the fact that by 2018, that drug had a kill ratio of 53%. Documented. Published. It was so deadly that the World Health Organization itself pulled the drug from consideration for ebola treatments. Ironically, inside the documents that nobody bothers reading, the death rate occurred regardless of viral load, which means that people were killed who didn't even have ebola. We murdered people. And by we, I mean the complacent and ignorant masses agreeing to let these things go unchecked. Murdered people in Africa. The death rate at 53%, and we let that publication of information in 2018 fail to inform our decision in the Spring of 2020 when Anthony Fauci, Ralph Baric, Peter Daszak, and others made the decision that we should inject Remdesivir into patients with COVID. We knew we were going to kill people. That's premeditated murder.*[29]

Although the drug Remdesivir was allegedly developed to treat Ebola, it "was subsequently proven to be lethal in human patients." The New England Journal of Medicine reported in 2019 that Remdesivir elicited the highest mortality rate of four therapies that were instigated for ebola in the Democratic Republic of Congo,[30] stating that the mortality rate was closer to 51% versus the 53% that was quoted by Martin in the above paragraph. Either way, that's pretty sorry odds for patients.

I've stated before that COVID-19 had a great PR and marketing team. But don't take my word for it. COVID-19 shined so brilliantly for its stakeholders that it literally obliterated the flu and other influenza viruses for nearly two years.

The graph below illustrates that right around the spring of 2020, the "flu" basically disappeared for two years.[31] Isn't that convenient? Where did it go? Could millions of people have been bamboozled into taking the death

29. https://rumble.com/v2029bk-we-murdered-people-Remdesivir-was-and-still-is-being-used-as-a-death-warran.html

30. https://www.nejm.org/doi/full/10.1056/NEJMoa1910993

31. https://worldhealthorg.shinyapps.io/flunetchart/

shot for the flu? Could billions of people have been locked down for the flu? People out of work, out of school, getting brainwashed at home by predictive programming on Netflix and TikTok... over the flu?

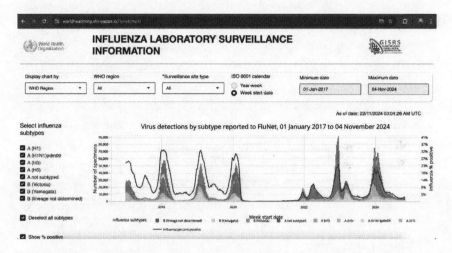

Dr. Michael Yeadon, former Pfizer executive, even goes as far as to state,

> *Based on a century of failure to demonstrate transmission of clinical symptoms from a person sick with any acute respiratory illness to a healthy recipient, it is clear that these acute illnesses aren't infectious in nature, nor are they contagious.*
>
> *We've been programmed to the contrary for so long and so effectively that many people simply will not accept the empirical evidence of the deception...*
>
> *Taken together, I call upon everyone to recognise finally that Occam's Razor slices well to reveal that EVERYTHING was propaganda. There was no new illness called COVID19. There is no SARS-CoV-2 "virus". This group of illnesses are not infectious or contagious.*
>
> *Acute respiratory illnesses are so common an occurrence that it has proven before to be easily weaponized and used in what can fairly be described as global terrorism by state authorities and institutions everywhere.*[32]

---

32. https://lionessofjudah.substack.com/p/dr-mike-yeadon-everything-was-propaganda

Military Murder

It wasn't only major medical systems that kowtowed to the NIH through bribery on COVID-19 protocols that were akin to genocide. Additionally, one military whistleblower with the pseudonym Daniel LeMay released a series of documents referred to as "The Remdesivir Papers," which he released to investigative journalist J.M. Phelps and later published in "The Gateway Pundit."[33]

The Remdesivir Papers detail how 601 military service members died following a series of fatal adverse events in Remdesivir clinical trials.[34]

The whistleblower "LeMay" illuminates the tragic news that some clinical trials were improperly run, informed consent for trial participants may have been nonexistent, and the results were never made public. The documents illustrate that the military began administering Remdesivir to service members ostensibly infected with COVID-19 months before the FDA approved the drug.

> *Data derived from the Department of Defense [DOD] Joint Trauma System ... by a military whistleblower offers a stark contrast to results of multiple clinical trials involving the liberal usage of Remdesivir in military treatment facilities and other civilian facilities, as well as its potential contribution to, at minimum, hundreds of untimely deaths.*

Brian Hooker, Ph.D., chief scientific officer for Children's Health Defense, stated:

> All of the information here needs to be made public and the public officials, including Tony Fauci, need to be held to account for the criminal acts associated with the fraudulent 'trials' of Ivermectin and hydroxychloroquine that were tainted in order to preclude their use,

---

33. https://www.thegatewaypundit.com/2024/10/Remdesivir-papers-did-service-members-deserve-die/

34. https://childrenshealthdefense.org/defender/gilead-falsely-advertised-Remdesivir-lawsuit/

and making Remdesivir the standard of care despite the obvious data showing that it kills people."[35] [36] [37]

Texas chairperson Gail Seiler of the FormerFedsGroup Freedom Foundation was administered Remdesivir in the hospital and lived to sound the alarm. She reported that although she and her family had stated wishes otherwise, she was administered the drug and listed as "Do Not Resuscitate." States Seiler, [The Remdesivir Papers] only "scratch the surface as to the homicide toll in military hospitals."[38] [39]

Of the 941 military service members who died between March 2020 and March 2024, 601, or 63.9%, were treated with Remdesivir. If 601 of our military service members were murdered by Remdesivir, primarily between November 2020 and July 2021, how many more were euthanized among the general public?

As of September 2023, the United States military comprised 1.29 million active-duty service members, with an additional 767,238 National Guard and Reserve members.[40] There are also approximately 346 million people in the United States.[41] [42] Using this information, it is possible that *if* the number of deaths from Remdesivir were consistent with the entire U.S. Population, that would mean that over 160,000 souls were euthanized from the drug. Of course, unlike all other statements in this book, my math is

---

35. https://childrenshealthdefense.org/

36. https://childrenshealthdefense.org/defender/fda-war-on-Ivermectin-doj-attorney-project-veritas/

37. https://childrenshealthdefense.org/defender/mechanisms-of-harm-lori-weintz-hydroxychloroquine-COVID-treatment/

38. https://formerfedsgroup.org/

39.

40. https://usafacts.org/articles/how-many-people-are-in-the-us-military-a-demographic-overview/

41. https://www.worldometers.info/world-population/us-population/

42. https://www.census.gov/popclock/?os=app&ref=app

purely conjecture for the purpose of illustrating the potential ratio from this Remdesivir genocide from the military data from LeMay.

With this information, do you still doubt that our government and even major medical systems are capable of genocide? By the end of this book, I will remove all doubt. We have more layers of the onion to peel. Thank you for the courage of being here.

A Prayer For Peace & Power

Heavenly Father,
As we read this book, please help us understand the power of your
protection in this dark time.
Please help us to keep perspective on the larger chess board on which
we're playing.
Please give us the opportunity to be players in this game, not passive
observers.
Raise us up in our respective Divine Calling, Abba.

Like your Son Yeshua illustrated when He calmed the storm, give us faith
that will settle the torrential seas of corruption on which we're wading.
We believe in your love, which also includes your gift of free will.

As we continue this book, grant us the peace that will be needed to
proceed with power and authority to rebuke the darkness and hold the
criminals accountable.
We love you Elohim, our Creator, and our Heavenly papa.

In Yeshua's mighty name, may the demonic agenda be cast out,
and may we be participants in your Holy Plan.

Amen.

Chapter Seven

Awakening The Lions with Dr. Kelly Victory

These front-line workers are the equivalent of our modern-day healthcare Paul Reveres. We have to listen to what they see and say.

Dr. Kelly Victory

One of the first intrepid doctors who learned that we were getting sold a bill of goods regarding COVID-19 was Dr. Kelly Victory. She stuck her neck out to expose oddities and red flags before some people had even gone into lockdown mode. In some ways, I see the story you're about to read as evidence of Divine Providence, and you'll see why in a moment.

Kelly Victory had foresight and wisdom coupled with extreme life circumstances that put her ahead of the rest of us who have since "woken up." Her voice has been paramount to helping many other healthcare professionals wake up for two reasons—her authority. Victory understood emergency medicine and was among the first humans I know who identified "monkey business" in the COVID-19 virus. In addition, Dr. Kelly is rational, logical and remarkably intuitive. She comes across with conviction and confidence. She donated many thousands of hours to podcasting and spreading what was then defined as "misinformation" and "conspiracy theory." Still, due to her brilliance and pedigree, she was the precise voice needed to wake up many other healthcare workers and doctors to the COVID-19 plandemic.

People listen to Dr. Kelly because she has, among other things, worked as a trauma and ER specialist for thirty years. She understands medicine both from the perspective of patient care, but also at a high administrative level. She was the CMO for Whole Health Management where she coordinated healthcare services for Fortune 500 companies.

There is no margin for error in this position, and expectations had to be sky-high. Recognizing her expertise and excellence, The Wellness Company recently asked her to come on board as the Chief of Disaster and Emergency Medicine. She works alongside longtime colleague Dr. Drew Pinsky and my good friend Dr. Peter McCullough. It was the founder of The Wellness Company, Foster Coulson, who called Steph and told her that we had a book about my story; TWC had already entrusted Stephanie with their book "The Next Wave is Brave" and their sister company "ZLabs" had worked with her on "Zelenko: How To Decapitate The Serpent," which I've been honored to promote alongside my book. You have almost certainly seen Dr. Kelly before, as she's a frequent co-host on the "Dr. Drew Podcast." In 2023, she and other authors released the book "Toxic Shock."

Dr. Kelly heard my story on X.com at least a couple of years ago. She has stated, "These front-line workers are the equivalent of our modern-day healthcare Paul Revere's. We have to listen to what they're seeing and saying." But I'm just a bum who rides around in ambulances and tries to make people not die.

Nonetheless, the attention and respect I received from Dr. Kelly Victory made me feel like I mattered and my story was important; she's been pretty good for my otherwise bruised ego during the pandemic when I struggling to save my marriage, watching people die in front of me and in my arms, and feeling so helpless that all I could do was post about it on X.com… and that was only after getting silenced on other platforms. I felt like I was being muzzled and gagged, but brave doctors like Dr. Kelly made me feel like there was a bigger plan, and that I could be a part of it.

"We're Experiencing Genocide…"

Dr. Kelly Victory first contacted me once after seeing a post I made about a cardiac arrest in a Pfizer line, which is a makeshift clinic you'd see anywhere from a gymnasium to a fairground, such as in Julie Threet's case in California. In the tweet I revealed that the patient, who wasn't elderly, collapsed after his or her shot with lethal arrhythmia. The patient was defibrillated multiple times but we weren't able to revive the patient. A nurse stated, "this is the second one in two weeks," and a story that I've been asked to tell on several occasions, including on the Alex Jones podcast, as well as earlier in this book.

Without giving away my location or the exact date of the occurrence, this now infamous event took place during a time when all we heard in the media was that this shot was safe. But when the nurse stated with exasperation that she had seen two such deaths in recent weeks, it sounded an alarm.

Pulmonary embolisms, heart attacks, and sudden deaths are more challenging to hide in a small community. A doctor pulled me aside and said, "Harry, we're experiencing genocide." I tried to share my story on TikTok, and the video got millions of views. However, my account was deleted for alleged "terrorist activity." That's when I moved to X.com, where I've struggled and been jailed or shadow-banned, but I've had more success communicating with curious followers and many trolls, too.

We healthcare workers were being propagandized along with the public with additional messages about the shot being "safe and effective." For instance, I was frequently told that "correlation doesn't equal causation" as a form of gaslighting me, telling me to tuck away what my eyes saw and pretend it wasn't real. Thankfully, around the time I woke up, there were guys much more intelligent than me, such as Ed Dowd and his superhero team of data analysts and insurance company professionals, who were analyzing some of the anecdotal abnormalities I was seeing to eventually prove that the correlation between shots and death that I witnessed was, indeed, empirically traceable. I'll pay homage to Ed in a later chapter.

As the months went by, the adverse events became more frequent in younger patients. Our children's hospitals used to be pretty empty, and most pediatric emergency calls had to do with trauma, but suddenly, I began seeing young heart attacks or young strokes.

As a paramedic, I must obtain a complete medical history. I ask whether the patient is on medications and if they've had a COVID shot. Therefore, I have heard countless parents state, "Well, yes, the child just had a COVID shot last week," for instance.

There isn't merely gaslighting involved with the healthcare community, but cognitive dissonance. I've walked into emergency rooms where doctors actually laughed at me when I reported to them that my young patient with heart failure recently had a COVID shot. "It can't be the shot," they'd state.

These doctors suffer from an inability to see what's right in front of their faces. They didn't seem capable, and some still aren't capable of reporting or even recognizing the facts, the physical bodies deteriorating before their eyes. Seeing as how most healthcare workers have taken the jabs, they're among the most unwilling minds to admit that not only have they downed this poison, but they've either recommended or administered it to others. In a later chapter, I'll propose a theory that's being tested by scientists much more intelligent than me, who suspect that the spike protein in the shots affects the hippocampus, which makes adherents to the jab more vulnerable to idiocy and propaganda.

"Monkey Business" and the Wuhan Flu

Dr. Kelly was never one of these doctors. In fact, she was way early to the party. Way before McCullough. Way before Malone. In fact, she was aware that there was something fishy going on before most people had ever heard the term "coronavirus" in their lives.

In January of 2020 Dr. Kelly heard that there was a "novel" virus that hadn't hit the U.S. at that point. Nobody was talking about it, but because she was in emergency medicine, she received a newsletter from the CDC… and smelled a rat. She indicated to me that an overzealous response from public health officials was one of many red flags she saw. Traditionally, public health officials want to keep the public in the dark until there's absolutely no way of hiding the truth; it's not in their best interest to create fear on top of managing response to a viral pandemic.

Apparently, with this "novel" virus eventually identified as "COVID-19," they were operating by a new plan… one that eliminated their tradition of critical thinking and caution, fueled fear rather than seeking answers, and assisted the public with operating intelligently.

Dr. Kelly saw that the discussions of wearing masks and using PPE were nonsensical, even for the fallible human resources in public health departments. During that time, she received calls from colleagues in the military and air force around the world, all asking her what she had heard. One pilot who called her was in Asia. "I don't know. You're at the epicenter of this thing. Are you seeing anything on the ground?"

He wasn't seeing people passing out in the streets like what we eventually saw on the televisions. That's when her lightbulb went off. The overzealous response wasn't in alignment with what doctors like Kelly were seeing clinically. The first time she was banned from every social media platform was the third week of February in 2020. At that time most people still had literally no idea whatsoever that there was a virus or anything out of the ordinary. She had simply stated, "this is a lab created virus, not a genetically occurring virus." Although Dr. Kelly is neither a geneticist nor biologist, she understood how to analyze the virus structure.

"This has the fingerprints of being lab generated," She began to share with other doctors and the public at-large.

And that was the last of Kelly's social media ministry… at least for a little while. Dr. Kelly wasn't going to sit down and shut up: she was going to shout.

Victory explains that what she saw in the COVID-19 virus was not genetically created. She explains that it was easy to spot: like she was looking at a Word document written in Times New Roman, but she caught a word every few sentences in Calibri; she knew they "cut and pasted and spliced" the genetic sequence in some regions of the virus.

Prior to actually studying the genetic sequencing, Dr. Kelly admits that she bought the wet market propaganda during January of 2020. Having spent some time at wet markets in China, she recalls that there are countless varieties of animals in various forms of horrific squalor. However, in February of 2020 when she saw the genetic sequencing, she knew the virus came from a lab. At that time, she was the only person who seemed to know about the lab-generated origins of COVID-19… aside, of course, from the death doctors and scientists behind it, such as Dr. Fauci.

Something downright miraculous happened in January 2020, and it wasn't merely that Dr. Kelly briefly got fooled by the virus story. During the third week of January, Kelly ruptured her Achilles tendon. This type of injury doesn't just hurt; it completely immobilizes you. She was stuck at home after a massive surgery to recover. Instead of binging on Netflix shows or chugging too much Lite beer, which I might have done in her seat, Dr. Kelly devoted this time to studying and reading. Having spent her career in medical management and emergencies, including mass casualties and pandemics, as well as her work with Continental, which has a massive footprint in Asia, she knew how a pandemic threat would be handled.

But what she saw didn't align with what she had done during her thirty-five year career. The masking and social distancing were foreign to her; even though she had been directly in charge with pandemics in the past and chiefly responsible for preventing as many deaths as possible. She called everybody she knew with a big platform and told them to give her the mic; she wanted somebody to find a single instance in history where "social distancing" was used, much less even mentioned in pandemic response.

She particularly seethed when officials such as Dr. Fauci talked about social distancing as if it were standard protocol. "It wasn't a thing, not ever," she told me, "but social distancing and masks were something to me: a talisman. You'd be better off putting a clove of garlic around your neck; it's pure kabuki."

As the director for many other emergencies including pandemics, she pointed out that lockdowns were never employed for good reason. They do far more harm than good; they aren't just a nuisance, but they penalize people who aren't at risk. In a common sense scenario you quarantine the few to protect the many, not quarantine the many to protect the few. What's more, she pointed out that lockdowns disrupt the supply chain. In fact, UNICEF estimates that a quarter million children would starve to death globally by a disruption in the food chain, according to Victory. Of course, that has been leveraged in today's media to propose that we send more money to the Ukraine. I can't make this up.[43]

In January 2020, healthcare professionals and doctors experienced in emergency response and pandemics, such as Dr. Kelly Victory, were confident that young people had *zero* risk from the COVID-19 virus. They understood that those with obesity, diabetes, and heart issues were the primary high-risk categories. Kelly knew early on that vitamin D deficiency would be a huge factor in survival.

Exposing Fraud

Dr. Kelly became the daily voice for the "doctor hour" on KABC 790 AM radio in California. "The John Phillips Show" in Los Angeles is a major-market radio talk show that covers a wide range of issues from local California to national politics. Phillips is also a frequent guest on cable news as a political commentator and writes for "The Orange County Register." Phillips granted Dr. Kelly a full hour of his show, which was on air from 1:00 - 3:00 Pacific Time. For eighteen months, Phillips gave Dr. Kelly half his show, from 1:00 - 2:00 p.m. Pacific Time.

Dr. Kelly could freely discuss what she saw daily on Phillips' show. She worked to expose everything that looked fishy (outside of the wet market) and spoke frankly about who was at risk, who wasn't, and what treatments for COVID-19 she knew of that were safe and effective. She discussed that the "vaccine" was coming and that it was a bad idea. Before COVID-19, people thought Dr. Kelly was a vaccine zealot! However, she had huge reservations about the shot that was coming down the pipeline for four main reasons:

1. There's a darn good reason we haven't had a vaccine for a respiratory virus; they mutate too quickly.

43. https://www.unicef.org/press-releases/global-hunger-crisis-pushing-one-child-severe-malnutrition-every-minute-15-crisis

2. mRNA is a dicey platform we've worked with for decades. Sometimes all the animals die in an experiment or clinical trial.
3. There's a reason vaccines take six to eight years to come to market. There are a lot of viruses for which we've never had a vaccine. There's no substitute for time - there's only one way to get twelve, twenty-four, or thirty-six months of safety data.
4. At that time the vaccine was predicated on the spike protein. That was insane to Dr. Kelly. She points out that the spike protein is the area of the virus that would immediately mutate. In short, the virus will have mutated out of that spike protein before anybody got jabbed; you'd be forever fighting last year's war. In a later chapter I'll go further into explaining how the spike protein plays into adverse events and, ultimately, the genocide.

Thanks to John Phillips and KABC Radio, every day Dr. Kelly was on air in California exposing the fraud around her saying that she smelled a rat. She freely called out that our American (and global) pandemic response was a scam. Although she wasn't getting paid for Phillips' show, she felt the satisfaction of knowing that she could wake people up, in California no less.

Cumulus Radio owned the station that aired Phillips' show. They said that they loved having Dr. Kelly on but that she couldn't say anything negative about the "vaccines." Victory believes that the station and its owners were genuinely deceived into thinking that they could be held liable for anything negative Dr. Kelly said about the "vaccine" if people died.

It was around this time that Dr. Kelly created the "Facts Not Fear" mantra and hashtag. She stood her ground stating that you can't lead from a place of fear; it goes against any biological capacity to make good decisions. Parents, teachers, political leaders, or doctors like Kelly must make decisions from their rational minds, not their monkey minds, when exercising anything from disciplining a toddler to leading mass casualty events, like Dr. Kelly.

Victory told the station that it was her responsibility to tell the honest, unvarnished truth. She stopped broadcasting in California but still receives emails, texts, and DMs weekly from people who share with her that they believe she saved their lives or the lives of their family members. With her Facts Over Fear message, she didn't just keep people from getting jabbed; she kept people sane.

Facts Not Fear

Nearly four years after Dr. Kelly began broadcasting, she's been wholly vindicated. She led Dr. Drew Pinsky to the light after appearing on his show and, at first, arguing and debating with him about her research. Even Dr. Fauci eventually admitted that the six-foot-distancing rule was made up. He has admitted that face masks don't stop anything and that asymptomatic people don't spread viruses. What's more, people finally realize that if they don't have symptoms of a virus, they shouldn't be shoving swabs up their noses. She admits, "if somebody healthy came in for a test I'd think they were loopy with a mental disorder."

Vindication doesn't undo the hurt Dr. Kelly feels for humanity. The mandates, lockdowns, masks, distancing, and nonstop COVID-19 PCR tests weren't merely a nuisance but dehumanizing. These measures aggravated people's asthma, allergies, upper respiratory issues, gingival disease, and dental disease, and we have an entire generation of children who have not learned to speak correctly because kids who are learning to speak need to see mouths move. They don't entirely learn to talk by what they hear but by mimicking mouth movements. Prohibiting the ability to see faces leads children to develop, among other things, social-emotional suppression as well. Kids must read facial and non-verbal cues to see what people are "really" saying.

In short, we won't know for decades how this psyop really impacted our kids and how many of them are going to have social anxiety or even versions of autism after having been masked, placed in front of high-stimulating cartoons and video games, and jabbed incessantly. There are people who, even today, won't give up the mask in airports, grocery stores, and for the particularly stupid ones, in restaurants.

The masks have become, for some people, like a swaddle is for a baby. When you take a newborn baby and wrap it up tightly, it loses the use of its arms and legs. It loses all autonomy. But with that loss of independence, the baby feels safe. That's normal for a newborn baby, but we aren't supposed to feel that way as adults. We aren't supposed to relish the feeling of losing autonomy. That shouldn't make people feel secure; it should cause alarm. However, a portion of the population has been so psychologically damaged that they won't sit in a seat that hasn't been swabbed down with alcohol or touch anything without hormone-disrupting hand sanitizers.

We've created a culture of people who bathe in Purell and wait for the government to make things safe for them. They're easy to control. They think they can sanitize life. In essence, this is a population of non-resilient people. Resilience is based on being able to face adversity and overcome it.

Some of these kids are stuck at a point in time. And that's a dangerous harbinger for the future.

Dr. Kelly has always been outspoken with a healthy distrust for authority and a tremendous distrust for the biopharmaceutical complex. She has understood long before COVID that the scientific training and labs are owned by pharmaceutical companies, as are the major medical journals such as the Lancet, JAMA, New England Journal of Medicine, etc. They're fundamentally the marketing arm for pharmaceutical companies. Even medical schools are owned by big pharma. So we're living in a propagandized system, and that makes it an uphill battle to get the truth.

For Victory, the COVID-19 pandemic represented an existential crisis. Because of COVID-19, she realized that so many other things she believed were fraudulent. She began asking, "What's the real story about other vaccines?"

She began asking why there was a rush to market for an mRNA vaccine based on a spike protein. She points out that there's a reason you don't rush out a vaccine program in the middle of a pandemic. It drives mutations. She went down the rabbit hole, reading books like "Turtles All The Way Down," and recognizing that it doesn't stop with vaccines, but it'll be oncology drugs and other treatments. The breadth of what she discovered and the implications for the future of medicine based on the sloppiness of our response to the COVID-19 plandemic shattered Dr. Kelly. Still, they invigorated her when she learned the importance of "Facts over Fear."

In 2024 Dr. Kelly joined The Wellness Company in hopes of helping other people who are trying to return some element of integrity to healthcare and reestablish people's confidence. It's said that less than 32% of people trust their doctors today, and for good reason. Doctors have become middle managers in a corporatocracy where insurance companies and hospital administrative staff with no medical training direct surgeons, doctors and nurses on hitting KPI's for the bottom line rather than for patient care and the directive of "doing no harm," and The Wellness Company wrote an entire book about this called "The Next Wave is Brave," which nobody should enter another hospital nor doctor's office without reading.

Dr. Kelly and I share a unique burden in seeing so many of our colleagues have started out with good intentions, motivated by healthcare, truth, sound science, and the Hippocratic Oath. So many of them, however, turned their backs on sound science truth and "doing no harm" because of the propaganda. Too few have woken up to say, "I promoted some things that were plain wrong; I was wrong. I feel remorse, and I will speak up about it." Instead, we see our colleagues bury their heads in the sand and comply.

In our introduction I briefly mentioned the concepts of mass formation psychosis, Stockholm Syndrome and cognitive dissonance. So as not to bore my readers, I haven't wrangled up every last term and historical event into one chapter, but I've dispersed them throughout the book, starting with the underlying psychological phenomena we've witnessed in recent years.

In the following chapter we'll look at a history of compliance in our country that gave the COVID-19 plandemic overlords and puppet masters the ability to bamboozle millions of healthcare workers to comply with a social experiment and untested gene therapy on our own American soil.

Chapter Eight
The Eighth Deadly Sin: Compliance

You give the whole world a shot, but you still got people starving?
Oh, you better take this shot you better take it! It's to save your life.
And it's free. We giving it free because it's to save everybody's life.
If it's to save lives, why ain't chemotherapy free? Why ain't insulin free?
If it's to save everybody's life.
So it's to save my life?
But you got people dying of malnutrition.
And we can't plant a garden over there?
But we can send shots everywhere around the world?!
Somebody better open their eyes!"

Apostle Herman L. Murray

In the fourteenth century, poet Dante Alighieri penned "The Divine Comedy," an imaginative narrative describing the afterlife, today considered one of the most significant pieces of literature in the Western world. In this poem he identifies "seven deadly vices" that tempt the soul due to the fall of man. These vices include: pride or vanity; envy or jealousy; wrath or anger; sloth or laziness; avarice (greed); gluttony; and lust.

In my book, there's an eighth deadly vice, like intellectual sloth and stupidity. It afflicts the ignorant, which, as recent history proves, is the majority of society both on U.S. soil and abroad. That deadly vice is compliance.

Throughout history, bad actors have recruited others to manifest their deadly schemes through compliance. Although there could be (and probably are) many volumes detailing compliance throughout history, I'll quickly breeze through just a handful that rightfully come up almost daily in conversations between me and my "non-compliant" peers.

Third Reich Compliance

Compliance is a huge deal and in a later chapter we'll dive into more evidence of censorship and threats having fueled the COVID-19 genocide. Having your "soldiers," "doctors," and even "pastors" comply with evil is nothing new. This didn't start with the Third Reich, but it didn't end there either.

One of the stories that breaks my heart more than any story on earth is the story of German worshippers one Sunday standing and singing in a church. As the story goes, when the train went by carry Jews in cattle cars towards the torture chambers, the parishoner asked the organist to turn up the music so that the worshippers wouldn't be distracted by the screaming of the Jews on the train.

This happened during COVID-19 as well when pastors told their congregations to comply—some forced masks. There were a lot of sheep and wayward shepherds in the churches who exposed themselves in 2020. Thankfully, there were some heroes, too. Steph's pastor, Jim Tarr, in Basalt, Colorado, fought the public health department to the point of being threatened with jail, not only himself but his entire brave staff at their Christian school.[44]

Throughout this chapter, I want you to remember that compliance isn't merely burying your head in the sand. It's being an accomplice to murder. Here are a few examples.

The Tuskegee Experiment

Also in the 1940's was the Tuskegee Syphilis Study, usually referred to as the "Tuskegee Experiment." U.S. Public Health Services (PHS) misled

---

44. https://www.youtube.com/@cornerstonechristiancenter7895/videos

African American men who were told that they were being treated for "bad blood" from syphilis. In truth, they weren't being treated for anything. The study aimed to track the natural progression of *untreated syphilis.*[45] The study participants were denied penicillin when it became the standard therapy for syphilis. When the men sought care from other doctors, PHS intervened so that they would suffer and remain without treatment. The study participants were offered meals, medical exams and burial insurance as incentives to make them more dependent and compliant for the duration of the study, which lasted from 1932 to 1972.

Tuskegee is a modern day example of what happens when people trust authority and put faith in their doctors. I'm a healthcare professional who aims to save lives every day. I would think that you, no matter who you are, will be safest in my hands. But do I trust other healthcare professionals? *Hell no.* Like the Tuskegee experiment, it is my understanding that when we put our health in the hands of medical "authorities," what we end up with is becoming the rats in a study about disease progression rather than disease management or healing.

If there was something really wrong with me or my kid, I would call one of The Wellness Company doctors, past or present or somebody who worked with AFLDS (America's Frontline Doctors) when they were first established; the doctors who went against the COVID-19 narrative and evacuated their traditional places of work. These doctors have the gumption and courage to break out of a system and they're probably getting paid in peanuts to do it compared to at major medical centers. They are men and women of conviction in their hippocratic oath.

Joe Blow surgeon or Gary the GP down the street? **He's not working for you**, your kids, nor your parents. He's working for the incentives he gets to jab as many people as possible or as a slave to corporate hospital and insurance company figureheads who give him KPIs that have nothing to do, I repeat, ***nothing to do with helping you get better.***

---

45. https://www.unicefusa.org/press/global-hunger-crisis-pushing-one-child-severe-malnutrition-every-minute-15-crisis-hit

Operation Paperclip

The Central Intelligence Agency or CIA hasn't been around since the Revolutionary War or even the Civil War. In fact, it's a relatively modern construct, and by construct I mean a satanic blight on our nation. In a moment, you'll see why.

The CIA, not yet eighty years old, was officially formed under the National Security Act of 1947, replacing the Office of Strategic Services (OSS), the previous intelligence agency that battled Axis powers. It was ostensibly formed to collect intelligence and inform national security, but the focus of its mention in this book will center around covert operations not against global threats, but against its own U.S. brethren.

Operation Paperclip was a secret program conducted by the United States after World War II. Prior to Operation Paperclip, the U.S. didn't have a bioweapons program, but that was going to change.

The U.S. Government recruited scientists, engineers, and technicians, many of whom had worked for Nazi Germany, mainly in the fields of technology, rocketry, aerospace, and chemical weapons. When the operation was authorized by President Harry Truman in 1945, officials were under the expectation not to recruit committed Nazi members; but that restriction was ignored. Over 1,600 German scientists and engineers were brought to the U.S., many of whom were known to have been involved in war crimes, including experimentation on humans. Some of these despicable doctors, including some brought to the U.S. from Japan, are reputed to have been performing surgeries that removed infected organs from patients without anesthesia. Then we got these soulless sickos to Fort Deitrich. From there, they became the heads of our American hospitals. Classic.

Operation Paperclip is credited with helping American advancements in aerospace, defense, and nuclear technology, the U.S. missile program, and the establishment of NASA. Does that also mean they recruited German videographers and filmmakers? There sure was a lot of creative cinematic license during that time.

MKUltra

MKUltra was a secret CIA program that aimed to investigate and develop techniques for mind control, behavioral modification, and interrogation. It ran from the early 1950s until it was supposedly halted in 1973, although many high-profile celebrities claim that it is still being used in Hollywood and the claims surrounding MKUltra mind control and individuals like Beyonce (witch alter ego "Sasha Fierce") Jay-Z (warlock alter ego "Hova,") and Kanye West (who knows what he's called anymore, I left the conversation after he was "Ye,") are claimed to be under the CIA programming.

The roots run deep with MKUltra and Hollywood, and if you want to learn more you need to pick up the book "Weird Scenes Inside The Canyon" by David McGowan. This book details the dark, demonic side of the 1960s and 70s music scene with terrifying evidence that the Byrds, the Doors, Buffalo Springfield, the Monkees, the Beach Boys, the Turtles, the Eagles, the Flying Burrito Brothers, Frank Zappa and the Mothers of Invention, CSN, Three Dog night, Joni Mitchell, Judy Collins, James Tarylor and Carole King were all a part of blood-soaked psyops and murders, if not political operatives themselves. There is absolutely a reason so many of these and other celebrities in Hollywood and music die mysteriously, and die young.[46]

Among the preeminent whistleblowers on MKUltra mind control is Cathy O'Brien, author of "TRANCE Formation of America." From the book's description, "The book was released in 1995 after the 1947 National Security Act was invoked to censor this testimony from the US Congressional Permanent Select Committee on Intelligence Oversight. The book, now in its 16th English edition, is referenced in major universities and is in law libraries worldwide due to its continued relevance to global events."[47]

Cathy O'Brien's story surged in popularity in 2020 after people saw the blatant mind control being used, especially such things as "six foot distancing," which was too obviously a ritual taken directly from satanic rituals, or the CIA's "Operation Mockingbird" media manipulation, which

46. https://a.co/d/2wJeSPD

47. https://a.co/d/iN4PLTx

many people saw through when hearing news anchors and journalists all repeat some of the same mantras, such as the oversimplified and overused phrase "safe and effective," intentionally the title of this book because it served as a harbinger for so many who read between the lines and knew that the upcoming "vaccine" would prove to be neither safe nor effective. As a rule, with a media owned in large part by leftist organizations and personalities, it's "safe" to assume that nothing they tell you is safe actually is.

MKUltra involved the use of drugs, hypnosis, sensory deprivation and psychological manipulation. It allegedly started in 1953 during the height of the Cold War under the direction of former CIA director Allen Dulles. The CIA invested time experimenting on our own American citizens ways that they could control or manipulate human behavior under the guise of national security. LSD was used as a truth serum because it would make subjects more susceptible to suggestion provided they were being interrogated. Unfortunately, a gaggle of unknowing hippies would be the test dummies in the 1960's rock and roll movement, hence the tales of rampant murders and early deaths among young people in the rock and roll scene that are detailed in David McGowan's book previously mentioned, "Weird Scenes from Inside the Canyon."

What did MKULtra mind control experiments have in common with the COVID-19 jab? Neither relied on informed consent. As recently as October of 2024 I couldn't find a "vaccine insert" (or the insert was left blank) that accompanied the COVID-19 jabs which described risks of the inoculation. MKUltra experiments were conducted on prisoners, mental health patients, and even ordinary citizens. Many of the experiments took place in hospitals, prisons and universities.

Again, not much diversion from what we experienced in 2021.

I'm not a historian nor a PhD professor. But I can put some dots together. When the vast majority of physicians are employed by a large hospital or physician group and coerced to push "vaccines" or lose their jobs, unfortunately we saw what happened. The hospitals stayed in business. The doctors kept their jobs. The public received their jabs. All of these entities complied. And then, a lot of people died.

The real coup to manipulate physicians didn't even rely on mind control to an extent, but merely ignorance. "Well, if the CDC and NIH say this…" The naive trust in "authorities" at three-letter agencies plainly has to stop in this country.

Dr. Kelly Victory cites some of the psyops just mentioned, including the syphilis experiments, MKUltra, and the Tuskegee experiments, as evidence that our current epidemic of doctors who don't think critically is nothing new. She quotes John Milton, who said that untested virtue is not virtue. If you can't think critically, you shouldn't be in medicine. When she began speaking Facts Over Fear, Dr. Victory was trolled, criticized, slandered, and threatened. She had her license threatened seven times in places like Colorado, North Carolina, Ohio, and elsewhere. Dr. Harvey Risch, whom Stephanie worked with on "The Next Wave is Brave" and co-authored "Toxic Shock" with Victory, was paramount in talking Dr. Kelly off the edge and encouraging her to keep going.

Something that fueled Dr. Kelly Victory's purpose in the hard times was caring for her fellow physicians and focusing on those willing to wake up. One case in point is that of Dr. Drew Pinsky. Dr. Kelly and Dr. Drew have known one another for thirty-five years, and when Dr. Drew learned that Dr. Kelly was being egregiously censored, he invited her to be on his show weekly and then bi-weekly. He initially fell for some of the rhetoric around the "pandemic."

Victory brought Ed Dowd, Dr. Harvey Risch, Dr. Jessica Rose, Dr. Peter McCullough, and Senator Ron Johnson to Dr. Drew's show. Over eighteen months, he transitioned from being a fan of Remdesivir and three-time COVID-19 jabbed to being, well, where he is now: a doctor on staff at The Wellness Company and a voice in the resistance and awakening.

With gain of function being performed on "Bird Flu" in the United States, or H5N1, this is a smoking gun that bird flu will be the next bioweapon unleashed. The mutated virus from the gain of function lab in Athens, Georgia already caused three cases of bird flu, which Victory believes has to do with culling our food supply… which involves culling huge herds of birds or poultry. What herds they don't cull they are vaccinating with mRNA vaccines.

I don't mention bird flu, gain-of-function research, or even bioweapons to fuel fear. As mentioned in the previous chapter, Facts over Fear is the key to staying sane when the world turns upside down, which it will again. But like Dr. Kelly, I am surprised to see the slow roll of evil. Victor says, "I thought the end times would be a cataclysmic explosion; I didn't fathom that it could be this slow, insidious downward spiral."

Like me, Dr. Kelly's threats have extended to death threats. Like me, she is not suicidal; but she has been afraid for her life at times.

Please keep my friend and fellow warrior Kelly Victory in your prayers, as you have kept me in them, too.

Chapter Nine
A Dead Family

Shortly after the rollout of the death shots I was still in New York in a Manhattan hospital, sitting in a waiting room with a cup of watery Folgers Coffee in a styrofoam cup. I was exhausted, laying my head back with my body slumped over the chair where I saw, from a television in the corner of the waiting room, the President took the stage. He promised that the "vaccine" would soon be available for all ages. He urged Americans to reclaim their lives and freedom by heading out of their homes and getting jabbed immediately.

The President stated that people wouldn't get COVID if they had their shot, and they wouldn't die. Curiously, I wasn't seeing the same thing on the ground. In my line of work, it was *when* people took the shot that they were at the highest risk of death.

"This doesn't make sense," I thought. "These hospitals have been empty, but suddenly we're seeing people get these jabs and we're busy again with emergency calls?"

In the preceding several months, I was inundated with fear, myself. Every time I walked into a patient's home, the fear was palpable. Every time I walked into the ICU or ER, you could cut the fear with a knife. Fear has a presence. If you have an abusive parent, you're walking on eggshells. I wrestled with getting angry with my fellow healthcare workers for kowtowing to the government mandates and fear messaging, but ultimately settled on forgiving and having compassion for my colleagues and being mad at the parents for abusing them: at the government for creating this terrifying environment with media that was staying alive through blasting lies. The "news" has always stayed afloat with the Jonbenet Ramsey or homicide stories, but this was open season on gruesome clickbait. It's unconscionable to me that we would put a society of scared children in front of highly dramatized R-rated movies; but that's essentially what the media did. Rarely did you see the stories of doctors such as Vladimir Zelenko, MD, who had almost no deaths in his entire practice in New York due to his wise use of Hydroxychloroquine and the "Zelenko Protocol." In my estimation, Zelenko's story should have been Top News every night of the week and played on repeat in the hospitals so that the staff understood how to do their jobs: save patients.

Just weeks after a massive COVID "vaccine" push on the reservation where I was working, we had just intubated our nurse manager. The nurse developed multiple pulmonary embolisms and clots in her lungs.

Another nurse standing next to me held back tears as we life-flighted our colleague to what was hopefully going to be a higher level of care. The nurse next to me was understandably sad for her colleague, but also still wrecked after her husband was also lost just one day after his own "vaccine," to a heart attack.

One week later, this woman's brother-in-law also died of a heart attack.

Within one week of taking the shot, she lost her husband, her brother in-law, and now she was watching our nurse manager, her friend, life-flighted due to this poison.

After the chopper lifted and the dust settled, the nurse looked at me and said, "I still haven't taken the shot, and won't." The hospital eventually fired her for declining, even though she had lost and witnessed so much. This seasoned nurse had been with that hospital for over twenty years.

If you think that the powers that be didn't know that they were harming us, keep reading.

In watching this and so many deaths due to this shot, I witnessed America, "land of the free and home of the brave," die in my arms.

I watched what my grandfather fought and bled for burn to the ground.

A lot of middle-aged men and women died, but so did the unborn souls from within their mothers wombs. These mothers had one job: to keep those babies safe. Sadly, due to the rampant propaganda and psychological manipulation, they neglected their duty and their children paid the price, not to mention the psychological trauma induced to fathers, siblings, grandparents, and the mothers themselves.

Right after the "vaccine" was offered to pregnant women we saw a surge in spontaneous abortion, which means miscarriages. The amount of people losing their children was horrific. It was like a maternal holocaust.

As a paramedic I saw nine patients miscarry in just one shift. That's just one single shift; one day of hundreds. The bleeding was so bad that I had to have additional staff help clean up multiple times. To put it in perspective, I wasnt accustomed to seeing an emergency for a stillbirth or miscarriage more than once every four to six months. What I was seeing is *not* normal.

One time while working in an emergency room a Physician's Assistant (PA) approached me. I don't commonly complain on the job, much less reveal all my true thoughts about the jabs immediately ,but I started a conversation with the PA. "This shift has sucked ass. Have you ever seen this many miscarriages in one shift?"

He stated, "No, this is like nothing I've ever seen."

I admitted, "I've been asking them if they took their COVID vaccine. It seems these vaccines are the common theme."

To which the PA responded, "Yea, something is way way wrong, it's frightening."

"I've done CPR in a Pfizer line, so I know they're dangerous."

"Harry, to be honest, I'm going to just put my head in the sand here. This is just too big."

Hearing him literally admit to willful denial was a blow to the gut.

A short time later I find myself rushing to the scene of a stillbirth. A woman screams, "God bring back my baby! This can't be happening to us. This can't be real!"

I'm in the ambulance with the woman, who's wailing in grief and terror, having just given birth to a dead baby.

The woman is not wearing pants, so I've covered her with a blanket from the waist down. I initiated treatment for blood loss and possible shock before we entered the ambulance. The patient's baby is in the vehicle with us, but he is not viable. The woman's husband is driving behind the ambulance.

I'm seated on the bench seat close to the patient, with her hand in mine. Although her face is just two feet away, she yells, "I did everything right. Why did God do this to us?"

This is the same question I wrestled with in my son Harry's second year of life as he presented with more emotional distance and never began forming words. I don't tell her what I know, that God didn't do this to her and her husband. They did. We did this. It doesn't make it hurt any less, and there's no way I can bring comfort to this woman by telling her now.

"I'm very sorry," I replied.

"Have you had any other pregnancies? Any negative health history? Do you take any medications?"

The woman has softened her voice. She whimpers and replies, "Just my vitamins. No. My first pregnancy."

"Did you take any COVID vaccines?"

"No. But my husband had to for his job. I didn't take any."

"Did he take them before or after you were pregnant?"

"Before. Why… does that matter?"

"I have seen a lot of miscarriages since the release of the COVID shots."

The patient dropped her head and began crying more. She immediately referenced God when I brought her into the ambulance, so I asked her if she would like to pray. She nodded. I prayed for her strength, and I pray today that God has granted this couple a healthy child.

Most of the miscarriages I've seen since 2021 have been from "vaccinated" mothers. Still, it isn't unheard of to see miscarriages in women whose baby had a father "vaccinated" at the time of conception. Due to the tremendous amount of death among those who've taken these shots, I think that most abnormalities these days should be deemed mRNA-related until *proven* otherwise.

This new technology is dangerous and has not been adequately studied before being administered to billions on purpose. Rest in peace to all the murdered children—prayers of peace for the grieving parents.

When you consider the deaths from the shots, don't forget deaths of the unborn.

Poem: Harsh Reality

A nation in tatters, weary and worn.
Where the wealthy feast, yet the poor are left torn.
The wealthy grow richer, their pockets now swell,
While the needy whisper through their living hell.

Youth held captive on islands of gold,
Judicial secrets leaving clients untold.
Horrors kept hidden, justice unsung,
Though peasants wait in line for their turn to be hung.

Victims once hopeful, by this system betrayed.
In depths of despair, their fates are now weighed.
Awaiting the noose, in shadows they stand.
A grim dance of fate, at society's hand.

I am praying for the people. For all of us.

Part Two

Connecting The Dots

Chapter Ten

The Most Hated Doctor In America

Since the government controls the hospitals, it also controls the physicians. They don't care about healing people but about profit.

Dr. Jim Thorp

On May 8th, 2024, "InfoWars" posted an article in their Science & Tech section titled, "OBGYN Doctor Calls On Attorneys To Sue Institutions That Forced 'Dangerous' COVID Shots on Babies & Pregnant Women."

Dr. James Thorp states in the article, "This should make tobacco litigation look like chump change." Dr Thorp is a Board-Certified Obstetrician Gynecologist and Maternal Fetal Medicine Physician with over forty-three years of obstetrical experience and has served (and still serves) as a clinician. He has also produced approximately 200 publications and remains active in clinical research. In the past three years, at the time of this writing, Dr. Thorp has seen over 22,800 high-risk pregnancies. He has published several peer-reviewed scientific publications documenting the dangers of the vaccine in women of reproductive age and pregnancy, calling the COVID-19 "vaccination" experiment one of "the greatest disasters in the history of medicine."[48]

On June 24th, 2024, Preprints.org published a study that Dr. Thorp co-authored with highly esteemed colleagues in various capacities in healthcare titled "COVID-19 Vaccines in Pregnancy as Safe and Effective as the U.S.

---

48. https://www.americaoutloud.news/author/jim-thorp-md-and-maggie-thorp/

Government, Medical Organizations, and Pharmaceutical Industry Claim?"[49] Any good doctor in obstetrics should have been asking this question.

The contributors to this study all had not only expertise, but some of them had horrific firsthand experiences that compelled them to contribute to speaking out in hopes of awakening others. One such contributor is Albert Benavides, an expert on the Vaccine Adverse Event Reporting System[50] who has analyzed deficiencies in the VAERS system, concluding that these deficiencies contribute to a substantial underreporting of serious adverse events and death. Benavides has a background in HMO claims auditing, data analytics, medical billing and revenue cycle management and has claimed that VAERS operates with two parallel systems, only one of which is available to the public. It is because of Benavides' brave work that people like Denis Rancourt were able to compile the all-cause mortality data he presented and which we briefly analyze in a later chapter.

Also in the study is Maggie Thorp, JD, a commercial litigation attorney whose law practice has involved both corporate bad faith and corporate fraud. Dr. Daniel McDyer contributed to this study as well, a Board-Certified doctor of Obstetrics and Gynecology. Also contributing is Dr. Kimberly Biss, a board-certified OB-GYN who has once said of her involvement in speaking out against the shots, "I've never seen this before … the miscarriage rate doubled again in 2022, all the way up to a staggering 15%. After seeing what was happening with my patients, I just couldn't stay quiet anymore." Dr. Biss appeared before Congress in 2023 to address the miscarriages following the shots.

Julie Threet contributed to this study, as well. Threet is a former Silicon Valley HR executive who worked in partnership with California's Butte County Public health to serve hospitals for several years before the jabs rolled out in 2022. She received two Moderna shots and, sadly, had adverse events just afterwards, beginning with lesions in her brain.

---

49. https://www.preprints.org/manuscript/202406.2062/v1

50. https://vaers.hhs.gov/

Threet later learned of women having menstrual disruptions in the clinics where she worked. Then, she witnessed athletes from Chico State University coming in with seizures and fainting. An alarm went off: Threet knew the jab rollout program had far too many side effects. One day, a healthy young man entered the clinic where she worked to get his jabs because he wanted to run track. The young man began seizing the moment the shot entered his system. All around Julie in the clinic were thousands of other people getting shots. The young man was down for fifteen minutes, and, to Julie's horror, ambulances were not called. But from that moment forward, Julie began speaking with her daughter, who worked at the clinic at the Alameda County fairgrounds (Julie was at the fairgrounds in Chico), about the adverse events and reactions to the COVID-19 jabs they were both seeing. Her daughter was told that the response was expected. Still, Julie observed that based upon chatter amongst healthcare workers, the seizure and other immediate reactions to the shots, and the fact that no patient was offered informed consent, something was *not* expected.

Shortly after her shots, Julie experienced a detached retina, basal ganglia, blood clots in her brain, and tinnitus. Yes, something was definitely awry. When her mother suddenly died of cardiac arrest after her fourth shot, Julie looked up own batch number on "How Bad Is My Batch"[51] and found that her Moderna batch was at the top of the list for vaccine injuries. Julie began analyzing vaccine deaths with the help of the system coded and created by Albert Benavidez, who noticed that among the problems with the VAERS reporting system was the fact that 99% of vaccine injuries are allegedly not reported, and also that the system times out every 20 minutes, making it impossible for many of these reports to get published.[52] Threet has become an ardent activist in working to hold communities accountable for recognizing patterns in bad batches and warning their constituents.

The final contributor to this paper called, "Are COVID-19 Vaccines in Pregnancy as Safe and Effective as the U.S. Government,

51. www.hotbadismybatch.com

52. https://www.bitchute.com/channel/HEpBeuAz9n9P/

Medical Organizations, and Pharmaceutical Industry Claim?" is Dr. Peter McCullough, an internist, cardiologist, epidemiologist who has dozens of peer-reviewed publications on the infection and has commented extensively on the medical response to the COVID-19 crisis. Dr. McCullough testified multiple times in the US Senate, Texas Senate Committee on Health and Human Services, Arizona Senate and House of Representatives, Colorado General Assembly, New Hampshire Senate, Pennsylvania Senate, and South Carolina Senate concerning many aspects of the pandemic response and is one of the most widely published cardiologists of all time, worldwide.

These contributors and their stories represent not only intellectual gray matter behind the study, but celebrates the courageous humans who have chosen the path of hard work and becoming targets in the public eye to spread the truth.

I know many intelligent people who are awake but do nothing about it. You'll read a lot about that later in the book when I begin talking about fear porn and controlled opposition. Those who choose research and study instead of golfing on a Sunday afternoon are called "conspiracy theorists." Those who choose collaboration with other lions are called "grifters." I pause in this book to celebrate these conspiracy-theorizing misinformation spreaders because they didn't always choose golfing or fishing on the weekends; they are storing treasures in heaven. The people mentioned in this book would drop everything to take my call. The anti-COVID-19 "vaccine" personalities are different parts of the body. We are warriors against the "pharmaceutical industrial complex," as Dr. McCullough calls it. And we need every human to join that body so that we aren't merely "David against Goliath" but the truth-tellers and dissidents who destroy Goliath.

In the June 24, 2024 paper, Dr. Thorp et al., those badasses I just mentioned, collected data from the CDC, FDA, and VAERS from January 1, 1990, to April 26, 2024. They specifically queried adverse events involving pregnancy complications following COVID-19 "vaccination," but they compared it with all complications over a period of 412 months. They then also compared the data to adverse events after influenza vaccination and other vaccines administered to pregnant women.

The group found that the CDC/FDA's safety signals were breached for all 37 adverse events following COVID-19 vaccination in pregnancy, including miscarriage, fetal chromosomal abnormality, fetal malformation, cervical insufficiency, premature rupture of membranes, premature labor, premature delivery, placental calcification, placental infarction, placental thrombosis, placenta accreta, placental abruption, placental insufficiency, placental disorder, fetal maternal hemorrhage, fetal growth restriction, reduced amniotic fluid volume, preeclampsia, fetal heart rate abnormality, fetal cardiac disorder, fetal vascular mal-perfusion, fetal arrhythmia, fetal distress, fetal biophysical profile abnormal, hemorrhage in pregnancy, fetal cardiac arrest, fetal death (stillbirth), premature infant death, neonatal asphyxia, neonatal dyspnea, neonatal infection, neonatal hemorrhage, insufficient breast milk, neonatal pneumonia, neonatal respiratory distress, neonatal respiratory distress syndrome, and neonatal seizure.

The authors of this study call for an immediate global moratorium on COVID-19 vaccination during pregnancy, claiming that "the United States government, medical organizations, hospitals, and pharmaceutical companies have misled and/or deceived the public regarding the safety of COVID-19 vaccination in pregnancy. Promotion of these products must be immediately halted."[53]

Among the many statistics one may pull from Dr. Thorp's research include the following:

Cognitive disorders in the COVID-19 vaccine versus influenza vaccines have a risk ratio of 87.0. The FDA uses a risk ratio of 2.0 as a breach of safety signal. Suicide or suicidal ideation in the COVID-19 shot versus influenza vaccine has a risk ratio of 186, with 2.0 indicating a breach of safety signal as determined by the FDA. Psychiatric illness in the COVID-19 jab versus influenza vaccine has a risk ratio of 188, with 2.0 being a breach of safety signal as determined by the FDA.

53. https://www.preprints.org/manuscript/202406.2062/v1

Cognitive Disorders - Risk Ratio for COVID-19 Vaccines
Versus Other Vaccines by FDA Database
FDA Uses a Risk Ratio of 2 as a BREACH of Safety Signal

• COVID-19 versus Influenza vaccines the Risk Ratio is 87.0 with a
95% Confidence Interval of 60.5-125, with a Z Statistic of 24.2,
and a p-value < 0.0001

• COVID-19 versus ALL OTHER Vaccines the Risk Ratio is 23.7 with a
95% Confidence Interval of 16.8-33.7, with a Z Statistic of 17.8,
and a p-value < 0.0001

James A Thorp MD on X @jathorpMFM

In addition to cognitive disorders increasing among the COVID-19 vaccinated, Thorp et al. found that suicide or suicidal ideation increased at a risk ratio of 186, with the ratio of 2 being a breach of safety signal for the FDA.

Suicide or Suicidal Ideation - Risk Ratio for COVID-19
Vaccines vs Other Vaccines by USA FDA Database
FDA Uses a Risk Ratio of 2 as a Breach of Safety Signal

• COVID-19 versus Influenza vaccines the Risk Ratio is 186 with a
95% Confidence Interval of 120-287, a Z Statistic of 23.6, and a p-
value < 0.0001

• COVID-19 versus ALL OTHER Vaccines the Risk Ratio is 47.6 with a
95% Confidence Interval of 32.8-68.9, with a Z Statistic of 20.4,
and a p-value < 0.0001

James A Thorp MD on X @jathorp

And finally, psychiatric illnesses increased with a risk ratio of 188, with the FDA breach of safety signal being at a risk ratio of 2. In a later chapter, you'll learn more about psychosis post-vaccination, so tuck these statistics away in your memory bank for just a few more minutes.

> **Psychiatric Illnesses** - Risk Ratio (RR) for COVID-19 Vaccines Versus Other Vaccines by FDA Database
> FDA Uses a <u>Risk Ratio of 2</u> as a BREACH of Safety Signal
>
> • COVID-19 versus Influenza vaccines the <u>Risk Ratio is 188</u> with a 95% Confidence Interval of 129-275, Z Statistic 27.0, p-value < 0.0001
>
> • COVID-19 versus ALL OTHER Vaccines the <u>Risk Ratio is 23.8</u> with a 95% Confidence Interval of 16.9-33.8, Z Statistic 17.8, p-value < 0.0001
>
> James A Thorp MD on X @jathorpMFM

Dr. Thorp isn't merely a brilliant clinician and scientist but a dear friend. In June of 2024, an antagonistic doctor named Ryan Marino, MD posted the following message on X.com:

> *If anyone knows where alleged EMT, antivaxxer Harry Fisher, works please let me know! His tweets violate legal scope of practice & basic ethics. Paramedics are literally THE front line against death/disease, & we should not allow bad actors to risk their ability to hold that line.*[54][55]

My friend Steve Kirsch immediately responded, "Hey @RyanMarino, I know Harry very well and we talk every day. He'd be happy to have a live X discussion with you for all to hear. If you want to accept, please respond to the DM that I just sent you and I'll set it up."

---

54. https://x.com/stkirsch/status/1822312613247615484?s=46&t=U0tkjwiWCBpCRHF1YrzMrg

55. https://x.com/ryanmarino/status/1802171821136978051?s=46&t=U0tkjwiWCBpCRHF1YrzMrg

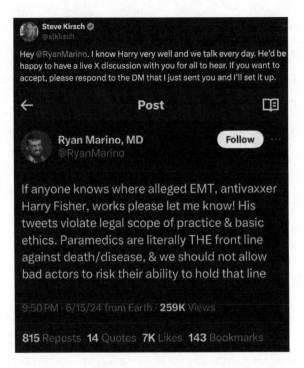

Then Dr. Jim Thorp brought out the big guns, stating,

> *It would appear that Dr Ryan Marino of Ohio did not declare major conflicts of interests.*
>
> *"Ryan's article failed to disclose that his employer, UH Cleveland, ran clinical trials for Pfizer on their COVID-19 vaccine."*
>
> *It appears that Dr Ryan Marino violated medical ethics by not disclosing his significant conflict of interest.*
>
> *It would appear that Dr Ryan Marino is unaware that The Cleveland Clinic likely entered into a cooperative care agreement receiving $431,032,935 from HHS.* [56]

---

56. https://t.co/gY4d9vYASw

It would appear that Dr Ryan Marino is unaware that Brooke Jackson documented likely fraud in the COVID-19 vaccine trials as published in the British Medical Journal while working for Pfizer's outsourced research contractor, Ventavia.

PART I

Are COVID-19 Vaccines in Pregnancy as Safe and Effective as the U.S. Government, Medical Organizations, and Pharmaceutical Industry Claim? Part I[v1] [57]

PART II

Are COVID-19 Vaccines in Pregnancy as Safe and Effective as the U.S. Government, Medical Organizations, and Pharmaceutical Industry Claim? Part II[v1][58]

It appears that Dr Ryan Marino is ignorant or unaware that Pfizer's own data documented the COVID-19 vaccine to be the deadliest most injurious data ever rolled out with 42,086 casualties including 1,223 deaths in just 10 weeks after rollout.

It appears that Dr. Ryan Marino of Ohio is ignorant or willfully ignoring the U.S. government's own VAERS database documenting extreme numbers of safety signals breached by the COVID-19 database.

It appears that Dr Ryan Marino has not reviewed the peer-reviewed medical literature that to date document 3,580 injuries and deaths associated with the COVID-19 vaccines [59]

It appears that Dr Ryan Marino is unaware or ignorant of the fact that the Czech Republic released their citizens de-identified COVID-19 case-time cohort data

---

57. https://t.co/4x4pMO4379

58. https://t.co/NMaFnOoXBz

59. https://t.co/GANUDyYc9z

of individuals vax date & death date data. The Czech data irrefutably documents that the COVID-19 vaccines have killed many of their citizens.

Apparently Dr Ryan Marino is unaware that Americans are no longer believing his propaganda or the government's propaganda as of Q1 2024 only 1% are taking the COVID-19 vaccines.

Dr Ryan Marino owes Harry Fisher, Ohioans, his patients, and the American people an apology. He needs to publicly repent.

Dr Ryan Marino and others who appear to have major conflicts of interests and who were responsible for being aware of the data reviewed above and have continued to push the injurious and lethal COVID-19 vaccines should undergo harsh repercussions - potentially including civil lawsuits and criminal prosecution.[60]

Damn. It's good to have friends like that in your corner. If you want to see more of Dr. Ryan's tweets, please visit https://x.com/RyanMarino. But please, be kind. (wink)

---

60. https://t.co/HOidsVK6NH

Poem: Like It's The Last

By Harry Fisher

Said I'm sorry again today,
another friend's loved one has passed away.
"The vaccine killed them" is what he said,
then cried out "my father's dead."

When during genocide does sorry not sway?
Eventually all evil will have to pay.
I say this not for vengeance's sake,
but God, we crave your wrath to take.

So hold your loved ones like it's the last;
The sea of loss is now wide and vast.

Cherish each moment, let no time slip by.
In this fragile life, we love, till we die.

Chapter Eleven
Blood Money

Medical school should be renamed Pharma school. Doctors only learn to treat symptoms with drugs while ignoring the cause. Real health won't be found inside a doctor's office.
Brandy Vaughan, ex-Merck Pharma rep & LearnTheRisk. org founder

I don't think there was ever a way even the most well-executed CIA psyop was going to suck in Dr. Jim Thorp. He didn't fall for the plandemic for a minute because he was well-versed in corruption in the medical profession due to pharmaceutical companies tampering with the system, the studies, the journals, and the government grants and funding they siphon and control.

Jim has known for decades, as many doctors probably do, that the pharmaceutical industry frequently writes scientific publications and puts doctors names on them. Why don't most doctors do anything about it? They're usually wimps, frankly, in my experience.

Not Thorp. He's a veteran who took his punches for this country and now lives with permanent paralysis. He's had about twenty back surgeries and in the hundreds of hours we've spent together, he's never complained about his condition once. He thanks God for his wife Maggie and his "number two" best friend after his wife, his dog. Jim's a fighter, he's my brother from another mother, and he's brilliant. But his story exposing COVID-19 fraud hasn't been all high profile podcasts and celebrity appearances; it's been, well, a fight.

When the New England Journal of Medicine reported in June 2021 that the "vaccine" was safe for pregnant women, Jim knew he couldn't politely keep quiet about what he saw. Naturally, this article was written by Pfizer, and they essentially slapped the names of twenty-one physicians and researchers who happened to be federal employees on it. This type of fraud has been going on in medicine for a long time.

The United States spends $4.1 trillion on healthcare each year, and yet we still have some of the highest rates of cancer, dementia and heart disease in the world. To put it in perspective, that's $12,000 in spending by the U.S. Government per person, per year. Where is that money going? A majority of it is being siphoned back into the hands of the pharmaceutical companies who incentivize doctors with just enough bread crumbs and bonuses to keep them in the racket. In India their government spends just $64 per person per year, and they're much healthier. In fact, the USA constituted half of the global deaths from COVID-19. Where is our money going?

First of all, nearly every member of congress has taken money from Pfizer. This has caused some doctors like Dr. Jim Thorp, who is a conservative Christian veteran, to wonder why even participate anymore. Many others like him appreciate President Donald Trump's stance on abortion or other Biblical values, but can't stand the way he and his administration bent over during Operation Warp Speed, and for good reason. It's hard for a veteran like Dr. Thorp to realize that our country's system is almost irreversibly evil. He suggests that we are, in essence, the "global beast system." Author Naomi Klein describes this well in her book "The Shock Doctrine," which is where the term "disaster capitalism" derives.

In an earlier chapter, you saw how Dr. Thorp had my back and stood up for me against the troll Dr. Ryan Marino. Then Jim gets trolled by those who say, "You're a follower of Jesus Christ, but you attack people? What a hypocrite!"

Nay. Thorp goes against people who are killing pregnant women, preborns, and newborns. He stands up to the medical industrial and pharmaceutical industrial complex. He stands up for doctors in a system that has made them slaves to insurance companies and hospital administration; who work for their pharmaceutical company incentives and kickbacks. Thorp goes after them voraciously to expose the truth.

In 2003 the Bush Administration asked Dr. Thorp to testify in front of the Senate. He had done more closed field surgeries at that time than just about any other maternal fetal medicine doctor. He treated the fetus as a *separate patient* from the mother. He accomplished this ultrasonographically with instruments, neeles, catheters and stents. Thorp's testimony was successful. In fact, following that testimony as well as the photograph "The Hand of Hope" photograph, partial birth abortion became illegal in the U.S.A. until Obama reinstated it in one of the very first things he did in office. Those sick leftists love killing; the DNC garners tremendous voting fuel from pro-abortionists.

The "Hand of Hope" photograph is a 1999 medical photograph taken by Micahel Clancy during an open fetal surgery. It depicts the hand of a fetus reaching out from an incision in the mother's uterus, seeming to grab the surgeon's finger. The baby, Samuel Alexander Armas, was delivered approximately three and a half months after this photograph was taken on August 19th, 1999, with his birthdate being December 2nd, 1999. During the surgery, performed by Dr. Joseph Bruner and Dr. Noel Tulipan, the procedure aimed to fix the spina bifida of the 21-week-old preborn baby, which was successful.

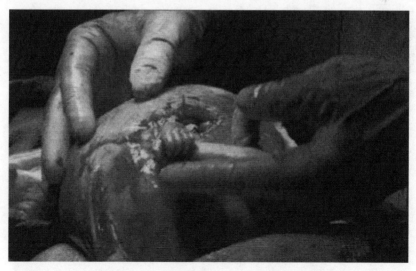

Photograph by Micahel Clancy, 19 August 1999
Nashville, Tennessee

EUA and Lancet Fraud

A pivotal moment in the heroic story of Jim and Maggie Thorp comes from a famous Lancet article with the lead author "Mandeep Mehra, MD." Mehra is a leading cardiologist at one of the most captured medical centers in the world: Harvard University. The article, which was allegedly fraudulently ghostwritten with Mehra's name slapped on it, falsely impugned hydroxychloroquine. It was published five months into the plandemic with the claim that there had been a large global study involving 95,000 participant patients treated with hydroxychloroquine (HCQ). The article proposed the HCQ was unsafe and ineffective. This was the red flag for Thorp, who had been using HCQ for forty-three years in pregnant women at that time, alongside the majority of his peers. It was not just safe for pregnant women but those who were breastfeeding and women of reproductive age. HCQ was the mainstay of therapy for autoimmune disease in women of reproductive age; the conceived while on HCQ and could remain on HCQ during the most vulnerable time period of pregnancy, during the first trimester. That's how safe and effective HCQ was.

There's another layer to this "red flag" experience Thorp had when he read the alleged study of 95,000 patients in the Lancet article that was allegedly spearheaded by Mehra. Thorp has published extensively in his speciality. He has been a reviewer for major journals as well, including the New England Journal of Medicine and many others. He has tremendous familiarity with the review process for medical journals and believes that it was absolutely impossible "they" could have wrangled 95,000 patients, treated them with anything in five months, analyzed that data and then published it in just five months. As it turns out, the data was all fraudulent, made up by a company called Surgisphere." Thorp personally exposed that fraud.

But why did they do it?

To acquire the "vaccine's" emergency use authorization (EUA), they had to impugn HCQ falsely. If there were an actual *safe and effective* treatment for COVID-19, that being HCQ, then the EUA wouldn't have been granted.

Exposing The American College of Obstetricians and Gynecologists

By some miracle, Thorp stayed on staff with SSM Health until mid-2023 despite all his whistleblowing. Dr. Thorp isn't just an OBGYN and is sub-specialized in maternal-fetal medicine (MFM). There are only about 1,200 of these MFM professionals in the entire country. At the turn of the century, that number was closer to 2,200, which means that despite population growth, our government has lost nearly half of our MFM doctors. That said, Thorp was valuable. It's almost too valuable to lose. Almost…

Additionally, Dr. Thorp was admired by his peers and a model employee. He was senior at a very large group; SSM had purchased St. Louis University and Dr. Thorp was not only the number one MFM doctor in terms of excellence, but in his prolific output. He read over 27,500 high risk OB scans in just four and a half years. SSM health treated him royally and he loved his patients and colleagues. By working remotely, Thorp saved time by contributing publications which were fed to SSM Health. Jim's military mindset gave him an understanding of the chain of command. Everything he published, he gave to his division director, Dr. Gil Gross, who was actually Jim's resident at St. Luke's Hospital. Sadly, everything Jim produced got squelched. He begged anybody in the world since late 2020 to debate him, but nobody has ever accepted that offer.

At this point in the story we'll bring in Maggie Thorp, JD. Brilliantly, Maggie got a Freedom of Information Act (FOIA) request to the HHS and CDC. Maggie reviewed all the communications between the parties, and then the American College of Obstetricians and Gynecologists.[61] Maggie developed a relationship with a woman who was high up at HHS and acquired 1,400 pages of evidence proving that HHS and the CDC bought out the entire American College of Gynecologists (ACOG), who control 60,000 OBGYN's. HHS and CDC then subcontracted with their sister organization, the American Board of OBGYN's (ABOG). This is important because ABOG has the punitive power to destroy people's careers. Also corrupted was the Society for Maternal Fetal Medicine (SMFM), who

---

61. https://www.americaoutloud.news/foia-reveals-troubling-relationship-between-hhs-cdc-the-american-college-of-obstetricians-and-gynecologists/

also colluded in putting out a letter on September 27, 2021 stating that if you deviate and spread misinformation that goes against the mainstream COVID-19 narrative that they would destroy your career. They would take away your licenses and board certifications.

So there you have it. It's all about the money. A *lot* of money.

In total, from what we can identify, $186 *billion* went to over 400,000 hospitals and clinics in the United States, and SSM health was one of them. SSM took $306,900,000 and signed the same "cooperative care agreement" as the other 400,000 hospitals and clinics.

These "care providers" sold their souls.

Later in this book I'll talk about Jim and my mutual friend Dr. Mary Bowden who worked for Houston Methodist, which was a hospital that was targeted. They mandated shots for all of their employees and took approximately $350 million in this "blood money."

These boards and societies are shooting themselves in the foot. Jim Thorp is plainly irreplaceable. One thing they had in Dr. Jim Thorp isn't solely the uniqueness of his specialty and his prolific output, but his respect and esteem among his peers. This man is a fighter. And he doesn't quit.

The first time Jim testified in front of the Senate was in 2003, during which time he stated:

> *The first fetal surgery is credited to Sir Albert William Liley in 1963. He developed the technique for diagnosing and treating fetuses suffering from anemia as a result of Rh disease. He is known as ``the father of fetology" and was an advocate for the rights of the child within the womb. Dr. Liley said, ``As a doctor, I regard the unborn child as my patient and protect and respect his life as I would the life of any other patient. From my clinical experience, I am convinced that unborn children are individuals and human beings who are capable of receiving and responding to medical care and who should have legal protection." It is extremely difficult not to see the fetus as a child before birth with the same value as a child after birth, especially after one considers her smiling, grimacing, moving, sleeping, yawning, stretching, sucking a thumb, as well as responding to pain from needle sticks.[62]*

62. https://www.govinfo.gov/content/pkg/CHRG-108shrg87755/html/CHRG-108shrg87755.htm

Long before COVID-19, Jim was awakened to the value of every child, choosing to refer to fetuses as "unborn children" worthy of respect as any other patient. Jim has watched in horror for these unborn children and their mothers as, over the past twenty years since that first Senate testimony, he has seen hospitals collapsing. In the daftest decision ever, his hospital fired him a year ago, shortly after he appeared on Tucker Carlson Tonight, stating:

> *One can make a very strong argument, Tucker, that the pushing of these experimental COVID-19 vaccines globally is the greatest violation of medical ethics in the history of modern medicine, maybe humanity. We have never, ever broken the sacrosanct golden rule of pregnancy; never ever.*[63]

To their credit, SSM held out and held on to Dr. Jim Thorp for a long time after they had received $307 million to push the vaccine on their patients and employees, even though Jim refused to comply and spoke openly and publicly about that decision.[64] They put that blood money on the line… but at some point they couldn't risk holding Jim on staff for another minute.

You might be surprised to have learned in an earlier chapter that hospitals are all about the money. Dr. Kelly and my collaboration in Chapter Six detailed the fact that doctors are a bit like "middle managers" with the insurance companies and hospital administrators calling most of the shots. But here's something that might shock you: in terms of square inch per capita, their profit is the highest in the neonatal intensive care nursery. They make more money in neonatal intensive care than any other square inch in the hospital. What's more, a maternal fetal medicine doctor has to be on staff for high risk obstetrics as a matter of legislation. In other words, if a hospital doesn't have a maternal fetal medicine doctor, their NICU will no longer exist. No hospital perceives they can afford to lose that profit center. Shortly after he got canned by SSM Health I asked Jim if he thought it was because he testified around the world, if it's because he was on Tucker, or

---

63. https://www.realclearpolitics.com/video/2023/02/24/dr_james_thorp_the_pushing_of_the_experimental_COVID_vaccines_is_the_greatest_violation_of_medical_ethics_in_history.html

64. https://www.americaoutloud.news/COVID-19-government-relief-funds-turned-the-healthcare-industry-on-its-head/

because he has been on thousands of platforms, even testifying in front of the U.S. Senate. He imagines that it was all of the above. SSM likely got a call from HHS and the CDC that said, "look, Thorp is a problem. You're violating the cooperative care agreement we paid you over three hundred million dollars to make. Terminate this bloke or give us back the money."

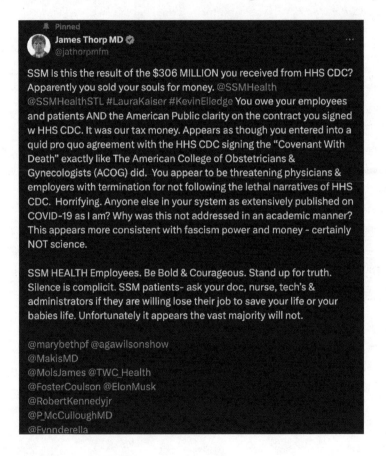

In a post on X.com, Thorp wrote:

SSM Is this the result of the $306 MILLION you received from HHS CDC? Apparently you sold your souls for money. @SSMHealth @SSMHealthSTL #LauraKaiser #KevinElledge You owe your employees and patients AND the American Public clarity on the contract you signed with HHS CDC. It was *our tax money. Appears as though you entered into a quid pro quo agreement with the HHS CDC signing the "Covenant With Death" exactly like The American College of Obstetricians & Gynecologists (ACOG) did. You appear to be threatening physicians & employers with termination for not following the lethal narratives of HHS CDC. Horrifying. Anyone else in your system as extensively published on COVID-19 as I am? Why was this not addressed in an academic manner? This appears more consistent with fascism power and money - certainly NOT science.[65]*

Jim Thorp has a message for my readers and the remaining SSM Health employees. He says, "Be bold and courageous. Stand up for truth. Silence is compliance. SSM patients, ask your doctors, nurses, technicians, and administrators if they are willing to lose their jobs to save your life or your baby's life. Unfortunately, it appears the vast majority will not."

SSM Health is one of the largest Catholic healthcare systems and the 35th largest hospital system in the United States. They span across five different states. Jim knew Laura Kaiser personally because when he worked in Pensacola, he was recruited from Kansas City St. Luke's, and Laura was his CEO; she was the CEO of SSM Health when Thorp was fired. He says:

She didn't have the ethical, moral and intellectual courage to execute me so she hired on one of her underling CEO's by the name of Kevin Elledge. Elledge called me up on a Thursday, June 29, 2023 and had a forty-five minute conversation which we didn't record because that's illegal. For the first thirty minutes he honored me as a model physician, saying everybody loved me, including patients. But quite frankly, he didn't. He said that they were having financial problems and were invoking a "no cause termination."

To add insult to injury, Elledge proposed that Thorp sign a $100,000 separation agreement that was essentially an NDA. Jim turned it down, saying kindly, "In good faith, I can't take that because you are having financial problems, and I don't need the money, so you should keep it."

---

65. https://x.com/jathorpmfm/status/1693815290407072085

Elledge pressured Jim, saying, "but you have five grandchildren. Take the money and sign the agreement."

But he knew it was blood money.

In seven minutes after that call, Thorp received an email indicating that SSM would break their contract, never paying Thorp what was owed him for the remainder of his contract, and then they proceeded to defame him by emailing his colleagues, who were shocked and forwarded the email to Jim. By refusing to take a $100,000 bribe by SSM, he was treated like a child predator or somebody who committed a gross felony. The email stated that Thorp would no longer see patients, effective immediately, and he was no longer a part of that team.

God bless Dr. Thorp for refusing that blood money. God created Dr. Thorp and Maggie for a purpose to see patients and save the lives of women and their unborn babies. He states that he hopes to be doing his work in MFM for at least another ten years.

Thanks to Jim Thorp, Maggie Thorp, and people writing our stories like Stephanie Pierucci, the uptake of the COVID-19 booster shot in 2024 is pathetic, with 99% of people having woken up to the fact that hospitals and the government have lied to them.

Is it up to Anthony Fauci, Kamala Harris, Barack Obama, or Joe Biden to repent? No. It's up to the Church to repent. Dr. Thorp brought to my attention a subtle Scripture from the Old Testament.

In Ezekiel Chapter 18, Verse 30 of the NKJV, it reads, "'Therefore I will judge you, O house of Israel, every one according to his ways,' says the Lord God. 'Repent, and turn from all your transgressions, so that iniquity will not be your ruin.'"

Throughout Scriptures we see that God told HIS people to repent, and he would spare the rest. If the Jews repented, His people, then he would spare the Gentiles, the athiests, and the godless ones.

If we don't repent, we will be destroyed.

Doctors aren't always empathetic. In fact, on a scale of one to ten, it's really bad for a doctor to be a ten empath. Dr. Thorp and I are alike in that we're empathetic healthcare professionals and men. We feel our patients' pain. Thorp calls it our double-edged sword. We know it's good and Godly, but Jim knows that he can't sit on his hands and resist the calling to speak out aggressively. But, too, didn't Jesus get kicked out of every place he preached? Our Lord was not passive, He called the Pharisees a brood of vipers.

It is my prayer that the Church will join me in this sacred prayer:

The Spirit of the Lord God is upon Me,
Because the Lord has anointed Me
To preach good tidings to the poor;
He has sent Me to heal the brokenhearted,
To proclaim liberty to the captives,
And the opening of the prison to those who are bound;

To proclaim the acceptable year of the Lord,
And the day of vengeance of our God;
To comfort all who mourn,

To console those who mourn in Zion,
To give them beauty for ashes,
The oil of joy for mourning,
The garment of praise for the spirit of heaviness;
That they may be called trees of righteousness,
The planting of the Lord, that He may be glorified."

And they shall rebuild the old ruins,
They shall raise up the former desolations,
And they shall repair the ruined cities,
The desolations of many generations;

Strangers shall stand and feed your flocks,
And the sons of the foreigner
Shall be your plowmen and your vinedressers.

But you shall be named the priests of the Lord,
They shall call you the servants of our God.
You shall eat the riches of the Gentiles,
And in their glory you shall boast.

Instead of your shame you shall have double honor,
And instead of confusion they shall rejoice in their portion.
Therefore in their land they shall possess double;
Everlasting joy shall be theirs.

Isaiah 61:1-7, NKJV

When this Scripture appears in the New Testament in the book of Luke (who was a doctor, coincidentally), here is the context in Luke 4, verses 14-30 in the New King James Version.

Then Jesus returned in the power of the Spirit to Galilee, and news of Him went out through all the surrounding region. And He taught in their synagogues, being glorified by all.

So He came to Nazareth, where He had been brought up. And as His custom was, He went into the synagogue on the Sabbath day and stood up to read. And He was handed the book of the prophet Isaiah. And when He had opened the book, He found the place where it was written:

"The Spirit of the Lord is upon Me,
Because He has anointed Me
To preach the gospel to the poor;
He has sent Me to heal the brokenhearted,
To proclaim liberty to the captives
And recovery of sight to the blind,
To set at liberty those who are oppressed;
To proclaim the acceptable year of the Lord."

Then He closed the book, and gave it back to the attendant and sat down. And the eyes of all who were in the synagogue were fixed on Him. And He began to say to them, 'Today this Scripture is fulfilled in your hearing.' So all bore witness to Him, and marveled at the gracious words which proceeded out of His mouth. And they said, 'Is this not Joseph's son?'

He said to them, "You will surely say this proverb to Me, 'Physician, heal yourself! Whatever we have heard done in Capernaum, do also here in Your country.'"

Then He said, 'Assuredly, I say to you, no prophet is accepted in his own country. But I tell you truly, many widows were in Israel in the days of Elijah, when the heaven was shut up three years and six months, and there was a great famine throughout all the land; but to none of them was Elijah sent except to Zarephath, in the region of Sidon, to a woman who was a widow. And many lepers were in Israel in the time of Elisha the prophet, and none of them was cleansed except Naaman the Syrian.'

So all those in the synagogue, when they heard these things, were filled with wrath, and rose up and thrust Him out of the city; and they led Him to the brow of the hill on which their city was built, that they might throw Him down over the cliff. Then passing through the midst of them, He went His way.

They led the Lord to the brow of the hill on which their city was built that they might throw Him over the cliff. No prophet, He reminded us, is accepted in his own country.

Poem: Fallen Cradles

I wrote this poem one night after seeing one mom-to-be after another come into the ER. They were "vaccinated" women miscarrying their children. They were told their babies would be safe; but one after another, those babies were dying.

Another blood soaked chair, screams fill the air.
Waiting their turn, does anyone care?
Emergencies plenty, in a room that holds twenty.
Lives are not covered under a warranty.
Experimental bough broke, the cradle did fall,
Now, 911 is the number they call.
Spontaneously courted, innocence distorted,
Hemorrhaged the life that's now been aborted.
Programmed are the masses, from grade school classes,
Billions of dollars on propagandized glasses.
The FDA to CDC, they snarl and laugh for all to see.
Greedy gargoyles on Pharma's foundation,
Sank teeth in the womb of God's greatest creation.
Through halls of power, the clock strikes the hour,
Decisions are made in an ivory tower.
The people, mere numbers, in ledgers not kept,
Innocence lost as Jesus wept.

Chapter Twelve
Unexpected "Adverse Events" Begin To Emerge

I arrived at a house with a parent on scene screaming, "there's something wrong!" The parent screamed over and over, "Something's wrong with them. Something's wrong with them!"

My partner and I were escorted into home by the parent after that parent denied having any weapons. The parent continued repeating "there's something wrong."

We notified the police department of the situation, but didn't know how long it would be before they arrived on scene. Upon entering the home, the patient is standing at the bathroom sink looking into the mirror. We noted a needle and thread in the patient's hand. One of the patient's eyes was already sewn shut. The patient was currently sawing their mouth shut.

I requested for them to stop. The patient glared at me with the one eye that was currently capable of opening. They continue sewing their mouth shut.

Due to active self-harm, the inability to answer questions appropriately, and an unwillingness to stop, we elected immediate transport under implied consent with parental consent as well. The patient was now growling and moaning through a sewn-shut mouth while being placed on the cot and restrained with soft restraints.

The sutures were immediately removed from the mouth due to probable airway obstruction.

This was a vaccinated patient that "was usually normal" per the parent on scene. They had no other psychiatric history. They were young with no other medical problems reported.

The difficulty with these "vaccines" and the evil protocols makes it hard to tell what causes these psychological breaks. We know the vaccines cause mental problems according to many reputable doctors. We also know the protocols, lockdowns, and all the abuse placed on the population caused mental issues as well.

All we can do at this point is ask about vaccination status, and collect that data. Real. Raw. Data.

I can say at this point that most of the significant cases of cancer, heart problems, strokes, and extreme psych that I run are vaccinated individuals. However, a large portion of our population took this dangerous substance so it's complicated to pin down cause when the shots aren't allowed to be genuinely studied. As Dr Ryan Cole has said, "You don't find what you're not looking for."

I'm seeing what I would call a dramatic spike in psychological and mental health medications. Some scientists in Japan are linking the correlation between the "vaccine" to mental health, including cognition and depression. Even hamsters, when introduced to gene therapy such as what is in the COVID-19 jab, experienced hyper aggression. These jabs mess with your mind, without question.

In the next chapter I'll dive deeper into psychosis. For the time being, here are my observations. Since the rollout of the jabs I've seen an uptick in suicides, evidence of patients who are hyper-aggressive, and both colleagues and patients who have become assertively mean. I've worked with some of my colleagues in Oklahoma City for years; we've shared laughter as well as held one another through life's various tragedies. Some of these same individuals, once like family to me, looked me dead in the eyes after their shots and said, "don't you dare let your fucking unvaccinated kids near mine." I can't tell you if the mental health deterioration and abusive behavior (not to mention illogical) is due to the jabs, or due to the stress of so many years of abuse by our government. A third option is that these individuals are so bitter, stuffing down so many negative emotions for their weak-willed compliance that they are retaliating against me because they are both ashamed, but also jealous.

Remember another thing about the lockdowns and subsequent mental health state of our country. Alcohol use increased. Methamphetamine use increased. Psychiatric medication use increased. And now these individuals have allowed a new technology to be intravenously introduced to their bodies... a new technology that we don't yet nor might ever fully understand. It's almost like these folks turned into zombies; they're docile and passive until they're not... and then they're bloodthirsty assholes, almost like sociopaths.

Our government abused the hell out of all of us; the jabbed and unjabbed alike. We have all been abused. The result of that seems to follow one of three trajectories. Either A: you become weak, passive, compliant, submissive, and even codependent on the abuser. B: You become an abuser yourself. Or C: you do what I'm doing and what you folks reading this book are probably doing or setting to do.

We fight back. We grab the slingshot fixin' to take down Goliath. We unite together from all walks of life and philosophies. I don't agree with everything said or done by the friends I've introduced to you in this book. Steve Kirsch has had to have a talkin' to me on more than one occasion about spouting off Second Amendment supportive tirades on his broadcasts. He doesn't think the government is out to kill us. But I'd be damned if I wouldn't take a bullet for that guy.

Jim Thorp and his wife are downright incredibly disciplined Christians who don't think highly of my smoking habits, but I'll be damned if you're gonna tell me Jim Thorp wouldn't take a bullet for me; a man who is already a paralyzed veteran and who has lived his entire life in service to this country and its families.

These folks aren't perfect, but we're the Justice League. We all have different superpowers, and what makes us special is that we aren't a bunch of clones sitting in an echo chamber stroking one another's egos. We have the conviction to stand up and resist evil, which allows us to put some differences aside and truly unite. There is no family like the medical freedom family.

Poem: As The World Burns

Children are dying,
Men lying,
The bias subsides,
For devils complying.
Freedom thwarted,
Only truth now deported,
Wait in line for your chance to be sorted.
Masking the science,
Robotic compliance,
God looking down on all this defiance.
Sudden death on the rise,
To no one's surprise,
An experimental thorn left tattered and torn.
Question not,
Fact check that thought,
Hold out your hand for your chance to be bought.
Now kneel world servant,
On the mount where just once stood,
And take your medicine,
For the greater good.

Listen to "As The World Burns" here:

https://twitter.com/harryfisherEMTP/status/1729890613360046382

Chapter Thirteen

Psychosis

The media is silent about a whole lot;
No medical history,
They get these shots, and suddenly, they get these brain tumors,
And they try to kill their entire family.
Everyone is going to be seeing things that they never thought they
would see,
You do hear, "It's not them, this isn't like them…"
I can't believe someone would do that to themselves.
They're staring at me after they bit their hand.
That was, for lack of a better word, demonic.
It just seemed demonic.
I think we're in for a really dark time ahead.
A really dark time.

Harry Fisher, July 2024

In October of 2024 after a well-deserved afternoon of sunbathing and soaking in hot mineral waters, Stephanie changed in the locker room of her local hot springs pool in Colorado. Suddenly, a little girl began to scream in one of the showers.

"Mommy the soap won't come out! It's burning my eyes! It hurts! It hurts!"

We all remember those moments with our kids when something hurt; a skinned knee, soap in the eyes, or getting bullied at school. We hurt with our kids. Their pain can break our hearts. There's nothing more acute than feeling the pain of your child.

Stephanie recalled to me the first time she saw her son's heart break outside of a physical boo-boo, when his heart ached with empathy. It was for the "killer whale" Keiko, the star character (an orca) in the movie "Free Willy." Hunter was six at the time and obsessed with orcas. He cried so hard that Stephanie said she began crying with Hunter. Stephanie kept coaxing her son, "don't worry, they're going to help Willy. It's going to be okay. Just wait for the end."

Stephanie recalls that it was the longest movie of her life. That little orca wailed and whined for about forty minutes. It was torture to listen to the killer whale in pain for the audience, especially a six-year-old orca-obsessed boy. Stephanie recalls that she wept herself to sleep that night, remembering her son's tears and whimpers, who also exhausted himself with empathy for "Keiko" and went to sleep without brushing his teeth. Steph recalls thinking, "It hurt so bad to see Hunter hurting, but I love to see his sweet and empathetic heart."

Our sweet children. How we wish we could prevent them from crying or hurting in any way. In His Divine love, God gave us the ability to choose Him; He provided us with free will. We *get to* choose His love. We *get to* fall in love with Him. We *get to* receive the comfort and nurturing presence of His Spirit. But it must break His heart to have given us the gift of choosing Him. He could have forced us to love and serve Him, like a tyrannical ruler. But instead He gave us the adventure of discovering Him and falling in love through free will. Damn that must be so hard; watching his children hurt one another, or hurt themselves...

During the writing of this book Stephanie's friend took his life in his garage; he hung himself. The man was only thirty-one years old. He had everything going for him. He was successful, in fact even before the age of thirty, just recently, he had been published in reputable journals for his work as an engineer. He invested his money wisely in real estate. He did yoga and by all appearances looked to be in perfect health with sculpted muscles, a great tan, and constant stories of adventures mountaineering. He had tickets to leave for Japan and ski in just a few weeks before he took his life.

Stephanie knew this young man was going to a facility recently for mental health. Each day she and her partner passed his house and wondered when his truck would be home. And then one day it was there. But the young man was not.

"So he did it... there?" Stephanie asked her partner, who was close with the young man.

"Yes, in the garage."

They heard the news just minutes before driving past his house; a friend found him in the garage. A note on the door said, "don't come in. Call 911."

The woman went in. He was cold. He had probably hung himself Wednesday night; he was found on Thursday morning.

There's another layer to this story and to the man's recent mental illness. The death of his mother hit him hard when he was nineteen. He had several aunts die before age fifty of cancer; he felt that he was doomed. Just before he took his life he learned that he had the same "cancer gene" as his mother and aunts.

Another layer is that when the jabs rolled out, he was dating one of the several stunning young women he dated over the years who stood with him in resisting the jab. However, at Thanksgiving his dad and brother told him he was not invited. Then his dad threatened to disown him. The young man caved and got two shots.

To our knowledge, the man had never taken psychiatric medication. According to a letter he wrote less than thirty days before his death, he knew that he was loved and that the world would be a better place if he remained alive.

However, this man's dad, despite his compliance with the jabs, disowned him for not complying sooner. Recently, he visited his brother, and a huge brawl broke out. The young man stood back and took the punches. His heart was shattered. His dad fueled the hatred between the two brothers.

The young man, age thirty-one when he took his own life, was still grieving the loss of his mother acutely when he lost the remaining family he had over an experimental gene therapy he didn't feel comfortable taking. We don't know where this man is now. We don't know how God judges these things.

I tend to think that suicide is the most selfish thing you can do to those you leave behind—those who will be forever plagued with guilt that they could have done something. I also know through the dozens of suicides I've witnessed in the military and as a veteran that once a man makes up his mind to end things, you can't talk him out of it.

But the final layer is this: I don't think the man committed suicide.

For at least a year before his death the man suffered from tinnitus, one adverse even we'll discuss later in this chapter. For that he began taking a low dose of a sleeping pill, which later prompted a doctor to prescribe Lexapro. For three weeks prior to his death, the man had been in a hospital detoxing SSRI's, which had caused a myriad of adverse reactions. He felt psychotic. He knew that he wasn't himself. He felt like the drugs had "killed" him and he couldn't feel any emotions. He was having, by all accounts, a psychotic meltdown. At one point he lamented, "I can't feel anything. I'll never have children. My body is numb below the waist." As you'll read later in this chapter, all of these symptoms coincide with potential viral spike protein side effects from the mRNA jab.

By all accounts, between the SSRIs and the jab, I think this was not a suicide but a prominent pHARMa homicide. A remarkable, brilliant, beautiful, healthy, and wealthy young man took his own life because he was experiencing psychosis. He had too many pharmaceuticals in his system, and he wanted to break free, but the drugs wouldn't let him go.

Stephanie shared, "But right now all I want is to think that this boy is finally in his Father's arms. The Father who will never disown him. The Father who says, "I love you my sweet boy. Oh, how I love you! I will never leave you nor forsake you. Please stay here in my arms. I will take your pain away."

During the writing of this book in late 2024, Stephanie witnessed her community shook with horror as three young men in her small community committed suicide within a week, two on the same day, and both by hanging. It felt like we couldn't leave this story, however unsettling, out of this book.

From Marina Zhang with the Epoch Times:

Suicide cases have been rising in the United States since the pandemic. In 2020, the CDC reported up to 46,000 suicides.[66] This number increased to over 48,000 in 2021,[67] and 2022, nearly 50,000 people died by suicide. While pandemic restrictions like lockdowns and long COVID have been linked with suicides, no studies currently link increasing suicide rates with the COVID-19 vaccine.[68] [69]

What I've seen post "vaccination" is plainly terrifying. There was the patient who sewed together their eyes and mouth, as detailed in an earlier chapter.

There was one patient who bit off a chunk of their hand while staring me in the eyes, smiling while bleeding profusely from the wound. I've witnessed an array of various forms of self-mutilation and even a suicide by gunshot while I stood witness.

Interestingly, I wouldn't have been in the room during these instances unless somebody had called 911. That is to say two things. First of all, these people are acting out in front of a loved one. That's horrific in and of itself. Secondly, there's a witness. And sadly, most of these witnesses have shared the same thing: "that's not who he or she is. That's not normal. This isn't my loved one. This isn't how he or she acts."

With vaccinated individuals who have these psychotic episodes, the vast majority if not all of them who didn't have a previous medical history of psychiatric distress *were "vaccinated."*

I'm often gaslighted by folks who say, "Well, correlation doesn't equal causation."

And to that I say, "how do you think we do science?" Jim Thorp discussed this gaslighting in an earlier chapter.

I want to know what prompted these psychotic episodes.

I want to know why the media doesn't cover these events.

66. https://www.cdc.gov/nchs/data/databriefs/db433-tables.pdf#1

67. https://www.cdc.gov/media/releases/2023/s0810-US-Suicide-Deaths-2022.html

68. https://www.nimh.nih.gov/news/science-news/2023/youth-suicide-rates-increased-during-the-COVID-19-pandemic

69. https://www.theepochtimes.com/article/psychosis-panic-attacks-hallucinations-bizarre-psychiatric-cases-among-the-COVID-vaccinated-5500128

And if it wasn't for my sounding the alarm about a potential correlation, we might never know where to look to uncover the cause… which is fundamentally how we do science.

We get a tip.

We explore that tip.

We develop hypotheses.

We test the hypothesis.

Because I'm the first guy on scene for 911 calls, I see the worst scenes imaginable.

My prayer is that because of my yelling and screaming about this genocide, the murderers will one day go to jail, if not hell. I often say that it's always darkest before dawn. I remain mildly optimistic, but with trepidation. We're in for a really dark time ahead.

Psychosis From The Spike Protein

Laura Aboli is a writer, speaker, and freedom fighter who was recently selected as "Top Global Freedom Fighter and Advocate of the Year for 2024" by the International Association of Top Professionals (IAOTP) for her outstanding leadership, dedication, and commitment to the industry.[70] Aboli is the co-founder of World-Check, "a database of Politically Exposed Persons (PEPs) and heightened risk individuals and organizations, which soon became the de facto standard for identifying and managing financial, regulatory, and reputational risk within the world's financial and legal institutions. Following World-Check's success, she co-founded Wealth-X in 2010, which went on to become the leading provider of intelligence on ultra-high-net-worth individuals."[71] During the plandemic, Aboli founded the United Democratic International Movement for Awareness and Freedom

---

70. http://www.iaotp.com/award-gala

71. https://www.westco.coop/markets/stocks.php?article=getnews-2024-3-18-laura-aboli-selected-as-top-global-freedom-fighter-and-advocate-of-the-year-by-iaotp

(UDIMAF), an organization dedicated to creating a better world through awareness, inspiration, and the relentless pursuit of truth.[72] [73]

Steph was recently scrolling social media and saw a clip of Laura speaking with Andrew Tate on the subject of psychosis. In the clip, Aboli stated:

> *The spike protein in the vaccines because it can actually transfer the blood brain barrier, what it causes once it's in your brain is neuroinflammation. Now what happens when we have neuroinflammation is that the hippocampus, which is our biological memory center, what tells us that you are you because it's based on all your experience from the time you are born, is that it stops producing new nerve cells. When it stops producing these new nerve cells the hippocampus has to decide to erase your memory in order to store new memories. We're using our personality, our individuality, our ability to think because of this process. And you might have seen this in people where suddenly they appear very different and you can't even talk to them rationally about things. The narrative is the narrative.*

The psychological distress of the plandemic is what Aboli credits to her founding of UDIMAF. It was one thing to know that COVID-19 was a potentially deadly virus in those early days (although we found out that it wasn't very fatal to the vast majority of people) but another to know that my livelihood might be drastically crippled if I didn't comply.

This was compounded on top of the fact that I was actually watching people suffer harm or even death for the shot, an experimental gene therapy that I saw kill people early on in the Pfizer shot lines. Everything around us during 2020-2022 felt unfair; and it was. It was unconstitutional and the mandates were never in alignment with our nation's laws. In every way, it felt like we were living in a slave state. The trauma of being forced to wear masks in order to enter buildings or even walk down streets was one thing; but then certain counties required vaccine cards to enter public spaces and it was beyond Orwellian. This drove people mad.

---

72. https://www.udimaf.org/

73. https://www.lauraaboli.com/

But Aboli brings up an even deeper question: did the jabs actually make people psychiatrically and neurologically mad?

You tell me.

I got a call one summer afternoon. 911: active labor.

I arrived to find a patient screaming in her closet. "You can't have it, I hate you!" She was screaming at somebody from the local fire department who was already on-scene.

The fireman stated, "we can't get her out of the closet. I think she's in labor. She just keeps screaming at us."

I walked into the closet and realized that the light in the closet wouldn't work. The fireman held a flashlight so that I could see what we were working with.

"Ma'am, how far along are you?" I asked.

The patient was lying on her back, partially obstructed from my view due to clothes hanging in the closet. There were fresh cuts on both of her arms and I noted heavy bleeding.

"Fuck you! You can't have it! We are going to die!" The patient screamed at me.

"I don't want either of you to die; I'm here to help. Can you tell me what year it is?"

"1764."

Due to the patient's inability to give the correct year, fresh cuts to her arms and active labor, we deemed the patient altered and endangering life. Care was initiated under implied consent.

"I'm going to help you and your baby," I stated calmly.

I noted crowing, which means that I could see the baby's head. The fire department personnel assisted with holding a light as well as the patient's hands, lest she hit me.

I noted that I was unable to move the patient at that time due to imminent delivery and concerns of trauma to both the patient and the baby. The newborn was delivered in the closet, suctioned, and the cord was clamped, only cutting it after pulsation. The delivery protocols were initiated. When the baby had a good cry we noted that it had movement, healthy color, and seemed to be in good condition. The baby was given to my partner, who stood with a blanket ready, for warmth and safety.

"What happened? Is my baby okay?"

"Yes, your baby is fine. It's right outside the closet with my partner waiting on you. Can we please move you to my cot for transport to the hospital? We still have to deliver the placenta en route and you've lost a lot of blood. You need fluids and I should monitor both of you on the way to the hospital."

"Yes, thank you. What happened?"

I explained the situation again to the woman and placed her on my cot for transport.

On the way to the hospital the woman was fully alert, providing the appropriate answers to all my questions. She denied suicidal ideation. We provided care for her wounds and initiated an IV with fluids.

"Ma'am do you have any medical history? Take any medications daily?"

"Just the normal stuff for pregnancy. I don't have any other medical problems."

"Do you remember getting into the closet? Did you cut yourself?"

"I don't remember. I have been having trouble remembering things lately. The other day I woke up walking outside of my home."

"What do you mean woke up?"

"It was like one moment I was watching TV and the next moment I was outside."

"Have you taken any of those COVID vaccines?"

"Yes, I'm completely protected. I just got my second Pfizer shot three days ago. I wasn't supposed to have my baby this early.

Later I attributed the early birth to possible "vaccine" complications. Thankfully this child lived. Many didn't.

It wasn't until several months later when doctors and scientists began speaking about mental problems in connection to the "vaccine" that I connected the dots.

Mental problems, brain fog, suicide, suicidal ideation, and others are among the many other horrible side effects that are said to be possibly caused by the "vaccine."

The mRNA technology is dangerous. On many levels. Its death by a thousand cuts.

After hearing Laura Aboli's remarks to Andrew Tate, I did a little bit of digging and found that there is ample evidence that the COVID-19 jab causes mental illness. One paper entitled, "Psychiatric Adverse Events Following COVID-19 Vaccination: A Population Based Cohort Study in Seoul, South Korea," finalized with the authors concluding that COVID-19 "vaccination" increases the risk of depression, anxiety, dissociation, stress-related and somatoform disorders, and sleep disorders.[74]

Being deprived of sleep is like being drunk. It's been said that operating a vehicle when you're sleep-deprived is as dangerous as driving drunk. Those who are already vulnerable to psychiatric events, warns the authors, may be susceptible to psychiatric adverse events.

The paper wasn't a hand-selected group of participants with a clear objective to prove a certain point. I say that because we often read skewed studies in medicine, even though that goes against science. There is a lot of money riding on scientific papers. Hence, James Thorp carefully explained how ghostwriters through Pharma use government-funded institutions like Harvard to conduct completely bogus studies. A more in-depth dive into this subject can be found in "The Next Wave is Brave" by doctors Richard Amerling, Heather Gessling, Harvey Risch, Peter McCullough, Jana Schmidt, and Jen Van De Water. [75]

This study, however, apparently includes a randomly selected cohort of 50% of Seoul's population, over 4 million individuals over nineteen. In regards to the study, Vernon Coleman states, "If you find me any scientific

74. https://www.nature.com/articles/s41380-024-02627-0

75. https://amzn.to/4aUXinE

study performed by a vaccine manufacturer which involved over four million people, I will eat my second best hat."[76]

As of October of 2024, Vernon Coleman is still censored from X, Facebook, Instagram, Linkedin, and all other social media. Please support Coleman by visiting www.vernoncoleman.com and take a look at books of his under the heading "COVID Books And The Great Reset." His first book about COVID and "the coming apocalypse" was published in April of 2020. You might call him prolific. I call him an oracle.

Zombie Vibes

"There's nothing there. Try to remain calm. You are going to pass out if you keep breathing that fast." 911. A young person, under twenty-one years of age.

"The demons are after me. I can see their eyes change! THEIR EYES ARE FUCKING BLACK!!" They were in hysterics; terrified. What this person saw was real, to them.

"Please sit on my cot; I will take you for help. I can pray with you, too, if you like?" This question is pretty routine these days. The suggestion alone seems to calm my hysterical patients. Unlike some, this person seemed to receive even a little comfort in the thought of prayer. They sat on the cot.

"Please don't let them get me." They whimpered. I secured the patient to the cot for transport.

"When did you start seeing these things? Do you have a history of depression or any other psych history? Take any medications?" I ask as a matter of routine. The patient was coherent, although nervous.

"No, I don't take medications. I started seeing them about a month ago. It was just one or two people a day with black eyes. Like their eyeballs are black as tar!"

---

76. https://lionessofjudah.substack.com/p/dr-vernon-coleman-proof-that-the?utm_source=post-email-title&publication_id=581065&post_id=149837027&utm_campaign=email-post-title&isFreemail=true&r=tluyu&triedRedirect=true&utm_medium=email

"Have you been under a lot of stress in the last month? Have you taken any drugs or alcohol?"

"No, I don't do drugs. I'm not old enough to drink!" The way the patient responded led me to believe that they were pretty straight-laced.

"Ok. Did you take the COVID vaccine?" I pried gently.

"Yes."

"When did you take that? Which one did you take?"

"About three months ago. It was my booster of Pfizer. I've had three now."

The patient's vitals were stable. Although his heart rate was slightly elevated, he had a normal sinus rhythm.

I was right about the hint of comfort in my question for prayer. The patient and I prayed on the way to the hospital. After some conversation, the patient seemed to honestly believe that certain people were "demons" based on their "black-colored eyes."

"Rebuke them."

First hand accounts from "vaccinated" individuals report psychosis shortly after COVID-19 "vaccination," including brain fog, hallucinations, dementia, suicidal ideation, self-mutilation, and blackouts. What has plagued me since seeing this starting in 2021 was the vast number of these individuals who have no medical history and, prior to "vaccination," were considered healthy and fit, even remarkably stable and grounded.

One of the reasons for writing this book was to get things off my chest, which is, frankly, a selfish goal. But Stephanie was able to twist my arm and get the ideas into a manuscript, a grueling task in and of itself because we wondered over many hours of conversation if telling my story could help the families of the "vaccine—" injured cope with what is about to come.

I don't think we've seen the full breadth of what this shot will do. I believe the immune system is rapidly and steadily decreasing among the "vaccinated." We are already seeing turbo-cancers soar and we are still seeing young people and even professional athletes dying suddenly.

What's more, the episodes of psychosis are increasing, not waning. The reason I want to expose this genocide isn't to one day see retribution for the bad guys (although that would be great), but because you absolutely must prepare. Preparation includes basic survival. You need to consider what you have to survive another bioweapon or cyberattack. If "they" did this over a flu in 2020, what will they do in 2025 or 2026? Or 2030? What we know from history is that dictatorial regimes don't take over fast... they slowly seep into power through a multi-pronged approach, usually starting with mind control.

On the subject of mind control, I've seen some horrifying adverse events that were so gruesome that we hesitated to include them in this book. It's now known in the medical community, even by those who are working to keep their heads in the sand, that "post-vaccination" psychosis has been well-documented. The media isn't covering these cases widely, but "Frontiers In Psychiatry" wrote, "It's important to acknowledge the potential for side effects, including rare cases like psychosis, which may increase with the rising number of vaccinations."[77]

In a study entitled "New-onset psychosis following COVID-19 vaccination: a systematic review," case reports, and studies were reviewed wherein the patient experienced new-onset psychosis following COVID-19 "vaccination" between December 1st, 2019, and November 21, 2023, using PubMed MEDLINE, ClinicalKey, and ScienceDirect. From the paper, "the Joanna Briggs Institute quality assessment tools were employed for included studies, revealing no significant publication bias."[78]

Thirteen of the twenty-four cases analyzed were female with a median age of thirty-six years. Twenty-two of the twenty-four patients had no history of somatic illness nor comorbidities, meaning over 90% had no medical history that might have predicted these results. In 45.8% of cases, psychotic symptoms were reported after the first jab, and in 50% after the

77. https://www.frontiersin.org/journals/psychiatry/articles/10.3389/fpsyt.2024.1360338/full

78. https://www.frontiersin.org/journals/psychiatry/articles/10.3389/fpsyt.2024.1360338/full

second shot. One-third of the patients reported receiving the Pfizer mRNA shot and 25% received the AstraZeneca jab.

In 83.3% of cases, the patient experienced motor disturbances, such as increased or decreased motor activity and "bizarre behavior." Most sadly, only half of the 24 patients made a full recovery after antipsychotics, steroids, and other treatment methods were administered. The remaining half suffered from "residual symptoms such as decreased emotional expressions, low affect, or residual psychotic symptoms."

Marina Zheng for the Epoch Times details a variety of psychotic events among people from whom you wouldn't expect such episodes. A 60-year-old neurotologist came down with cerebellar ataxia, preventing him from going to the bathroom or even feeding himself without assistance. The doctor claims that he would have panic attacks following his mRNA shot, confessing that he thought about killing himself many times after experiencing panic attacks nightly that would leave him in "abject terror." The symptoms first started after his second dose of the jab. By the time he had his third shot, he stated that "there was no question in my mind."

Other doctors and a nurse practitioner confess in Zheng's well-researched article that they witnessed various levels of psychiatric illness post "vaccination," with hallucinations and suicidality being among those symptoms. Zheng learned:

The Vaccine Adverse Event Reporting System (VAERS) is a self-reporting database co-managed by the U.S. Centers for Disease Control and Prevention (CDC) and the U.S. Food and Drug Administration (FDA), used to surveil for early warning signs of potential adverse reactions. VAERS has documented over 9,400 and 1,600 cases of anxiety and depression, respectively, in relation to the COVID-19 vaccines. The vaccines comprise, respectively, over 60 percent and up to 50 percent of all anxiety and depression reports on VAERS.

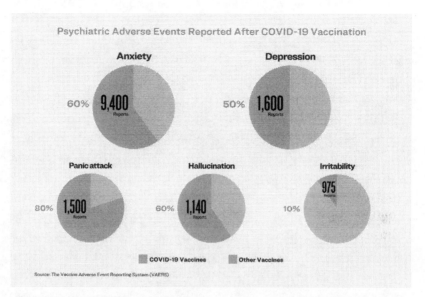

Psychiatric adverse reactions reported to VAERS after COVID-19 vaccination.

The NIH, ScienceDirect, and IBICT out of Brazil have reported cases of psychosis lasting several days, weeks, and even months. The image below shows screenshots from major medical journals, courtesy of The Epoch Times, illustrating three patients' psychotic events: the first from a woman in Brazil, the second a girl in India, and the third report from a Taiwanese boy.

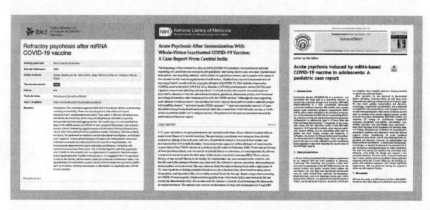

Screenshots of reports on psychotic adverse events in a Brazilian woman (L), an Indian girl (C), and a Taiwanese boy. Screenshots via The Epoch Times.

Dr. Diane Ryder Counce is a board-certified neurologist and neuroradiologist practicing in Birmingham, Alabama. She has been active in clinical research and is a principal investigator at Accel Research Sites, contributing to studies on neurological disorders, including Alzheimer's, stroke, Parkinson's disease, and migraines. [79] [80]

Dr. Counce suggests that the atrophy of the hippocampus, which is crucial for memory, may also impact the neighboring limbic system, the region associated with emotional processing. She reasons that as memory-related areas of the brain degrade, nearby systems linked to emotions might be affected. This could lead to decreased emotional regulation. Counce reports that several of her COVID-19 jabbed patients developed brain atrophy, including one who had hippocampal atrophy, which included symptoms of memory loss and a change in personality.

Doctors speculate that this drastic and sudden change in mental status and personality may be a result of the viral spike protein. The spike protein may cause inflammation, which is often associated with depression.[81] Marina Zhang also uncovered from Dr. Aruna Tummula that even pre-2020 research shows that mRNA "vaccines" are highly inflammatory.[82] Curiously, anti-inflammatory drugs and therapeutics such as Ivermectin and Hydroxychloroquine have been viciously attacked,[83] as was detailed in a previous chapter by Dr. Jim Thorp. I pray that everybody I love is currently stocked with Ivermectin. If your local compound pharmacist stops prescribing it, you can go to The Wellness Company for a prescription or even have a friend head south of the border to grab it quickly in Mexico.

PubMed speculated in September of 2022 that, "An mRNA-based COVID-19 vaccine can cause mild to moderate side effects. A number of

79. https://www.accelresearchsites.com

80. https://www.councemd.com

81. https://onlinelibrary.wiley.com/doi/full/10.1002/wps.20723#:~:text=Increased%20inflammation%20also%20exists%20in,inflammation%20is%20agnostic%20to%20diagnosis.

82. https://www.nature.com/articles/nrd.2017.243#Sec3

83. https://www.theepochtimes.com/article/psychosis-panic-attacks-hallucinations-bizarre-psychiatric-cases-among-the-COVID-vaccinated-5500128

cases of cardiac, gastrointestinal, and psychiatric side effects have been reported as rare side effects associated with the COVID-19 vaccine,"[84] as an abstract in the image below reveals.

PMID: 36170703
Free article

Abstract

Vaccines are crucial to ending the COVID-19 pandemic. An mRNA-based COVID-19 vaccine can cause mild to moderate side effects. A number of cases of cardiac, gastrointestinal, and psychiatric side effects have been reported as rare side effects associated with the COVID-19 vaccine. This article presents a patient, who after the second injection of the mRNA-based COVID-19 vaccine, immediately developed anxiety, nonspecific fear, and insomnia as the prodromal phase of psychosis. Starting from the second week, the patient manifested delusions of persecution, delusions of influence, thoughts insertion, and delusional behaviour, culminating in the suicide attempt. The duration of psychosis was eight weeks, and symptom reduction was observed only after the gradual administration of antipsychotics over four weeks. The investigations of the patient did not support any structural changes of the brain, any severe medical conditions, a neurological abnormality, a confusion or a state of unconsciousness or alterations in laboratory tests. Psychosis due to the use of alcohol or psychoactive substances was excluded. The psychological assessment of the patient demonstrated the endogenous type of thinking, and the patient had schizoid and paranoid personality traits strongly associated with schizophrenia. This case indicates a strong causal relationship between the mRNA-based COVID-19 vaccine injection and the onset of psychosis. We intend to follow up this case for possible development of schizophrenia and understand that the COVID-19 vaccine could possible play a trigger role in the development of primary psychosis. Longer-term supporting evidence is needed to estimate the prevalence of psychosis following vaccination with the mRNA-based COVID-19 vaccine.

The Israeli Health Ministry censored a doctor after she implied that there could be a connection between the jabs and the murder of a woman named Diana Raz by her husband. Dr. Rotem Inbar stated, "As for the murder... as strange as it sounds, there are psychotic or neurological situations because of the vaccine," according to the Jerusalem Post.[85]

Another study published on the NIH website speculates that the jab triggers an immune response that includes the release of proinflammatory cytokines. The authors of a study entitled, "Can new onset psychosis occur after mRNA based COVID-19 vaccine administration? A case report hypothesized that a cytokine storm may increase the risk of psychosis.[86]

---

84. https://pubmed.ncbi.nlm.nih.gov/36170703/

85. https://www.jpost.com/israel-news/doctor-who-hinted-coronavirus-vaccine-connected-to-murder-censured-658848

86. https://pmc.ncbi.nlm.nih.gov/articles/PMC8349391/#bib0002

The viral spike protein in the mRNA jab has long been a concern of leading doctors, including cardiologist Dr. Peter McCullough, who is on staff with The Wellness Company, one of the companies who has provided a Spike Protein Detox for both adults and kids. Stephanie even has her son taking the supplement during prolonged visits with "vaccinated" family members and she takes it herself as a defense against sweating, shedding yogis in her hot yoga studio. We'll include information in the graphic at the end of this book where you can find more information about The Wellness Company supplements, or you can get 10% off by using the code www.twc. health/stephanie where you can use the Spike Protein Support developed by TWC doctors that includes nattokinase, an ingredient that has been successful in treating some patients with spike protein related symptoms.

Other dangers of the spike protein may include:

- Neuroinflammation[87]
- Inflammation (with which depression often coincides, among many other diseases and discomforts);
- Blood clotting, which reduces the oxygenation of tissues, forcing them to age;
- Blood clotting in the brain, which may cause cognitive impairments such as psychosis;
- Anxiety, erectile dysfunction, and visual impairment from the clotting;
- Lowered immunity;
- Disturbance in brain activity (increasing likelihood of psychosis);
- Nerve irritation and neuroinflammation (linked to suicidality);
- Activation of human endogenous retroviruses (HERVs), which are linked to psychiatric symptoms like schizophrenia;[88]

---

87. https://pubmed.ncbi.nlm.nih.gov/26223957/

88. https://www.cell.com/iscience/fulltext/S2589-0042(23)00681-8?_returnURL=https%3A%2F%2Flinkinghub.elsevier.com%2Fretrieve%2Fpii%2FS2589004223006818%3Fshowall%3Dtrue

- Reactivation of Epstein-Barr virus (EBV), which is linked to psychosis;[89]
- Damage to the gut microbiome (also leading to psychiatric symptoms; your gut is your second brain) [90]

I've seen a lot of weird shit in the army as well as in my everyday life as an EMT. But a patient sewing their eyes and mouth shut with a needle and thread or a patient biting into his hand while staring me dead in the eye were, to put it lightly, fodder for my most horrific nightmares.

Sometimes, considering what I've seen, I don't honestly know how I'm still here; how I haven't, too, succumbed to psychosis or psychiatric illness. There were more nights than I can count during the writing of this book that Steph called and said, "hey, are you okay?" Wading through what I've seen and penning it in this book was pretty traumatic for Steph. It's traumatic for the majority of you to read it. But imagine seeing it.

I don't sleep well.

I often wonder how our Heavenly Father feels witnessing sin. How it feels to see man, with whom He shared the garden before the fall, do shit like we do with the gift of our free will.

God help us.

89. https://www.ncbi.nlm.nih.gov/pmc/articles/PMC6737467/

90. https://www.theepochtimes.com/article/psychosis-panic-attacks-hallucinations-bizarre-psychiatric-cases-among-the-COVID-vaccinated-5500128

Part Three

Planned Extermination

Chapter Fourteen
For The Greater Good

Due to the fact that I've done CPR in a Pfizer line, I cannot in good conscience put this substance into my body. Give to Caesar what is his, and to God what is God's. This body belongs to God.

Harry Fisher, from his medical exemption letter, 2021

"When were you first diagnosed with cancer?" I asked a patient recently.

"Six weeks ago. They say it's already stage four."

"I'm so sorry," I responded. "Did you take any of those COVID "vaccines?""

"No. I've heard of the turbo cancers those shots can cause."

I paused for a breath and admitted to the patient, "it sounds like you are experiencing turbo cancer now, though. What do the doctors say?"

The patient didn't mind the prying. He said, "I was low on hemoglobin about 10 weeks ago, was feeling weak and they gave me a blood transfusion at the hospital. The cancer wasn't present then. I'm betting I received vaccinated blood. Was diagnosed with stage four cancer just a few weeks after that."

Just weeks later I spoke with another patient who was suffering from what appeared to be a "vaccine" adverse event. The patient wasn't jabbed, but had been intimate with somebody who had.

Curious about the experience, I did a basic online search and found the low hemoglobin after an mRNA COVID-19 shot could be caused by autoimmune hemolytic anemia, which is an acquired hemolysis that has been reported after the jab.

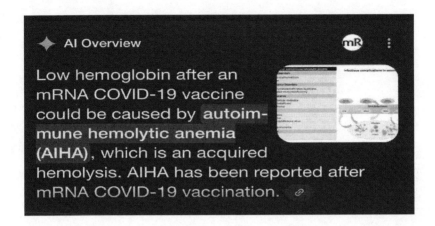

When posting my story on X, comments poured in from people who had lost loved ones who were un-jabbed after blood transfusions, underscoring the need for untainted blood lest we eventually poison the entire global population.

A researcher with the handle @NotOpCue in the comments of that post did an even more exciting dig, finding now-censored data from the "Wayback Machine" indicating that researchers at the Sloan Kettering Cancer Center found that changes in an information-carrying molecule called "messenger RNA" (mRNA) can inactivate tumor-suppressing proteins, therapy promoting cancer. About forty days later Sloan Kettering added a disclaimer to that summary organized under the location detail "scientists find cancer drivers hiding ma no DNA" that stated, "It's important to note that mRNAs are a normal component of all cells and the specific ones discussed here are not involved in mRNA-based vaccines, like the ones developed against SARS COV-2." See the image below for the screen capture of the Memorial Sloan Kettering Cancer Center summary and subsequent disclaimer.[91]

---

91. https://x.com/NotOpCue/status/1633700970365427712

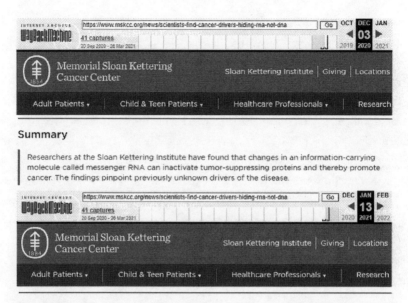

Summary

Researchers at the Sloan Kettering Institute have found that changes in an information-carrying molecule called messenger RNA can inactivate tumor-suppressing proteins and thereby promote cancer. The findings pinpoint previously unknown drivers of the disease.

Summary

Researchers at the Sloan Kettering Institute have found that changes in an information-carrying molecule called messenger RNA can inactivate tumor-suppressing proteins and thereby promote cancer. The findings pinpoint previously unknown drivers of the disease. **It's important to note that mRNAs are a normal component of all cells and the specific ones discussed here are not involved in mRNA-based vaccines, like the one developed against SARS-CoV-2.**

In the same thread, another man admitted,

> *The woman that I was supposed to marry, had to take the jab to work, then they sent them home to work. She developed stage 4 bone cancer and I just heard from her and sadly, she's close to the end... Plus the chemo has done to her what it does to many, gave her false hope, and weakened her immune system and her blood vessels.*

The Nuremberg Code

The Nuremberg Code is a set of ethical principles for conducting human experimentation. It was established after World War II during the infamous "Nuremberg Trials" in 1947. During the Nuremberg Trials, the public learned about inhumane experiments conducted by Nazi doctors on concentration camp prisoners. The Code laid the foundation for modern ethical standards in medical research and human rights. Or did it?

The Nuremberg Military Tribunal's decision in the case of the United States v Karl Brandt et al. includes what is now called the Nuremberg Code, a ten-point statement delimiting permissible medical experimentation on human subjects. According to this statement, humane experimentation is justified only if its results benefit society and it is carried out in accord with basic principles that "satisfy moral, ethical, and legal concepts."[92]

Sadly, the Nuremberg Code is not legally binding. It has significantly influenced international and national regulations governing human experimentation, a cornerstone in bioethics and the framework for ensuring the protection of human subjects in research. At best, the COVID jabs are a violation of the Nuremberg Code, mainly the following four of ten statutes, including (abbreviated):

1. **Voluntary Consent:** *Participation in medical experiments must be voluntary, and participants must give informed consent without coercion, deceit, or undue influence. They should have sufficient knowledge of the experiment's nature, purpose, and potential risks.*

4. **Avoidance of Unnecessary Harm:** *The experiment should be conducted to avoid all unnecessary physical or mental suffering and injury.*

6. **Risk Aversion:** *The degree of risk to be taken should never exceed that determined by the humanitarian importance of the problem to be solved by the experiment.*

10. **Willingness To Terminate:** *During the experiment, the scientist in charge must be prepared to terminate the experiment at any stage if he has probable cause to believe, in the exercise of the good faith, superior skill, and careful judgment required of him, that a continuation of the experiment is likely to result in injury, disability, or death to the experimental subject.*[93]

92. "Permissible Medical Experiments." Trials of War Criminals before the Nuremberg Military Tribunals under Control Council Law No. 10. Nuremberg October 1946 – April 1949, Washington. U.S. Government Printing Office (n.d.), vol. 2., pp. 181-182.

93. https://research.unc.edu/human-research-ethics/resources/ccm3_019064/

The Nuremberg Code (1947)

Permissible Medical Experiments

The great weight of the evidence before us to effect that certain types of medical experiments on human beings, when kept within reasonably well-defined bounds, conform to the ethics of the medical profession generally. The protagonists of the practice of human experimentation justify their views on the basis that such experiments yield results for the good of society that are unprocurable by other methods or means of study. All agree, however, that certain basic principles must be observed in order to satisfy moral, ethical and legal concepts:

1. The voluntary consent of the human subject is absolutely essential. This means that the person involved should have legal capacity to give consent; should be so situated as to be able to exercise free power of choice, without the intervention of any element of force, fraud, deceit, duress, overreaching, or other ulterior form of constraint or coercion; and should have sufficient knowledge and comprehension of the elements of the subject matter involved as to enable him to make an understanding and enlightened decision. This latter element requires that before the acceptance of an affirmative decision by the experimental subject there should be made known to him the nature, duration, and purpose of the experiment; the method and means by which it is to be conducted; all inconveniences and hazards reasonably to be expected; and the effects upon his health or person which may possibly come from his participation in the experiment.

   The duty and responsibility for ascertaining the quality of the consent rests upon each individual who initiates, directs, or engages in the experiment. It is a personal duty and responsibility which may not be delegated to another with impunity.
2. The experiment should be such as to yield fruitful results for the good of society, unprocurable by other methods or means of study, and not random and unnecessary in nature.
3. The experiment should be so designed and based on the results of animal experimentation and a knowledge of the natural history of the disease or other problem under study that the anticipated results justify the performance of the experiment.
4. The experiment should be so conducted as to avoid all unnecessary physical and mental suffering and injury.
5. No experiment should be conducted where there is an a priori reason to believe that death or disabling injury will occur; except, perhaps, in those experiments where the experimental physicians also serve as subjects.
6. The degree of risk to be taken should never exceed that determined by the humanitarian importance of the problem to be solved by the experiment.
7. Proper preparations should be made and adequate facilities provided to protect the experimental subject against even remote possibilities of injury, disability or death.
8. The experiment should be conducted only by scientifically qualified persons. The highest degree of skill and care should be required through all stages of the experiment of those who conduct or engage in the experiment.
9. During the course of the experiment the human subject should be at liberty to bring the experiment to an end if he has reached the physical or mental state where continuation of the experiment seems to him to be impossible.
10. During the course of the experiment the scientist in charge must be prepared to terminate the experiment at any stage, if he has probable cause to believe, in the exercise of the good faith, superior skill and careful judgment required of him, that a continuation of the experiment is likely to result in injury, disability, or death to the experimental subject.

Image of "The Nuremberg Code" with highlights courtesy of
@NotOpCue on X.com

When I was a kid in 1985, babies between 0 and 12 months old in the U.S. were given approximately five vaccines. In 2004, babies twelve months and younger were given an average of thirty-two vaccines. So why are today's kids sicker than any generation since the age of cholera or tuberculosis, in the late 1800's? It doesn't say much about scientific advancement.

Dr. Vernon Coleman posits that vaccines did not eliminate the risk of death due to infectious disease, but that cleaner water, better food, better housing and improved sewage disposal fostered better health and less deadly infections.[94]

When my four children were under one year of age, I dutifully took each one of them to their pediatrician for vaccination during what is called a "wellness visit." Little did I know that these pediatricians stay in business purely because of the wellness visits. The foot traffic and cross-selling during those "check-ups" account for the vast majority of pediatrician income; not treating sick patients, but treating well ones.

In his book "Anyone Who Tells You That Vaccines Are Safe and Effective is Lying," which we'll cover again later in this book, Coleman proposes that mass vaccination campaigns are doing more harm than good. I'm going to put words in Coleman's mouth to suggest that based off the evidence he presents, the words "mass vaccination" and "genocide" are essentially interchangeable.

You can find Dr. Coleman's book on Amazon, but get the physical copy as soon as humanly possible and guard it carefully in a fireproof safe. Ideally a blue one (DEW joke). Joe Biden's Administration, coincidentally, tried to have Coleman's book banned[95]

Shortly after I began noticing adverse events post "vaccination," I began to question the jab. I knew pretty early on that I would resist until I saw more medical data and results; and the results I witnessed were not comforting.

The sight of one's government orchestrating the demise of its citizens is a chilling spectacle. My initial response was to raise my voice in protest. I created a TikTok video that went viral but I was soon banned from the platform. Before good ol' Elon freed the bird I created a new Twitter

---

94. https://www.vernoncoleman.com/main.htm

95 https://www.amazon.co.uk/Anyone-Tells-Vaccines-Effective-Lying/dp/1091757712/ ref=sr_1_1?crid=3N88VRZLR5OVQ&dib=eyJ2IjoiMSJ9.Llal-Tbq6khZ3OXmT6HB- dg.fb7N-B_hEzKGd9N5q7jS2hUE43rNzO9C4cC9XJTs5_w&dib_tag=se&key- words=anyone+who+tells+you+vaccines+are+safe+and+effective+is+ly- ing&qid=1726517185&sprefix=%2Caps%2C126&sr=8-1

account just about daily. I felt compelled to speak out, but I wasn't sure if I was ready to shout... I felt scared. I knew that I was tough; but the enemy is dark, dirty, and out for blood.

As I began to scroll through social media looking for others who would validate that I wasn't crazy, somebody quoted Coleman. I thought he sounded like a genius and he had to be very brave to say what he was saying in this era of censorship. When I learned that he had been sounding the alarm for many years about vaccines, I was humbled. How did I let my beautiful son Harry succumb to vaccine injury when he was just an infant when the information was out there?

At that point, knowing that the information I needed was out there but I hadn't sought it out, I felt a tremendous wave of guilt wash over me. I had drunk the Kool-aid, and now my child was never going to live an everyday life. He is very, very sick.

So I got drunk—a lot.

As the burden of silence and censorship grew heavy, I sought refuge in the numbing embrace of alcohol. At the time of this writing I don't drink anymore, and I never will again. More on the reasons why later... let's just say that I almost ended up in a body bag myself, and I'll detail that moment towards the end of this book.

It is safe to say that drinking gallons of beer on an empty stomach was my attempt to escape the fact that genocide was brewing before my eyes, unfolding at a rapid rate. The booze was my attempt at a shield. But it didn't make me more robust; I was equipping myself with poison to get rid of the images of dead men, women, children, and preborn babies because of yet another poison. In some ironic twist, I was using poison to forget about poison. I was buying into the propaganda that beer is a good time; it's the nightcap I deserve after a long day. It even made me more fun when I tumbled and wrestled with my two youngest children, both little boys. I reasoned that because booze is easy to pick up without a prescription, it isn't a "drug." I later learned that I was very, very mistaken.

My connections began to fray under the strain of what I witnessed and the reality of the genocide unfolding before me. Before long, my life resembled a rudderless ship, adrift in a sea of the departed. I couldn't look out ahead of me to chart a course without seeing their faces; the images of the slain haunted me. And so I stopped trying to move forward. I drank, treading water, and contributed little outside of clocking in and trying to keep people alive. The bottle felt safe for a time. The opening was narrow. I only saw a sliver of reality when I looked up or out. At this time, I couldn't handle more truth than what filled my blood-soaked day job. My shifts were between twelve and twenty-four hours, with very long days in between shifts. During the times when I was away from my family, and sometimes even when they were there, drinking was my only way to cope and blur the images in my head. One day, I was told that if I didn't comply with the jab, there would be no more grace extended to me, even though without me,e there would be even fewer emergency personnel during a time when we were already short-handed. But, short-sighted as it was, the administration in charge of my ambulance unit decided to strongarm me. I didn't cave.

My wife at that time was livid. She didn't want me to get the shot, but she worried about paying bills. We had already been living paycheck-to-paycheck. The mama bear in her lashed out. She was angry with the plandemic. I was enraged at the hospitals. I was furious that I was one of too few to stand up and hold out without the jab. She was angry at me because she didn't know where else to put her anger. She was furious at my social media videos, the only productive work I had the motivation to do. And looking back a couple of years, I wonder if she was also mad that she couldn't be the person to whom I confided.

My social media presence became essential to me because it was the virtual "pub" where I could go and mingle with other healthcare workers. Every time I pressed record, I prayed a life could be saved, but my wife wasn't getting that attention or my vulnerability; I wonder now if it made her jealous. That was never my intention. I just needed a place to vent. With two toddlers in tow, she didn't need my bitchin'.

For every friendly healthcare worker or anti-vaxxer online there were ten haters. I was being mocked for being anti-vax, threatened constantly, and demonized as a murderer. I wasn't scrolling Twitter all day; I called every ambulance service within a hundred miles. They were all desperate for personnel, but each one claimed that they wouldn't hire me until I took the jab. They all, without a doubt, had managed their fair share of patients dying from the shot. When they said, even apologetically sometimes, that I was unwelcome until I took the shot, they sounded plainly Satanic to me. Like the witch in Snow White holding the poisoned apple. "Here, sweetie. Take a bite. It's good for you." They knew it was poison.

At one point, I asked the Stillwater Oklahoma Ambulance Service, "What are your call times?" They explained that their call times were much longer than normal. This means that they were short on personnel, and the people in their community were dying due to the lack of staff.

Call times are critical in my line of work. Too much time elapsing equals less lives saved. Minutes can be the difference between life and death. Yet these EMS services were underperforming to the point of killing people due to mandated tyranny. I was spent; I vocalized this to Stillwater Oklahoma Ambulance Service. They actually agreed, but still wouldn't hire me.

Those who understand that the "vaccines" were deadly can quickly identify these stories as genocidal or democidal behaviors. However, many still don't know why I'm angry. "You had a choice, Harry. You weren't being forced to take the shot. You could choose to find another job. Don't be melodramatic. Nobody was tied down and poked." Well, that's not actually true; there is a video of a young serviceman who was tied down, restrained, and jabbed. But that's beside the point. I was told that I needed to stop being so dramatic about the mandates because I wasn't physically restrained.

But it didn't feel like I had a choice. I put my family at risk of homelessness. I was forced to lose my job and I called every ambulance service within a two hour radius to no avail. I lost my marriage due, I imagine, to the strain and stress put on me and my wife. I also take responsibility for being a beer guzzling slob, mind you. But what nobody seems to comprehend when I repeat this story is the fact that *your communities didn't have a choice.* You lost EMS services because of the mandates. Your dad or aunt might have died because a call took too long. Services didn't arrive in time to save him or her. Accepting this tyranny for EMS services cost us lives. Your community lost a great baseball coach or a prayer warrior in your church. You lost key players on your team. You lost members of your town who were critical to the fabric that protects and loves your children. You actually didn't have a choice in that. That mandate was murder.

It took months before I finally found a service that hired me by accepting my exemption. The pay cut was staggering; I had to work double the shifts to compensate for my financial loss. I was never a slacker; I used to work 60-hour work weeks. I started working 120 hours a week. This was the final straw in my marriage; the "d" word was spoken, and it was hard to turn that ship around. I reasoned that my wife was young and better going and finding somebody now than in ten years from then. She had a whole life ahead of her. I was on the verge of having two ex-wives and four kids. I wasn't feeling as hopeful for myself. That allowed me, in some ways, to be highly present in my work. I had nothing else to distract me from all the dots I was connecting.

Once I got back to work I was on one contract in Oklahoma where I'd already witnessed many young deaths from heart attacks, strokes, and miscarriages shortly after "vaccination." And that was just after one week back on the job. One afternoon I got a call to see a patient. They had developed drastic, lethal side effects. Among them was chest pain. "Did you take a shot?" I asked the patient.

They responded, "yes, Pfizer."

The individual was in their early twenties and didn't live another hour after our conversation. An aortic aneurysm took the life of someone that just wanted to do their part "for the greater good."

One after another, we witnessed bodies succumb to this deadly shot. For a minute I wished I was back at home saddled up to a six-pack again posting on socials about my anger. "Safe and effective," rang in my ears. The men and women working around me definitely knew that we were up against a failed experiment. "Safe and effective," I muttered once in an ambulance with a patient having passed on before we reached the ER.

"Something like that," my colleague muttered.

This became like a code. I knew who "knew" what was up in these little codes.

In some ways, it was like being surrounded by the Gestapo. I had to be careful who I spoke with and what I revealed about what I knew. I felt like a double agent when I muttered something like, "We're all in this together," the response was a snicker or even a blatant, "as long as Pfizer turns a profit." Then I knew I'd found somebody who was awake. I didn't see many of them, though.

"Can you believe all this?" I remember asking a physician's assistant once in the ER after a long night of prominent "vaccine" injuries and death.

"I'm just putting my head in the sand," she said.

"This problem is too big." She concluded.

She kept her head down, scribbling notes in the most recent deceased patient's medical record before crossing the room to tidy up equipment and clean the treatment area. I stood, watching her. I didn't even have the energy to leave the room. The PA began setting up equipment for the next patient that might come in, perhaps one that I would deliver to her. I saw that she was processing through keeping busy, never allowing a single limb to settle. If her arms weren't both moving, both her legs were. Even as she penned notes in the chart her head followed her hands. Her wedding ring dangled off her finger and I noticed that her scrubs were abnormally large on her.

"You getting enough sleep?"

I knew better than to ask her about food or diet, despite my being on the verge of losing my second marriage to one of the fairer sex.

"I'm hanging in there. Thank you. Take care."

She walked out of the room. Busy, busy, busy. She had to distract herself in her own way.

There was no doubt in my mind that she was jabbed, too. The hospitals were less motivated to accept nurses or other personnel who didn't comply. There were a few hold-outs. There are some fake cards here and there. However, the hospital staff was threatened; the administration would even bring in attorneys to battle anybody who claimed religious exemption. Some of those religious exemptions included not wanting to take the shots due to the use of aborted fetuses in the product. The attorney gave a list of products that use "HEK Cells," or aborted babies—anything from sodas to potato chips, Advil to Albuterol. The attorneys were tongue-in-cheek, mocking staff and their request for exemptions by daring them to claim they didn't use any of the products, including HEK Cells.

HEK Cells is short for "Human Embryonic Kidney 293 Cells" or HEK293. These are a specific cell line derived from human embryonic kidney cells. Initially generated in the early 1970s by Dutch scientist Dr. Alex van der Eb, HEK Cells were used in biological and medical research for various purposes, especially in molecular biology, biotechnology, and pharmacology. They're easy to culture in a lab and proliferate.

HEK Cells aren't actually in sodas, but have been used in food and beverage R&D to study taste receptors on a molecular level. They can be engineered to express human taste receptors, allowing researchers to screen compounds to see how they react with those receptors. We all know we like sugar, and it tastes just about the same to everybody: sweet. So if you want to avoid HEK Cell usage, anything with low-calorie or "natural" sweeteners should be avoided. HEK Cells are used in research, not in the actual sodas or potato chips.

That said, the attorneys engaged in mental abuse and a form of gaslighting healthcare personnel to get them to take the jabs. It was, indeed, a new low for humanity.

Thankfully, I received my religious exemption. I wrote "due to the fact that I've done CPR in a Pfizer line, I cannot in good conscience put this substance into my body. Give to Caesar what is his, and to God what is God's. This body belongs to God." The exemption was approved, but the hospital canceled the rest of my contract and sent me home. What a terrible pandemic that we could risk losing critical hospital staff, eh?

I have many times dreamt that the hospital which took me out of commission would write a letter to the community apologizing for removing a valuable asset to the health and lives of their people.

But that wouldn't be necessary unless they felt contrition.

That wouldn't be necessary if this was intentional after all, now would it?

Censorship

Some time ago, I was speaking with a friend who works for the NIH. I understand that at the time of this writing, the NIH provides 19,000 jobs to Americans, but when RFK Jr. has his way, it will employ substantially fewer.

"Man, they banned be from TikTok. They labeled me a "terrorist." Me! A veteran who swore an oath to this country."

"Brutal, man," my friend stated compassionately, genuinely bummed.

"They said I'm banned for 'terroristic activity,' I continued, "all because I said, 'I'm a paramedic that did CPR IN PFIZER LINE!' This is fucking insane!"

My courageous friend responded, "I've been trying to get as much information out anonymously as possible, I keep getting censored, too. Yes. This is all so crazy. It's like living in a bad horror film or the twilight zone!"

"How can this be happening? You know this is mass murder, right?"

The friend was silent. He knew. I knew he knew but asked the question somewhat rhetorically; I was frustrated. Sometimes insanity is doing the same thing time and again, and expecting different results. As the plandemic waned, I grew increasingly insane asking the same questions over and over, sometimes multiple times a minute. "You work at the NIH and you know what they're pushing. You know it is killing our people. You have to come out and tell everyone where you work, who you are, and what you're experiencing," I pled, in vain.

My friend confirmed what I already knew. "I can't, Harry. I'm scared for my family. They'll just fire me and ruin my life. Or worse. It's all too big. These people don't mess around. You really need to be more careful too, Harry."

Imagine having this information confirmed by somebody at the NIH while you're going to work every day seeing children harmed, people murdered, and lives ruined by an experimental substance that was mandated by the President of the United States.

Isn't he held to an oath, too?

No oath is too ironclad to quell greed.

At this time, it wasn't just TikTok that banned me, but all other major platforms—until X.com, that is.

I can't justify censorship. I went from the ultimate troll laboring to block holistic health practitioners and label them as "nutjobs" while working with The Daily Show to getting a swift kick in the behind from karma for my previous choices. For the record, I don't believe in karma. I believe in consequences. The consequence of a divided nation that has glorified division instead of listening, a mob I was once part of, came back for me once I tried to leave their "gang."

The division in this information war will forever inform the decisions of adults who have been awake during the past few years. The paradox of everybody embracing "their" truth and fighting to the death to defend it is tragic. Of course, one side is armed with information while the other is armed with propaganda.

Interestingly, those authentically seeking truth don't waste time name-calling, discriminating against others for their beliefs (in freedom, bodily autonomy, and personal sovereignty, no less), and vehement disrespect online. We are too busy pinpointing where our intuition leads us and digging up supporting facts among papers, testimonials, and accurate word data. Those who aren't digging generally resort to doubling down on their ignorance, resulting in vicious trolling.

The battle for belief is fierce, with both sides willing to endure emotional turmoil to defend their perceived truths. This struggle has taught me that reality cannot be imposed in large doses. Instead, it must be presented in digestible portions to avoid overwhelming rejection. This approach mirrors the tale of Jack and the Beanstalk, a story of choice and consequence. Despite mockery, Jack's decision to trade his cow for magic beans led to an unexpected ascent to a realm of knowledge and adventure.

In our current information war, we offer seeds of wisdom, but only those open to the possibility will trade their comfort for growth. Many are content with their current state, unable to envision the potential value of change. This complacency is often intentional, as those in power seek to stifle our spiritual and physical potential, confining us within self-constructed barriers.

Yet, they fail to acknowledge that we possess the key to our liberation. It is always within our grasp. The choice to use it or ignore it rests solely with us. Whether we choose to sow the seeds, climb the beanstalk, reach new heights, or remain confined is ultimately our decision.

When I heard that nurse say that the patient I was trying to resuscitate was "the second one in two weeks," that moment catapulted not only my passion as a social media truth warrior, but it also sprung the warrior within me into action. Knowing how many people probably succumbed to this experiment was weighing heavily on my mind from that moment; it's become the pivot in my hero's journey. Even today, that simple, dark moment still haunts my thoughts, even though I've seen much darker ones since. People walked into these clinics like sheep to the slaughter hoping to save themselves or their loved ones. Lord, please let my story bring hope that when we all get cornered and incensed about evil that we will be more effective in bringing about more good.

It truly felt like we had a domestic enemy that was intentionally trying to murder our fellow Americans. But this wasn't just an American murder scene but a global one. An international cabal was deliberately blocking much-needed warnings from the front line.

Imagine being in a war, and your medic comes to you saying, "The enemy is killing our soldiers." do you tell the medic to shut up? Do you cut out the tongue of the person trying to warn you? I would hope not. But that is precisely what has happened. It's still happening on most platforms.

Why?

I asked "why" a lot in the first couple years after the "vaccine" rollouts until I settled on a simple answer that is very personal to me and my story. I took an oath to defend my nation against enemies foreign and domestic and didn't take that oath lightly. No, I wasn't a Republican at that time and up until the writing of this book I have never even voted in a Presidential election. But I've always loved my country, even while being suspicious and unimpressed with its politicians.

I don't like taking oaths. The Bible says we shouldn't. However, I did. And knowing people are being murdered en masse weighs heavily on my conscience; I took an oath to protect you.

In the original wrestling and turmoil within I was angry, as most of you were, too. I wanted to destroy anyone willing to knowingly kill people, and frankly, a firing squad seemed like a reasonable consequence for treason. However, the situation of retribution for COVID criminals is too deeply entrenched to merely hand out death sentences. The recovery will require a scalpel, not a sword.

Going forward, we must find the cabal in charge of this genocide; the puppetmasters at the tippy top. Don't rely on the President to enact justice; it has to be a widespread, immutable demand from the People. In a perfect scenario we will have trials to make examples of the criminals. Drag those trials out slowly like the Depp-Heard soap opera or the O.J. Simpson shenanigans. This gives the public time they'll need to wake up; if they are capable. If we, however, allow this horrific genocide to go unpunished, then our children will experience it, and perhaps on an even more gruesome scale. The caskets will keep getting smaller and smaller. Over the years, if we sweep these crimes under the rug, we will consequently see more of our freedoms and our voice continue to get smaller, more censored, and less powerful. I don't want to live in that world, and neither should you.

Poem: A Witches Brew

A witch's brew you can't undo.
Potions of death, most without clue.
Turning children to martyrs, experimental fodder.
Crying mother, denying father.
Nurses dancing on Tok while fleecing the flock.
Broken the time on the humanities clock.
Taking their shot, what mad scientists wrought,
white coats were once sought, but all have been bought.

In halls of power, the hour grows sour,
The tree of liberty stripped of its flower.
Voices of reason, now voices of dread,
As the light of the dawn is replaced with blood red.

And in this twilight, where truth is a lie,
The silent majority just kneel as they die.
For every choice, now made in fear,
The end we watch, for it draws near.

Chapter Fifteen

I'm A Bad Man

"How can you be so chipper when the world is turning to shit?"

"How can you see people dying all day and still smoke cigarettes?" Stephanie responds.

"Do you like me?" I ask.

"Of course. I consider you one of my dearest friends. I know you'd come out here and give a lickin' to anybody who hurt me or my boy, even if you had to take a helicopter to get here." Steph knows of my aversion to helicopters and my recent fear of flying after the revolutionary cancer doctors were sent soaring to their deaths in a passenger flight of 62 souls over Brazil.

"If you like me, then why do you sound so damned chipper when you ask me if I'm scared of lung cancer?"

"I'm not chipper about the idea of your lungs turning into ash. I'm chipper..." She stops for a second, considering why she's chipper.

"I've never thought of myself as chipper, actually. Thank you. I take that as a compliment."

"It wasn't a compliment! I think you're insane!" I say. "What's wrong with you?"

"I think it's a tremendous compliment. On a day when one of my dear friends just ran into a pillar on I-35 and I'm devastated about losing him and feeling the weight of that loss, it's interesting to me that you see me as chipper, even today."

"You're always chipper. And you do this a lot, 'mm-hmm,' and that pisses me off."

"Harry, everything pisses you off. You're just a bad man." Steph says it teasingly, but she doesn't overdo the sarcasm. This forty-something year old woman can still count on one hand the men she's slept with in her life. She doesn't drink, doesn't do drugs, to my knowledge doesn't touch cigarettes. She goes to church on Sundays and any other day she finds time. She's giving. Trusting. Even naive. I'll never be like her.

"I'll never be like you, and that's a good thing. You're going to be caught by surprise."

"No, Harry. I know damn well what's happening in the world. I know that there's probably going to be another bioweapon. I've read the same pages as you have from the globalist playbook. I know there are men and women plotting our demise as we speak. I've spent years closing my blinds at night, scared every time some kid passes by with a light on his bicycle, wondering if "they" are coming after me for my own activism. I know there's an enemy. I'm just not letting him live inside my head rent free."

"They are coming after you. They are plotting your demise. You should be terrified."

"Anger is like drinking poison expecting another person to die. That's not something my nervous system can handle precisely because I know how bad things are, how shitty they're going to be, and how terrified my child will be. Don't you ever wonder if your sons will be in war?"

I don't think they're going to draft either one of my sons. Drafting a non-verbal autistic child is even more unimaginable than drafting girls. And my youngest boy has Type 1 Diabetes. Even in the End Times, he'd be too much of a liability. Chatty Cathy continues to expound on her irritating chipperness.

"Today when I spoke with another friend about Ron dying, he told me 'he'd pray.' I told him he's an idiot. Why would you pray for him? His fate is sealed. I felt angry for a moment. I've had lots of conversations with Ron about God but recently he got really into aliens and started talking about connecting with some Pleidian brothers or relatives from the planet Cookoo. In an instant, I felt terrified that my friend was going to spend time in hell."

"Spend time? Like a vacation?" I haven't heard anybody describe an eternity of hopelessness as 'spending time in hell."

"The jury is still out on hell. I wonder if even those captives will be released."

"No way God is releasing murderers and child rapists. No way He should."

I'm one of those guys who can't imagine sharing space with pedos in heaven, call me crazy.

"But the reason you think I'm chipper is because I've dealt with my own death and reconciled it. Well, Christ did all the work. I know where I'm going. I've been through hell, and I've got an insurance plan in place to get into heaven, first-class. Maybe it is peace that passeth understanding. Maybe it's naivete. Maybe I'm like those doctors you talk to who refuse to draw the parallel between miscarriages and the 'vaccine.' Maybe it's cognitive dissonance. Whatever it is, I have peace."

"See, there you go again. I know you're telling me the truth. I even agree with you. But the way you say it is pissing me off. See, I am a bad man. I'm a jerk."

"Well, Harry, you have some King David tendencies…"

"What part of David? Dancing around naked while praising the Lord?"

"I was thinking more that you're a great man with some serious darkness, too," she responds.

"Do you know what I want to do?" I ask her.

"Don't tell me. Virgin ears." She laughs. I'm happy for the comic relief, as well.

"I just want to find a remote plot of land with a fridge full of cold beer and a carton of cigarettes. Then I don't want to see a soul. I just want to watch sunsets."

"Bet you'll tweet," she quips.

"Aren't you funny? I'd never touch a phone again. I'd never give the haters another syllable of fodder. I don't want to be the guy starting a revolution. I don't want to be the guy speaking up. I don't want attention. I don't want to see other humans ever again as long as I live. This world is shit and it's full of shitty people, including psychopaths intent on genocide. And as for the cigarettes, I'm going to die. Why die without pleasure? I feel like that would be the ultimate slap in Christ's face."

"Harry, don't you think you're abusing grace? Paul asked us if we should go on sinning because of grace. His answer was no. Remember, Christ didn't come to abolish the law, He came to fulfill it. Fornication, lying, drunkenness, murder: God hates these things. And so should we, like our eternal lives depend on it."

"There's no way in hell I'm not going to heaven," I responded, happy with my little play on words.

"And when you get there, I bet the Lord will be standing there hand-in-hand with your Grandma Josie, ready to greet you."

"I can't wait to go home. I want to sit in her lap and hear her sing "Blessed Assurance" more than anything in the world," I said.

"I love your assurance. I love how assured you are of God's love. I love how much you believe in your salvation, with no hints of ego or a sense of your having earned it. You, indeed, have blessed assurance. The Bible says that when Adam and Eve ate from the knowledge of good and evil that it was only then they realized they were naked. Do you remember what they did?"

"The hid," I said.

"Right. But you don't hide. You made a smoothie out of every single fruit from the tree of knowledge and now God is walking down the path towards you. What do you do?"

"What?" I asked.

"You're standing in the path waving your arms naked as can be and you're saying, hey Lord, look at me! You won't believe what I found. That tree you told me not to eat from? The fruit is wild. Is it laced? This is fun!"

Now Steph and I are both laughing. Best laugh I've had all week, in fact. The image is ridiculous, but accurate.

I begin to stitch something together in my head. "You know what I hate more than anything?"

"Helicopters," she guesses.

"Good point. Probably true. But there's something I might hate even more than helicopters." I paused.

"I hate being alone. When I'm alone all I do is look at the walls and see images in my head from all the terrifying things I've seen."

"I can only imagine," she responded quietly. It seems to be the trump card, although I didn't mean to shut her up. We sit for a moment in silence.

"Seth Holehouse has interviewed every single high-profile man and woman in the truth movement," she piped up. "And today he said that you're the bravest man he's ever met. I can't erase what you've seen. But for what it's worth, I don't want my son to grow up in a world without men like you in it. You're not a bad man, you're a real one. Get some sleep."

Poem: A Whisper of Hope

One sacrifice, two, now at the gate,
Parents walk children to meet their fate.
Mainstream lies, a child cries,
Destroying the body and mind as parent complies.
In shadows deep, where truth is veiled,
A silent scream, a future derailed.
With hearts heavy, they march in line,
To a fate unknown, a dark design.
But in the night, a spark ignites,
A whisper of hope, a call to fight.
For every tear, a voice will rise,
To challenge the dark, to seek the skies.

Chapter Sixteen
Increasingly Odd Calls

Almost everyone who promotes vaccination is paid to do so. The supporters of vaccination have a personal interest in promoting vaccination. On the other hand, just about everyone who questions vaccination does so at a significant personal cost. Vaccination is big business, and many of those who promote it and make money out of it do everything they can to protect an intellectually vulnerable but enormously profitable exercise.

Vernon Coleman, August 2011

We're plagued with an epidemic in this nation of people who refuse to admit the reality in front of their very faces. It's self-absorption; people are too busy to stop and think. It's laziness: people are fried after a day at work or with their kids and they zone out to Netflix while stuffing down trauma with drugs; especially food or booze. It's pride: people don't want to admit they were duped. Mark Twain is attributed with a sentiment that goes something like, "it's easier to fool people than to convince them that they've been fooled."

Another favorite of mine is by Leo Tolstoy, who wrote:

I know that most men—not only those considered clever, but even those who are very clever and capable of understanding most difficult scientific, mathematical problems—can seldom discern even the most straightforward and most obvious truth if it is such as to oblige them to admit the falsity of conclusions they have formed, perhaps with great difficulty—conclusions of which they are proud, which they have taught to others, and on which they have built their lives.

I am consistently reminded that pride led to the fall of man and the Scripture from Revelation 12:4 that indicates that 'a third of the stars' were swept from heaven by the dragon's tail, commonly referenced to illustrate that a third of the angels were cast out with Satan. This verse has led some to believe that one-third of all angels joined Lucifer's rebellion and were banished.

I've been taught, and it proves to be true in my experience, that pride leads to denial and destruction. For this reason I pray regularly for eyes to see and ears to hear; lest I be bamboozled by pride, too.

One afternoon I arrived to a scene to find a pediatric patient with signs of shock. They had sustained a gunshot wound to the chest. The police department was on scene, and one officer stated, "it appears to be self-inflicted. The parent said the patient hasn't been acting normal the last couple days. Today they heard screaming in the child's room and walked in. The child had the parents' gun pointed at themself… and pulled the trigger."

I approached the child. "Talk to me, tell me your name," I said calmly as I placed occlusive dressing on the wound. The entry and exit were noted and covered.

The patient didn't respond. Their eyes were open, their pupils were equal and reactive. Their breathing was rapid. Their skin was diaphoretic. Their blood pressure was hypotensive. Saturations 76%. Suddenly I heard screaming from the other room. It was the child's parent. "That's not them! That's nothing like them!"

I remained with the patient. "Can you tell me your name?"

The child was unable to speak at that time.

Upon exiting the residence with the patient secured for transport, an EMT partner obtained the patient history from the parent while I continued to administer immediate care. The parent shared that there was no prior history of mental illness. No current medications. Two COVID shots. Last one within a month.

The patient was transported emergent to the nearest appropriate medical facility. Interventions en route to the ER included:

- Chest needle decompression;
- Bringing SATS up to 96%;

- BVM via intubation after the patient became unresponsive;
- Fluids WO with two large bore IVs.

The child had a pulse upon arrival to the ER but died in surgery.

It's calls like this that bother me the most. Not just because it's a kid who dies, which is enough to upset anyone, but knowing the COVID-19 shots can alter a person psychologically pains me. The probability that their family will never get honest answers that could help keep this from happening again pains me, too, not only for this family but for others… the future families who will experience this trauma.

I actually got into a heated debate with a nurse over this call. When I gave them the report, including the fact that the patient had their COVID-19 shots, the nurse got angry, told me it wasn't relevant information and called me insensitive.

Prior to the vaccines I would run calls consisting of heart attacks, strokes, seizures, miscarriages, stubbed toes, cuts and falls; these were all the typical calls.

What changed after the rollout was the age groups and frequency. The strokes were now often occurring in young patients. Heart attacks and chest pain calls in young age groups growing in numbers by the day. Multiple new onset seizure calls demanding ambulances to high schools and middle schools. The common denominator, the "vaccines." I would ask the patients, and they would answer affirmatively; every time.

Many realized that the shots could be the cause of their new ailments. Many remained in the clutches of denial. The parents that gave this experiment to their children held blank stairs listening to the possibility. Sometimes I was met with anger at the mention of the possibility. Who wants to know that they harmed their kid by believing something they were told? Nobody.

It's a tough conversation, especially with a younger patient and their parents. I was explaining that this safe shot wasn't safe at all. At times, I wouldn't bring it up, and I could tell it wouldn't make a difference to those suffering at the time, but I tried holding myself to a standard. If this isn't known, it will only happen again and again. They are claiming more victims.

As the days turned into weeks and weeks into months, the pattern became more evident, and the weight of knowledge grew heavier. The calls were not just numbers but names and stories that would stay with me long after my shift ended. The young, vibrant lives, once full of potential, now faced uncertain futures. Their eyes, once bright with dreams, now clouded with confusion and fear. It was a silent epidemic, spreading through whispers of doubt and confirmed by the sorrowful nods of my colleagues. We were on the front lines, not just of a health crisis, but of a crisis of faith in what we were told was the pinnacle of medical achievement.

The conversations in the back of the ambulance were no longer just about symptoms and medical history. They were about life choices, trust, and the delicate balance of hope and despair. As I administered aid, I couldn't help but wonder about the long-term effects of these decisions made in moments of fear—the trust we placed in higher powers, the trust that was now broken for so many. As I looked into the eyes of those I served, I knew that this was not just a physical ailment; it was a wound to the soul of our society, one that would take more than medicine to heal. It was about restoring faith, not just in vaccines or treatments, but in the institutions allegedly protecting us.

Most days of my life I see things that others can't fathom. I may share it online, but I receive death threats, shadow bans, and I'll battle censorship.

Since 1997, I've been in the business of helping people not die. But that's also required me to see a lot of death. I rarely meet another human who has seen as much death as me. However, this frightens me. We are living in a society that's largely removed from death. We don't know the pig or cow slaughtered for our evening meal, nor do we treat or tend to the wounds or the injuries of our own loved ones. If we see them die, it's generally from

Our governments want us to die. I'm not talking just to Americans, either.

It wasn't until I was censored as a paramedic on the ground that I could say this word: bioweapon. It came logically. If there wasn't *intent* of harm and genocide, why would the doctors who were successfully treating patients with protocols like the McCullough or Zelenko protocols be censored? Why was Jim Thorp fired from his job even recently; a physician at the top of his field working in a rare and super-specialized niche?

After my original viral TikTok videos were censored and I was labeled a "terrorist" by the app, I knew that my story was being censored because the powers that be didn't want me to blow the whistle on this one critical element of the COVID-19 pandemic: intent. Vaccine manufacturers have legal immunity and have enjoyed this for decades. So why would they care if I blow the whistle on "vaccine" injuries? It wasn't about the injuries. It was something more gruesome: there was intent to kill. The "vaccine" adverse events don't indicate big "whoopsies" by the pharmaceutical companies. They don't illustrate the complete daftness of Fauci and his minions. They represent something darker: intentional genocide.

Calls became more bizarre, and I began speaking out about them more. One of the most disturbing side effects I saw was something called "Fournier gangrene," in which male genitalia begins to rot off. Yet some doctors still weren't connecting the dots, not tracing anything back to the elephant in the room—young heart attacks, strokes, miscarriages… and even rotting genitals. I dropped off one patient with Foreman's Gangrene, only to run to a field where a twelve-year-old had a stroke playing kickball.

Another call touched me as a father, it was a "near syncopal" episode, meaning a man almost passed out. He was otherwise fit and healthy, but we arrived on scene to him sweating and saying, "I don't know what happened."

He went on to say, "I was about to stand up to get something, and my stomach started hurting. I felt dizzy and almost fell down."

I affixed a monitor to check the man's vitals and acquired an EKG. He was still complaining of slight abdominal pain. As I often keep people in conversation to ground them into reality and, of course, because I'm empathic and really care about their stories and medical history before carting them off to the E.R., the man finally agreed to allow me to transport him to the hospital. During that medical history assessment he denied taking any medications. In fact, he had no pertinent past medical history. However, he had received three of the Pfizer jabs.

The man and I had a heartwarming conversation about his family. He identified his young children as "his world." To my knowledge, the man stabilized and eventually returned home to his children.

However, months later I got a call. 911: weakness and nausea. The man's once strong frame had deteriorated; he was a fraction of the man I initially met. He was slight and weak; he could barely speak.

I was told that the first call I ran with him proved to be an aortic dissection. He had survived the surgery a few months earlier, but it had taken a significant toll on his body. He went from being robust, vital, and hopeful to being slight of frame and even gaunt. The man's children stood watching as my partner and I lifted the frail father onto my cot. That was the last time they saw their daddy alive.

Every Father's Day that's rolled around since this episode, I have wanted to visit that man and his children to say Happy Father's Day. I lament for the children he left behind. The world needs more dads like him who light up when speaking of their children. I wonder if my dad lit up when talking about me, but I can't fathom that it was so. The tragedy of children losing a father who really, genuinely relished in his role and honor of being a father compelled me to double up on my social media presence, sounding the alarm.

In fact, prior to the "vaccines" for COVID-19, aortic dissection and aneurysms were extremely rare. After the experimental shots, they weren't rare anymore.

> **Dr. Dawn Michael** ✓ @DawnsMission · May 10
> This is never before seen footage of me in Los Robles Hospital after losing my husband in the same hospital and how I was treated that day as a prisoner in my room, denined from seeing him the entire time I was in the hospital COVID ward. #NeverForget #Covid
>
> 1:33

Photo Courtesy of a screenshot on X.com by @dawnsmission[96]

---

96. https://twitter.com/i/status/1788951874982527112

The children who lost their father that day weren't much older than my own two youngest boys. I was shattered about my divorce. In truth, I would have done anything to stay married. No dating scene nor hope for a kinder mate could appeal more to me than the thought of being with my sons' mother. I fought, too. But I failed.

In the meantime as we managed the details of the divorce and discussed how we would tackle the caregiving of two sick children; one vaccine-injured and another with Type 1 Diabetes, I put one foot in front of the other. At this time in 2022 the conversation devolved from "if we see 'vaccine-'injured patients today," to "*when* we see 'vaccine-'injured patients today."

Each morning I wake up for work expecting to see people in their worst moments. I humbly recognize that each time I show up to do my job, that moment will be the one survivor's talk about on the couch, so to speak, processing with therapists or psychiatrists for years and even decades to come. That is, ideally, when the patient or the patient's surviving loved ones seek help for the trauma of a mortal emergency. With that in mind, I've always sought to be both empathic and grounded; the stable image of Christ is never far from mind. He was kind enough to draw crowds to his loving, magnetic presence. And he was emotionally regulated enough to get run out of just about every town he visited without going over the edge; a paramedic must be stable as well as gentle in these situations. As a default mode, many men do very well on the stability, even verging on "coldness." Not me. I have no chill. I readily embrace these people. My heart escapes through my voice. My prayer is that everywhere I go, they feel that they are God's beloved. And, too, I hope they know that even as I conduct my job with professionalism, I love them, too as my brothers and sisters in this crazy dysfunctional family called "humanity."

The roller coaster of waking up, preparing to see people at their worst and being the "guy in charge," saving lives, and following protocol with urgency and clarity are toggled with going to bed every night under the weight of incomprehensible exhaustion. From my pillow, I often stare at the ceiling, wondering what could've been done differently and how I could have improved. I suspect it's expected to be in continual self-criticism when lives are on the line. The unhealthy territory for first responders is when we internalize somebody's health and blame ourselves for not being good enough.

However, this self-consciousness dissipated in 2021 and 2022 when my critiques became externally focused: I started to let myself off the hook a little. I began to see an enemy, a body of corporate overlords intentionally harming people. I stopped shrugging things off and saying passive things like, It is what it is," and began to see that there was no "luck of the draw" in the fates of men and women around me. This was murder.

Life became like one big losing football game. We were down too many points, and there isn't enough time left on the clock to turn this game around. I might make a good play here and there, but the other team is bigger, stronger, and they've been charting their winning strategy for decades. Each morning I pull on my jersey and get back on the field. But each day the shoulder pads get heavier and heavier.

As a species, we are now merely postponing the inevitable. I don't see how we'll turn back the clock.

Having seen the death, trauma and heartache you've read about in this book, you'd think I am keen to be vindicated. After being threatened, censored and publicly ridiculed as well as privately bullied, you'd imagine I'm eager to post a "ha! Told you so!"

I'm not. Unlike the trolls haunting me and my children, I don't want revenge. I just want people to stop dying. I didn't want to witness a genocide from ventilators or the shots. But since we're here, let's continue to lay out a strategy to never let this happen again.

On July 6th, 2024, a study was published in the "New England Journal of Medicine," which is so groundbreaking that I'm sure it'll get buried. A group of scientists, including Dr. Stanley A. Plotkin and several other pro-vaccine ambassadors, have insisted for decades that vaccines are safe and effective; they've led the public to believe that vaccine products are well-studied and well-tested. As I'm sharing throughout this book, that couldn't be further from the truth. In a monumental backtrack, a study entitled "Funding Postauthorization Vaccine-Safety Science" reveals that these former vaccine evangelists have admitted that vaccines are not adequately studied both pre- and post-licensure.

In the study, published by the New England Journal of Medicine, the doctors admitted, "prelicensure clinical trials have limited sample sizes [and] follow-up durations" and that "there are no resources earmarked for post-authorization safety studies."[97]

All the death, dying, divorce, and drunkenness began to eat away at me. I started to see more and more of the dots connecting.

All this genocide around me… and even though I wasn't sleeping well at night, I began to really wake up. And I was pissed.

---

97. https://www.nejm.org/doi/full/10.1056/NEJMp2402379

Poem: Beware The "Vaccine"

In my field, I have to yield, let a higher authority take the wheel.
I ran a child, just five months old, couldnt regain what death had stole.
Tried so hard, as mother cried, dad stood screaming standing beside.
Compressions and breaths, drilled child's leg for the med,
No movement, no pulse; the baby was dead.
Eyes fixed, without life, no trauma in sight.
Why would God take this young one tonight?
No chance I'm calling this innocent soul on scene.
We leave for the hospital, my sirens they scream.
En route I pray for the parents and my team.
I wish this all was just a bad dream.

Chapter Seventeen
Fear Porn & Controlled Opposition

"Therefore, to him who knows to do good and does not do it, to him it is sin."

James 4:17, NKJV

My fellow paramedic and I were walking back to a hotel provided to us while we were contracted as paramedics. We had endured a long shift and an even longer conversation over the previous couple of weeks.

I was tired, but incensed by what I'd seen that day. "You know, you keep telling me that I should stop talking. But I'm not going to shut up about what I've seen. You know these shots are dangerous, too. You've seen the deaths first hand. Aren't you mad that you took the shots? They lied to you!"

My colleague responded, "It upsets me a little, I guess. But they'll just fire you, Harry. You're putting your neck out for no reason. You have kids. At some point you have to realize you're fighting a losing battle and just start thinking about your kids."

"I am thinking of my kids. If I stop talking... if we all give up... my kids will have nobody defending them from this evil invasion."

I could see that my friend was trying not to roll her eyes. "Oh God, there's no invasion. That sounds so crazy."

I wasn't relenting on that subject. "Evil forces have invaded our nation. Our entire world. Those running this system are pushing confusion and mandating deadly shots. Those in charge want us to submit or die. Actually: submit AND die; that's what's happening to a lot of people. You see it."

"Harry, what proof do you have of all this evil conspiracy theory stuff? I know the shots aren't as safe as they say they are, but people are trying to help others. That's good. That's not evil."

"What proof do I have? You just admitted to COVID shots not being safe, yet they're mandating them. That's 100% evil."

My friend doubled down. "But you're saying there's some massive conspiracy to basically warp the minds of everyone. I just don't see it. It's very far-fetched."

Irritated, I was a bit harsh with my following comment. "With all due respect, you are a biological female who cut off your breasts. You take dangerous medications because the evil system affirms your confusion at an early age. You have told me that you regret doing that to yourself. Do you not remember that? Evil has harmed you directly in many ways."

My friend was silent. We returned to the hotel but didn't talk any more during the walk. Later that evening, I heard a knock on my door. The paramedic friend had come to my room. I thought she was fixin' to argue some more. I knew I'd been harsh and felt terrible.

Instead, she came in and gave me a hug. I apologized for being callous. She cried on my shoulder, and then left.

We have yet to talk about it all again.

It's been said that it's always darkest before dawn, and living so much of the year in Alaska, I can tell you that it's the coldest, too. I want you to do something: visualize the dawn. Visualize a time when you can send your children to public school without fear of indoctrination. Without seed oils in their foods. Without gender-bending perverts at the head of the class. Visualize a time when you don't fear WW3, FEMA camps for political dissidents, and child molesters around every corner. Visualize a time when you can let your eight-year-old walk down the street without fear of kidnapping, when you can let your wife go on a run without checking your watch every five minutes to wonder when she'll be home again safely when you can open up a tab on your browser without bad news about cardiac events on the rise, turbo cancers eating away at your friends list, or death around every corner. Visualize a time when this world won't be so scary. I want to look my children in the eyes and talk about the dawn. But I also want them to be strong. They're going to need it, real soon.

For those of you, my friends, who are still here at this point in my story, you've gotta be sober about what's happening, and where it comes from. I believe that you who are awake are remarkable, and that's why I remind at least fifty people every day that I love them on X. I really do. But not because you pray for me nor because you stroke my ego - although I do need cheerleaders more often than not. I love the people I engage with who are action takers. Who are ready to face the darkness with me, and do. They participate in conscious parenting, attend school board meetings to fight perverts and political agendas in curriculum, and they resist medical tyranny in their hospitals and workplaces.

There are people who claim to be awake, however, whom I don't love. These are the folks who are watching the world fall to shit with popcorn like it's entertainment. They're the vermin that will be cast away, about whom I suspect the Lord will say - I knew you *not*. In the "truther" community, there are a lot of these rats. These are the folks who know the truth but do nothing about it. James 4:17 states, "Therefore, to him who knows to do good and does not do it, to him it is sin (NKJV)."

These people know that the government is run by a mob and the pandemic was a money grab at best and a genocide at worst, but they sit and watch. They can quote chapter and verse of current events, or maybe even the Good Book itself, but they aren't doing a damn thing to fight the darkness.

I see how they've been deceived. A torrent of material on social media, as well as from your politicians, tell you that you're relatively powerless, after all. We are pressured from every angle to watch and consume fear porn. Fear, after all, gets excellent ratings. But if I paid attention to even five percent of the videos or podcasts that are sent to me daily, I'd never do a damn good thing in life. I sometimes grab coffee and a bagel from a deli near my apartment. There's a guy in there who's a joy to chat with. He watches podcasts for hours every day. He knows every politician in every state, what is being voted on or not passed, and the ramifications for the country. He says he's MAGA and a "truther," and he brags about being unvaxxed. But this guy works in a bagel shop and spends weekends isolated on his parents' farm. He isn't DOING anything. He works out once or even twice a day. He periodically goes out with friends. He's sober, which is a killer and which I admire. But the dude is wasting space and consuming talk radio or podcasts but giving jack shit back to his community. I love the guy, and I hate him for the way he squanders truth with selfishness. It's almost like the verse in the Bible about being either hot or cold; those who are lukewarm are those whom the Lord detests.

All this is to say that I implore you not to get sucked into the circlejerk of information gathering combined with inaction. At some point, stop watching television, podcasts, or listening to radio and get off your ass and do something. If you don't know every detail about the unsuccessful sniper on the roof in Pennsylvania or who went through Trump's drive thru, you're better off for it.

In my mind there's an image that's almost as horrific as watching somebody watch kiddie porn in his basement. It's the guy (or gal) who sits in front of a phone or computer consuming information every night. At his local bowling alley, church, or synagogue, there are other concerned citizens meeting and discussing how they might help their community or, if not through political activity, how they can at least be a good role model for others. But then there's ol' Frank the Fear-Porn consumer. He sits and gets so randy about the globalist agenda, Luciferians starting World War Three, martial law, civil war, Venezuelan gangs raping every last woman in America. *Man, get off your ass and do something.* Be a man. Be a leader in your community. Get off your screen. Get a grip. Grow a pair. Take up your cross and march. It's darkest before dawn, and it's going to get even darker.

I've wondered how people get so paralyzed watching media when we need them out there on the front lines. I wonder how so many millions of people bought into the concept that the white hats are coming to castrate all the child predators and Hillary is in Gitmo and all that other hogwash.

Among a few other things, it's one of the most important things for you to take away from this book. It's a game. It's probably controlled opposition. You see, the term controlled opposition refers to the idea that a group or movement that appears to be opposing a dominant power or ideology is actually being secretly directed or manipulated by that same power to mislead or neutralize genuine opposition. Influential powers create or influence opposition groups to maintain control over dissent. The best example of this was QAnon.

I have a lot of intelligent Q friends who look outside the box at everything. They teach me many things I might only have found with them. I love their ability to see beyond red and blue. I appreciate their hunger for answers, searching deep, dark corners of the web for clues about what reality is and what fiction is. And, too, I've seen that they have also been captivated with a prolonged tease, continually believing that a climactic exposure is right around the corner. Perhaps we have Q's to thank for exposing Epstein or Diddy. However, I also suspect that controlled opposition has at least slightly co-opted the movement. This explains why some of my intelligent and well-intentioned Q friends stagnate in their influence on the world.

You see, the Q people were so convinced that Trump was or was the coming Messiah and that his secret military was going to lock up all the pedophilic politicians that they didn't see a need to do anything more than stock up some food, water, and walkie talkies and watch. Pay attention to a few of the most popular QAnon phrases and see how obvious it is:

"Where we go one, we go all" (WWG1WGA) – This is a central slogan of QAnon, symbolizing unity among followers.

"The Storm" – Refers to a predicted event where members of a supposed global cabal will be arrested and exposed.

"Trust the plan" – A call for followers to have faith in the process, believing that justice is inevitable despite setbacks.

"Nothing can stop what is coming" (NCSWIC) – Expresses the belief that the outcome of their cause is inevitable.

"The Great Awakening" – Refers to a future moment when the general public will realize the supposed truths that QAnon followers believe.

"Dark to light" – Symbolizes the transition from ignorance or deception to knowledge and truth, as seen by QAnon adherents.

"Follow the white rabbit" – This phrase is borrowed from *Alice in Wonderland* and suggests the idea of going down a rabbit hole of hidden knowledge or conspiracies.

"Red pill" – Derived from *The Matrix*, it signifies the moment someone becomes aware of the alleged hidden truths behind world events, a common concept in other movements as well.

These folks who called themselves "red-pilled" followed the "white rabbit" all the way to their basements where they "trusted the plan" and waited for "the storm" because "nothing can stop what is coming." If there was ever an example of controlled opposition, it has to be Q.

Controlled opposition didn't start with QAnon, although they crushed it in execution. It can be traced to authoritarian or totalitarian regimes. In Nazi Germany, the Gleichschaltung (coordination) involved eliminating or controlling organizations that could oppose the government, but at times, allowing limited forms of dissent or opposition that were carefully monitored. In the Soviet Union, Operation Trust (1921-1926) was a counterintelligence operation run by the Soviet secret police that created a fake anti-Bolshevik resistance movement to identify and neutralize natural opposition groups. These and others throughout history show that intelligence services use controlled opposition to disrupt genuinely dissenting movements either through fake organizations or co-opting existing ones.

All this is to say that there are real threats out there; real enemies and bad guys who want you dead. This book will detail more about them than you need to know. Don't be like Frank the Fear Porn consumer: be like the heroes in this book. Kelly Victory, Jim Thorp, Mary Bowden and Steve Kirsch. Get off your ass. Do something. Be a hero.

Poem: The Storm

Some woke as victims from parties with no end,
Advantage taken by those they called friend.
Fighting their demons, fearing the trend,
Truths, black and white, turned gray as they blended.
Covered one eye, pointing Baphomet's fingers,
Up and down, the truth always lingers.
Raging chaos, youth stolen away,
Drowned, the innocence under rainbows decay.
Threats and pizza held many at bay,
Now comes the time when veils fall away.
Shadows whisper secrets, darkness will fail,
In the heart of the storm, the truth will prevail.

Chapter Eighteen

Yes, There Are Definitely More People Dying

The...concern I have is the bioweapon that was released on us, the vaccines...That needs to be communicated effectively in the new administration—that something terrible happened...it was the greatest crime I've ever seen, the most significant fraud ever perpetrated on a populace.[98]

Ed Dowd

I arrived on scene where a patient's parent told me the patient had just been speaking, but then began puking and then collapsed. "I thought he was having a seizure, but he wouldn't come out of it," the parent shared.

"Does he have a history of seizures?" I asked the parent while assessing the patient. The patient was posturing inward. Their pupils were unequal with positive nystagmus. Their eyes were gazing up and to the right. Breathing was rapid and shallow. I noted immediate transport was a necessity and a possible CVA. There were no signs of trauma.

The parent stated "I caught him on his way to the floor and helped lay him down." We learned that the patient had no history of seizures.

---

98. https://lionessofjudah.substack.com/p/edward-dowd-it-was-the-greatest-crime?utm_source=post-email-title&publication_id=581065&post_id=151948554&utm_campaign=email-post-title&isFreemail=true&r=tluyu&triedRedirect=true&utm_medium=email

The parent requested to ride in the ambulance, which was approved by me.

We intubated the patient in the ambulance due to their unresponsive nature; their airway and breathing instability coupled with decreased O2 stats compelled this decision.

The parent was not praying while holding the patient's hand during the medical intervention. "Does your child take medications daily? Do they have any other medical history?" I asked.

"No, they are completely healthy."

"Has your child taken any of the COVID shots?"

"Yes, but they only had two. Do you think this could be from the COVID "vaccine?" Did the "vaccine" cause this?

"I don't know. I know there's been a lot of bad since those came out. Many doctors are saying they cause multiple problems. I'll tell the doctor at the hospital their vaccine status and hopefully they can get you definitive answers."

Hope springs eternal, they say.

The parent continued to hold the patient's hand while praying. "Please God, wake up! Please God, don't take my baby!"

Upon arrival at the emergency room we provided my report to the ER physician. I explained to the physician what interventions we'd performed and what we'd witnessed. I then informed the physician that the patient had no additional pertinent past history, but was experiencing CVA signs and symptoms post mRNA-"vaccination."

The physician smirked but replied harshly, "COVID "vaccines" are SAFE. Any other information?"

"We didn't see these types of issues in the young before these shots…"

"If that's it then goodbye."

I wish this episode were a one-time event. But it happened many times to other children at many different hospitals. Some doctors even laughed at the mention of possible "vaccine" injury. Doctors weren't documenting these victims as probable vaccine injuries. They weren't counting the deaths from the COVID shots, which means that the data we're allowed is bullshit.

As a portfolio analyst and formerly a Wall Street fund manager for BlackRock with billions of dollars under management, Ed Dowd has invested endless hours analyzing data regarding the COVID-19 event, especially mortality rates. When he met Dr. Robert Malone at a protest of unlawful mandates in Hawaii, where he lives where there was, as Dowd describes them, "draconian lockdowns and mandates."[99] That was October of 2021, and Dowd became acquainted with Malone then. Ed told Malone then that he was suspicious about the vaccine due to anecdotal evidence he'd picked up on the island of Maui. He points out that in the investment world, that's how many decisions are made. They start as anecdotal evidence that fuels more research. Then, the investor or manager can develop a thesis upon which he can decide on a specific position or security.

Using this methodology, Dowd paid close attention to the anecdotal evidence of vaccine injury and disability and began monitoring insurance companies and funeral homes to build a thesis. Dowd started to collaborate with a high-level insurance expert named Josh Stirling MBA, JD, who eventually went on to found "Insurance Collaboration to Save Lives."[100] Stirling assisted Dowd in evaluating insurance and CDC data before they brought two Portuguese PhD physicists on board who formed a firm with Dowd. They academically and objectively tackled the thesis that the vaccine was causing excess deaths, disabilities and injuries. Two PhDs, a retired insurance executive, and two other anonymous individuals joined Dowd, who became the face of a movement to bring attention to COVID-19 vaccine injury and awareness. Dowd eventually released the book "Cause Unknown: The Epidemic of Sudden Deaths in 2021, 2022, & 2023." The book description states,

> *2020 saw a spike in deaths in America, smaller than you might imagine during a pandemic, some of which could be attributed to COVID and to initial treatment strategies that were not effective. But then, in 2021, the stats people expected went off the rails. The CEO of the OneAmerica insurance company publicly disclosed*

---

99. https://rumble.com/v5jpv43-ed-dowd-on-COVID-shots-excess-deaths-disabilities-and-injuries-bret-weinste.html

100. https://www.linkedin.com/in/joshstirling/overlay/about-this-profile/

that during the third and fourth quarters of 2021, death in people of working age (18–64) was 40 percent higher than it was before the pandemic. Significantly, the majority of the deaths were not attributed to COVID. A 40 percent increase in deaths is literally earth-shaking. Even a 10 percent increase in excess deaths would have been a 1-in-200-year event. But this was 40 percent...

What has caused this historic spike in deaths among younger people?

What has caused the shift from old people, who are expected to die, to younger people, who are expeced to keep living?

*It isn't COVID, of course, because we know that COVID is not a significant cause of death in young people. Various stakeholders opine about what could be causing this epidemic of unexpected sudden deaths, but **"CAUSE UNKNOWN"** doesn't opine or speculate. The facts just are, and the math just is.[101]*

In an interview aired on October 22, 2024 with Bret Weinstein on the "Dark Horse Podcast," Dowd claims that COVID-19 vaccines have resulted in millions of deaths and disabilities globally, stating "... 5 billion people on the planet got a vaccine of some sort. If you apply the range of the death rate in the US that I gave you earlier, you get a range of globally, 7.3 million to 15 million died from the vaccine..."

However, those who lived might not have retained a high quality of life. Dowd also claims that there are between 29 and 60 million disabled globally. With up to 18% of the vaccinated suffering injuries, Dowd claims that "we get a range of, at the high end, 900 million, 500 million at the low end."[102]

If a regular shot had even two or three children injured, it would be pulled off the market, without question. In 2011, Vernon Coleman, author of "Anyone Who Tells You Vaccines Are Safe and Effective is Lying," pointed out that: "In April 2011, the US Health Department's National

---

101. https://a.co/d/cAfaSYz

102. https://rumble.com/v5jpv43-ed-dowd-on-COVID-shots-excess-deaths-disabilities-and-injuries-bret-weinste.html

Vaccine Injury Compensation Programme released its figures for 2010 the report showed that allegedly safe childhood vaccines officially killed or injured no less than 2,699 children in the year 2010 in America. The parents of those children received $110 million in damages. The US Government has reportedly also paid compensation to the parents of autistic children."[103]

For some odd reason… this wasn't the case with the COVID-19 shot.

For a virus that is relatively mild in every age category that has a very low risk of death to even patients with preexisting conditions or compromised immune systems, we were rushing out a shot that had a higher risk of death than even the oldest of patients simply catching the virus and powering through it.

The question is *why?*

The answer involves lies, mobsters, and even the potential of a depopulation agenda, let's look at a few more facts that we have the luxury of understanding now in hindsight.

What I've seen in the field as a first responder and healthcare worker is nothing less than carnage. In my estimation, although Dowd's statistics are severe and even verge on unbelievable, I agree with his analysis based on my first-hand experience on the ground actually ministering to and holding these patients in my arms.

As the graph below illustrates, when the shots became ubiquitous in 2021, miscarriages, stillbirths, and all deaths reported to VAERS skyrocketed; stillbirths went from a mere handful to nearly 3,500 reported to the Vaccine Adverse Event Reporting System from 2020 to 2021. All-cause deaths well exceeded 20,000 in 2021 from barely any in 2020. VAERS represents only a tiny fraction of the total adverse events that occur, because very few healthcare providers file the adverse event reports in VAERS, and when they try, it's remarkably difficult to finalize the report.

---

103. https://a.co/d/09GEydn

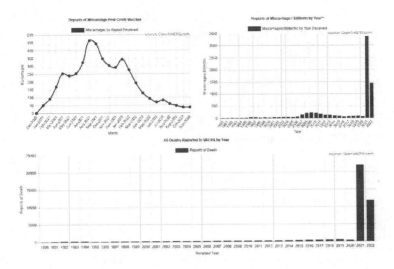

Evidence of heart attacks attributed to "vaccines" is also skyrocketing, as one peer-reviewed study found a 1,236% increase in excess heart attack deaths among King County, Washington's 2.2 million residents. The study reveals the following numbers by year:

2020: 11 excess heart attack deaths

2021: 75 excess heart attack deaths

2022: 111 excess heart attack deaths

2023: 147 excess heart attack deaths, a 1,236% increase compared to 2020.

In addition, cardiac arrest deaths, in general, rose about 25% from 2020 to 2023, during which time the population in King County, in the Seattle area, actually shrunk. In response to this news, Dr. Peter McCullough said:

So it looks like the vaccines are the smoking gun... This is now fully peer-reviewed in the emergency medicine literature. We've messaged the Medic One unit in Seattle. They clearly need to do more research to figure out how soon these vaccines were administered and to whom.[104]

---

104. https://x.com/VigilantFox/status/1859647125661024516?utm_source=substack&utm_medium=email

The image below is from the "Journal of Emergency Medicine: Open Access" in a detailed research article entitled, "Excess Cardiopulmonary Arrest and Mortality after COVID-19 Vaccination in King County, Washington."[105] The conclusion states:

We identified a significant ecological and temporal association between excess fatal cardiopulmonary arrests and the COVID-19 vaccination campaign. The increase in excess cardiopulmonary arrest deaths may also be attributed to COVID-19 infection and disruptions in emergency care during the pandemic. Urgent further research is needed to confirm our observations with attention to risk mitigation for incident events and improved survival with resuscitation.

ResearchArticle **Journal of Emergency Medicine: Open Access**

Excess Cardiopulmonary Arrest and Mortality after COVID-19 Vaccination in King County, Washington

Nicolas Hulscher[1*], Michael J. Cook[2], Raphael B. Stricker[3] and Peter A. McCullough[1]

[1]*McCullough Foundation, Dallas, TX, United States*

[2]*Vis a Vis Symposiums, Highcliffe, Dorset, United Kingdom*

[3]*Union Square Medical Associates, San Francisco, CA. United States*

*Corresponding Author
Nicolas Hulscher, McCullough Foundation, Dallas, TX, United States.

Submitted: 2024, Sep 23; Accepted: 2024, Oct 17; Published: 2024, Oct 24

Citation: Hulscher, N., Cook, M. J., Stricker, R. B., McCullough, P. A. (2024). Excess Cardiopulmonary Arrest and Mortality after COVID-19 Vaccination in King County, Washington. *J Emerg Med OA*, 2(1), 01-11.

Abstract
Introduction: Since the onset of widespread COVID-19 vaccination campaigns, there have been concerns about serious cardiovascular adverse events as a result of mass vaccination. This study aimed to estimate excess cardiopulmonary arrest mortality in King County, WA, and investigate any association with COVID-19 vaccination rates.

Methods: An exploratory data analysis was performed. Comparative analyses were performed to evaluate the changes in total EMS attendances over time. Excess deaths were calculated using the 2015-2020 cardiopulmonary arrest mortality trend line. The relationship between excess cardiopulmonary arrest mortality and vaccination rates was analyzed using polynomial regression analysis.

Results: Approximately 98% of the King County population received at least one dose of a COVID-19 vaccine by 2023. As of August 2nd, 2024, there have been approximately 589,247 confirmed COVID-19 cases in King County. In 2021-2022, Total EMS attendances in King County sharply increased by 35.34% from 2020 and by 11% from pre-pandemic years. Cases of 'obvious death' upon EMS arrival increased by 19.89% in 2020, 36.57% in 2021, and 53.80% in 2022 compared to the 2017-2019 average. We found a 25.7% increase in total cardiopulmonary arrests and a 25.4% increase in cardiopulmonary arrest mortality from 2020 to 2023 in King County, WA. Excess fatal cardiopulmonary arrests were estimated to have increased by 1,236% from 2020 to 2023, rising from 11 excess deaths (95% CI: -12, 34) in 2020 to 147 excess deaths (95% CI: 123, 170) in 2023. A quadratic increase in excess cardiopulmonary arrest mortality was observed with higher COVID-19 vaccination rates. The general population of King County sharply declined by 0.94% (21,300) in 2021, deviating from the expected population size. Applying our model from these data to the entire United States yielded 49,240 excess fatal cardiopulmonary arrests from 2021-2023.*

What do we make of this data and legions of other stories, articles, and studies?

I call it genocide: what we are experiencing is planned extermination. Imagine a system that was already limited on staff, already neglecting their patients. Now imagine that system telling the few capable employees still working that they have to take an experimental shot or be fired.

You can't tell me this wasn't a planned extermination. You can't tell me this wasn't intentional harm. Innocent people have been targeted and, frankly, I'm humiliated that I didn't see through it before I did with the "happy hypoxia" I describe in an earlier chapter.

More than humiliation, I feel angry. I've been chastised for this anger more than once. Nurses, paramedics, teachers, doctors, and politicians who saw through this extermination sat down and shut up for fear of losing their jobs. As a society we should *all* be ashamed. Not just those who are asleep, but those of us who woke up and still stayed silent… or at least those of us who weren't loud enough.

I was confused for the better part of late 2023 and most of 2024 when I saw a lot of Trump vs. Harris rhetoric and some mention of turbo cancers, but only some people paid attention to one of the most significant presentations in the past four years.

Dr. Denis Rancourt is a PhD who has made significant contributions to environmental science, measurement science, soil science, theoretical physics, allo physics, magnetism, planetary science, and bio-geochemistry. That last one I had to look that one up, it's the scientific study of the interactions between biological, geological, and chemical processes on Earth, as the term pretty clearly illustrates. It focuses on how organisms (biological components), minerals and rocks (geological components) and chemical elements and compounds interact and influence one another in the environment. In the real world, this might be study of the carbon cycle or nitrogen cycle). Dr. Rancourt directed an internationally recognized interdisciplinary research laboratory which was awarded significant research funding. Read: he has been given great responsibilities for his expertise and judgement. If he's trusted with big money, he's got the respect of the people with the deep pockets. What's more, Rancourt's articles have been cited more than 6,000 times in peer-reviewed scientific journals. This dude is a genius.

Dr. Rancourt gave a presentation on November 18th, 2023 in Bucharest, Romania that has been referred to as the "17 Million Excess Deaths" study by the few people I know who've quoted it, probably because, like me, they learned about it in a conversation between Bret Weinstein and Tucker Carlson.[106] During the conference in Bucharest, Rancourt begins his presentation by pointing out that death rates have declined dramatically over the past one hundred year, as is evidenced in the graph below.

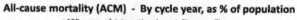
All-cause mortality (ACM) - By cycle year, as % of population

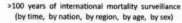
>100 years of international mortality surveillance
(by time, by nation, by region, by age, by sex)

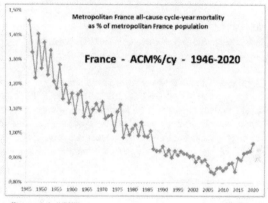

(Rancourt et al., 2020)

ICS

On average, approximately 1% of the population dies each year. Note that all-cause mortality crept upwards from about 2005 to 2020, when this chart ends. Rancourt points out that governments are very serious about counting deaths, and that it is a "legalistic" process. According to Rancourt, the main thing you see in All-Cause Mortality data are seasonal sources of mortality. These include seasonal variations (more people die in the winter than in summer,) war, economic collapse (Great Depression,) summer heat waves, earthquakes, the 1918 bacterial pneumonia outbreaks (in assaulted social classes, generally not the rich,) and COVID-period assaults, which

---

106. https://rumble.com/v45f6cl-tucker-carlson-x-ep.-60-dr.-bret-weinstein-exposes-the-world-health-organiz.html?mref=1bxo9j&mc=69gy3

include lockdowns, isolation, medical assaults, economic-sector closures, institutional and service closures, deprivation of usual social and medical treatments, and mass vaccination.)

The graph below also notes that CDC-declared pandemics, including H2N2, H3N2, and H1N1+, were not included in all-cause mortality spikes.

All-cause mortality (ACM)
>100 years of international mortality surveillance
(by time, by nation, by region, by age, by sex)

What is detected in ACM by time and by age group?

➢ Seasonal variations (hemispherically synchronous)
➢ War (WWII, Vietnam War in USA data...)
➢ Economic collapse (Great Depression USA, Dust Bowl USA, famine...)
➢ Summer heat waves (mid-latitude, temperate regions)
➢ Earthquakes (all-ages building occupants)
➢ Not the post-WWII CDC-declared pandemics:
       1957-58, "H2N2" / 1968, "H3N2" / 2009, "H1N1+"
➢ 1918 bacterial pneumonia outbreaks (in assaulted social classes)
➢ Covid-period assaults: Lockdowns, isolation, medical assaults, economic-sector closures, institutional closures, service closures, deprivation of usual social and medical treatments, mass vaccination

(e.g., Rancourt, 2023, "There Was No Pandemic")   ICS

These so-called CDC-declared pandemics caused no increase or rise in all-cause mortality. Mortality spiked initially in Canada, where the elderly were subject to aggressive measures to stop the spread or mortality of the virus allegedly. Another peak in mortality happened in geographic locations where these aggressive measures were taken, particularly in regions where mechanical ventilators were used or in more impoverished areas where, conveniently, "vaccine equity" was a priority, rolling out the shots to less affluent neighborhoods. These neighborhoods would have been better off with Jehovah's Witnesses banging down doors than with the government trying to enforce "equity" on the population. As you might have guessed, this "vaccine equity" was funded by, among others, the Gates Foundation.

Another interesting point from the Rancourt presentation in Bucharest is the age of those who died. During the 2022 spike that Rancourt discusses in his lecture, he includes the graph below, indicating that it wasn't the elderly who were dying more but an increase in younger populations, including 25-44-year-olds.

What's really concerning is the geographical data indicating that the virus happened to kill more poor people. That's not a signature of a virus, but a sign that these lower income neighborhoods were affected by something other than a virus. Viruses aren't selective.

Loss of jobs, loss of social activities, and loss of position in society increased stress. Mandates, institutional pressures, and other pressures from the regulatory side also increased anxiety on the population. In Peru, for instance, 10,000 so-called "military reservists" were commissioned to find everybody who would test positive for COVID-19, extracting them from their families and isolating them. This didn't reduce mortality, it resulted in more people dying. Aggressions such as these caused social isolation and psychological stress.

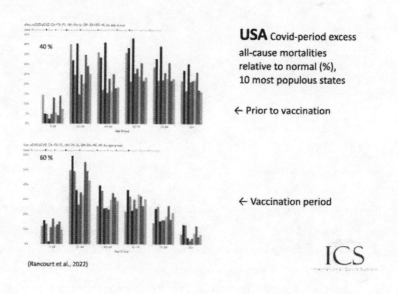

USA Covid-period excess all-cause mortalities relative to normal (%), 10 most populous states

← Prior to vaccination

← Vaccination period

(Rancourt et al., 2022)

ICS

The immune system is weakened under these stresses. In fact, an entire field of science is dedicated to researching this phenomenon. In a large population with that much-depressed immunity, the primary organ affected is the lungs; bacterial infections abound.

Rancourt proves with his data that the "vaccine" caused death. In the chart below, you'll see that every time a new dose was unleashed, death skyrocketed. The shot was a toxic substance that each body reacted to differently. With added doses of the jab, the toxicity increased in the body, which means that more shots resulted in higher mortality rates, as is illustrated in the chart below.

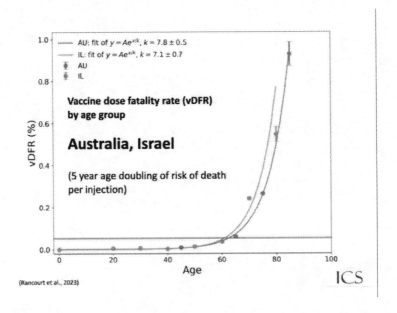

"Your risk of dying per injection doubles every four or five years in age," states Dr. Rancourt, who illustrates the spike in mortality based on age in the graph above. There was, for instance, almost a 1% chance of death following a shot for those in the 80+ age group. As you'll see in the following graph, it's around the fourth dose that you began seeing an exponential increase in mortality in many places, such as Peru and Chile. At this marker of four shots, the data indicates that there was approximately one death per twenty injections in the 90+ year-olds.

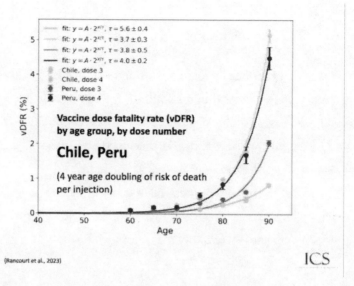

Photo Courtesy of the International COVID Summit

In short, elderly people were killed mainly by the shots in terms of all-cause mortality. Younger people were more affected by the stress and associated disease from that anxiety and their depressed immune systems.

Dr. Rancourt concludes the following from his research.

1. COVID-19 "vaccines" should be considered a toxic substance
2. Fatal toxicity is x1000, which is admitted by the industry
3. All-ages mean fatal toxicity: 1 "vaccine" death per 800 injections
4. Approximately 17.5 million "vaccine" deaths worldwide at the time of this presentation
5. Fatal toxicity is exponential with age, with the risk of death doubling every 4-5 years of age
6. Fatal risk attains one death per 20 injections in 90+-year-olds challenged with booster doses[107]

---

107. https://rumble.com/v45kw30-17-million-deaths-from-the-mrna-shot-denis-rancourt-bucharest-conference.html

COVID-19 VACCINES

➤ COVID-19 vaccines should be considered a toxic substance

➤ Fatal toxicity is X1000 that admitted by the industry

➤ All-ages mean fatal toxicity: 1 vaccine death per 800 injections

➤ 17 ± 0.5 million vaccine deaths worldwide, to present

➤ Fatal toxicity is exponential with age,

> with risk of death doubling every 4-5 years of age

➤ Fatal risk attains 1 death per 20 injections, in 90+ year olds

> challenged with booster doses

ICS

Slide Courtesy of the International COVID Summit

One of the countries that got the most homicidal by far about this shot was New Zealand. They pride themselves on being "fully vaxxed."

Late in 2023 it was discovered in leaks from the New Zealand government that the nation had an increase of about 3,000% in excess deaths between 2021 - 2023.[108] Residents of New Zealand were under heavy lockdown restrictions and it's been said that 95.8% of the country is "fully vaccinated," which means that people ages twelve and over have received at least one dose of the COVID-19 mRNA jabs and 94.7% having received two shots.[109]

Head of New Zealand Loyal, Liz Gunn, suspects that tens of thousands of kiwis have died from these jabs. New Zealand only has five million people identifying as permanent residents or citizens, there were 5,285 excess deaths in this otherwise small country during just a 49-week

---

108. https://lionessofjudah.substack.com/p/devastating-fully-vaxxed-new-zealand

109. https://en.wikipedia.org/wiki/COVID-19_vaccination_in_New_Zealand

period in 2022, which equals approximately a 3,203% increase over the figures for 2020.[110]

Said Gunn, formerly a TV host who became an investigative reporter:

The number of deaths is usually less than the number of those suffering from ill effects of the injections, then the extrapolation of the numbers that have been injured and killed starts to become, frankly, eye-watering… People who attended the same jab site, and were jabbed one after the other, at consecutive times on the same day… We saw their jab date and we saw their date of death.

The reason I bring up New Zealand is not because of the number of souls who appear to have died too early from the jabs nor the remarkable increase in deaths by percentage of the population, but because there is a part of this story that keeps me up at night and, in my discernment, illustrates to me that there is something fishy about New Zealand. Let me know if you think this is weird, too. Although the general public was beaten into submission to the tune of about 95% of the population, the New Zealand government issued over *11,000* exceptions to key staff. This is in a country where people who refused to obey lockdowns or get jabbed literally had their homes raided by government officials.[111]

This screams planned extermination—jabs for you, but not for we elite. There were myriads of videos on TikTok, many of which have been censored, of the Hollywood elite getting jabbed, but in some videos, it was clear that the shot was not even going into the arm of the celebrity. This type of hypocrisy isn't classism or elitism; it's murder. The public was forced to obey government powers and even deceived into thinking people like Joe Biden or Anthony Hopkins were receiving shots to garner more compliance. However, time and again, we're learning that many of these elites were putting on a show to say, "Hey man, I'm just like you. We're all in this together." Bullshit.

---

110. https://expose-news.com/2023/10/22/new-zealand-is-a-crime-scene/

111. https://x.com/kylenabecker/status/1710080478554837007?s=20

The icing on the cake is that New Zealand's former Prime Minister Jacinda Ardern's new role after stepping down from government office is, get this: the World Economic Forum's global "disinformation czar."[112]

THIS SCRIPT WRITES ITSELF.

---

112. https://lionessofjudah.substack.com/p/devastating-fully-vaxxed-new-zealand

Poem: The Cards They Dealt

In the depths of my mind, I sit and wait,
Hold tight to the hand which seals their fate.
Whispered softly me to self,
Should I play the cards they dealt?
Masking smiles soaked in the rain,
Faking joy through the pain.
To give or not, what should it be?
It's not my fault they cannot see.
Ethics and morals, ostracized are we,
Let them hang or let them be?
I did not grow it nor plant the seed,
They tie the rope to their own tree.
If I were cruel, I'd laugh with glee,
For they hated him, and now, they truly hate me.

Chapter Nineteen
Genocidal Byproduct

Bill Gates and Dr. Fraudci got pretty vocal during the plandemic. Where there are millions of people dying, you can bet that Bill Gates is nearby, caressing his hands in front of his face manically. Gates is one of the most vocal advocates of depopulation. He's given a slew of TED Talks, with the most recent one in 2022 praising the technology he stands behind that will deliver vaccines more quickly (even without the vaccinee knowing they're being inoculated.)[113]

Bill Gates didn't just pop up out of the computer lab as a boy genius; he was born into a family of eugenicists and he is merely carrying the torch. Perhaps like Mark Zuckerberg, he is simply the carrier of a CIA-derived technology, the frontman or face of something developed long before Gates could ride a bicycle. Although he's such a royal dweeb that I suspect he can code, but still can't ride a bike. Biden apparently can't.

Bill Gates' father, William H. Gates Sr., was on the board of Planned Parenthood. Like his son, Gates Sr. was billed as a philanthropist and civic rights activist. These sorts of charming terms are often used to describe the world's most homicidal idiots because they think *we* are the idiots; a lot of people fall for these psyops in the clown world.

In a Ted Talk Gates provided in February of 2010 titled, "Innovating to Zero!" Gates laughed and stated that if we are "successful" in vaccines and 'reproductive health,' i.e. contraception

---

113. https://www.ted.com/speakers/bill_gates

and abortion, that we might be able to reduce the population by 10-15%. Gates has been obsessed with reducing the number of people who are born for decades. He and his wife were among the first to step up in 2020 before many counties were even in lockdown saying that they were working hard on a vaccine and that we needed to make sure we complied with social distancing, masking and lockdowns. Melina Gates conveniently and *totally coincidentally* wore an upside down cross during their initial COVID-19 related interviews.

Fourteen years after that 2010 Ted Talk, Gates is still beating the depopulation drum, and he's not alone. In an article titled, "The Elites Feel They Don't Need 90% of Us On the Planet Anymore," former British MP Andrew Bridgen is on video stating:

> *It's clear that we have a depopulation agenda around the vaccines... and it will be through repeated pandemics, wars, and famines, and everything that they're arranging in the world is to ensure that we have plenty of wars ...And on top of that... governments are making bizarre decisions and legislation, which is making it very, very difficult for our farmers to produce food... Unless the people stand up, and we need to stand up together around the world... the future for humanity is looking very dark.* [114] [115]

Dr. Michael Palmer, MD, was a biochemistry professor at the University of Waterloo, Ontario, Canada, and was fired in 2022 when he refused the CV19 so-called "vaccine." He now helps run Doctors4COVIDEthics.org, a website dedicated to warning people of the dangers of the COVID-19 jabs. In his book "mRNA Vaccine Toxicity," Palmer claims that the COVID-19 jab was an "intentional murder program," stating"

> *It was evident in 2020 that the risks that were being taken were completely unreasonable. It normally takes many years to develop a vaccine. . . these years were condensed into just a few months. . . . If you combine the radical shortening*

---

114. https://t.me/RogerHodkinson/

115. https://substack.com/home/post/p-150202165

of time for testing, which on its own creates a huge risk, combined with a new technology (mRNA) that means the risk is incalculable. So, it's completely irresponsible. . . . After the beginning of the vaccination campaign, and the first few weeks with disastrous results, it would have been necessary to immediately stop this campaign… The technology is fundamentally flawed. It will always produce the outcome that the body will begin destroying itself. …We commonly see destruction of the blood vessels, and this causes blood clots. You destroy the blood vessels, and then you get strokes and heart attacks. …This is a deliberate agenda of killing, not by the person who applied the shots, they may be honestly deceived.…There is no other interpretation in my mind that this is deliberate murder, deliberate killing. The entire gene-based (mRNA) vaccine agenda is a deliberate poisoning and killing.[116]

The Depopulation Industrial Complex

I used to be the guy who said, "I'm not an anti-vaxxer" with a derogatory and defensive tone. All four of my kids are vaccinated, although under my watch they will never have another shot as long as they live. I used to trust traditional vaccines, as did Dr. Kelly Victory and other doctors you'll meet throughout this book. I thought that all vaccines were safe because, naturally, they're thoroughly tested and licensed by the FDA. And then, we got this. A franken-shot mRNA experimental gene therapy that failed in testing, only to be covered up by Pfizer and rushed under "emergency use authorization" by the FDA. What could go wrong?

However, the idea that traditional vaccines are "thoroughly tested" may have been incorrect from the start. The Package Inserts for traditional vaccines are listed on the FDA website. But what is that?

116. https://www.lulu.com/shop/david-rasnick-and-brian-hooker-and-margot-desbois-and-sucharit-bhakdi/mrna-vaccine-toxicity/paperback/product-6n68j9.html?page=1&pageSize=4

Photo Courtesy of a Screen Capture of FDA.GOV[117]

Some of these vaccines have *not* been evaluated for their carcinogenic potential, mutagenic potential, or potential for impairment of fertility. Case in point: the Hepatitis A Vaccine.[118]

STN: BL 103475
Proper Name: Hepatitis A Vaccine, Inactivated
Tradename: HAVRIX
Manufacturer: GlaxoSmithKline Biologicals
Indication:

- For active immunization against disease caused by hepatitis A virus in persons 12 months of age and older.

Product Information

- Package Insert - HAVRIX

Supporting Documents

117. https://www.fda.gov/vaccines-blood-biologics/vaccines/vaccines-licensed-use-united-states

118. https://www.fda.gov/vaccines-blood-biologics/vaccines/havrix

13   NONCLINICAL TOXICOLOGY

13.1   Carcinogenesis, Mutagenesis, Impairment of Fertility

HAVRIX has not been evaluated for its carcinogenic potential, mutagenic potential, or potential for impairment of fertility.

... Or the Hepatitis B Vaccine...

STN: 103239

Proper Name: Hepatitis B Vaccine (Recombinant)

Tradename: ENGERIX-B

Manufacturer: GlaxoSmithKline Biologicals

Indications: ENGERIX-B is a vaccine indicated for immunization against infection caused by all known subtypes of hepatitis B virus.

Product Information

- Package Insert - Engerix-B

Supporting Documents

13   NONCLINICAL TOXICOLOGY

13.1   Carcinogenesis, Mutagenesis, Impairment of Fertility

ENGERIX-B has not been evaluated for carcinogenic or mutagenic potential, or for impairment of male fertility in animals. Vaccination of female rats with TWINRIX, which contains the same HBsAg component and quantity as ENGERIX-B, had no effect on fertility. *[See Use in Specific Populations (8.1).]*

Photo Courtesy of FDA.Gov[119]

119. https://www.fda.gov/vaccines-blood-biologics/vaccines/engerix-b

Or the influenza virus…

STN: BL 125127
Proper Name: Influenza Virus Vaccine
Tradename: Fluarix
Manufacturer: GlaxoSmithKline Biologicals
Indication:

- For active immunization of persons 3 years of age and older for the prevention of disease caused by influenza virus subtypes A and type B contained in the vaccine.

Product Information

- Package Insert - Fluarix

Supporting Documents

299   13   NONCLINICAL TOXICOLOGY
300   13.1   Carcinogenesis, Mutagenesis, Impairment of Fertility
301   FLUARIX has not been evaluated for carcinogenic or mutagenic potential, or for impairment of
305   fertility.

Photo Courtesy of FDA.gov[120]

Was the mRNA "vaccine" rollout designed to fuel depopulation via vaccination? That sounds like a conspiracy theory. However, on August 17th and 18th, 1992, in Geneva, Switzerland, women's health advocates and scientists met to discuss " fertility-regulating vaccines." Obviously, this is a coincidence…

---

120. https://www.fda.gov/media/84804/download

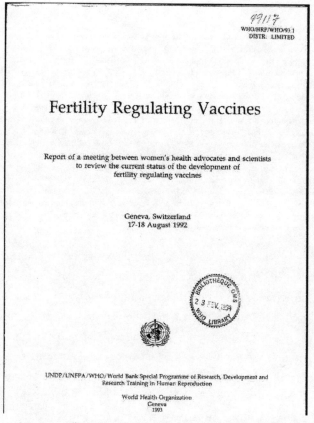

The entire report "Fertility Regulating Vaccines" can be found in the footnotes [121]

The National Institute for Health (NIH) reveals evidence of a depopulation agenda through vaccination programs, too. One report, "Vaccines for Immunological Control of Fertility," was published on NCBI in 2009 and states, "Vaccines have been proposed as one of the strategies for population control. Immunocontraceptive vaccines can be designed to inhibit (1) production of gametes (sperm and egg); (2) functions of gametes, leading to blocking of fertilization; and (3) gamete outcome (pregnancy)."[122]

---

121. https://drive.google.com/file/d/1FKMhagpd6bRZJ8la96bgH7UwQ8CmFNnI/view

122. https://www.ncbi.nlm.nih.gov/pmc/articles/PMC5904606/

Abstract   Go to: ▶

Vaccines have been proposed as one of the strategies for population control. Immunocontraceptive
vaccines can be designed to inhibit: (1) production of gametes (sperm and egg); (2) functions of
gametes, leading to blocking of fertilization; and (3) gamete outcome (pregnancy). Immunization with
gonadotropin-releasing hormone coupled to different carriers has shown curtailment in the production
of sperm with concomitant infertility in various species. Immunization of nonhuman primates and men
with ovine follicle stimulating hormone has also resulted in reduced sperm output. Various
spermatozoa-specific proteins such as FA1, PH-20, $LDH-C_4$, SP-10, SP-17, sp56, SPAG9, and Izumo
have been proposed as candidate antigens to develop contraceptive vaccines, which have shown efficacy
in inhibiting fertility in different animal models. Immunization with zona pellucida glycoproteins-based
immunogens also results in curtailment of fertility in a variety of species. However, ways to overcome
the observed oophoritis associated with zona proteins immunization have yet to be discovered, a
necessary step before their proposal for control of human population. Nonetheless, this is a very
promising approach to control wildlife animal population. Phase II clinical trials of β-human chorionic
gonadotropin-based vaccine in women have established the proof of principle that it is possible to
inhibit fertility without any untoward side-effects by vaccination. Further scientific inputs are required to
increase the efficacy of contraceptive vaccines and establish their safety beyond doubt, before they can
become applicable for control of fertility in humans.

Additionally, sperm counts are on the decline, prompting some entrepreneurs to say, "unvaccinated sperm is the new Bitcoin," which is obviously my personal retirement plan when they finally find a way to prevent me from working as an EMT any longer. From the report "Sperm Counts Are On The Decline. Is the Human Race in Danger?" We read that between 1973 and 2011, men's sperm counts fell by more than 50 percent.[123]

Earlier in this book, I mentioned Vernon Coleman and his prophetic book "Anybody Who Tells You That Vaccines Are Safe And Effective Is Lying."[124] What strikes me most about vaccines, not limited to the COVID-19 jab, is that I can't help but wonder what that patient's life would be like if they had just taken the risk of Hepatitis, the flu, or the Wuhan flu, i.e., COVID-19."

Catherine Austin Fitts claims that people are "literally being mind-controlled with very sophisticated technology and subliminal programming and media persuasion where people they really like and admire are encouraging them to do something. And they can't fathom that it could be dangerous. They just can't believe that the government would lie in a way that would kill millions of people or disable millions of people."

---

123. https://www.discovermagazine.com/health/sperm-counts-are-on-the-decline-is-the-human-race-in-danger

124. https://amzn.to/3YrlSaH

For CHD.TV, Mary Holland, Esq. and president of Children's Health Defense, states, "Most Americans and most people around the world would have had no idea that if you got a vaccine, you could become paralyzed. You could have a stroke. You could have a neurodegenerative injury. You could die."[125]

By any stretch of the imagination, the cure was worse than the disease when it comes to COVID-19.

There Was No Pandemic

"Slow the spread" was a phrase we heard nonstop in 2020 at the beginning of the unconstitutional lockdowns and mandates. But we didn't slow anything. In my estimation, we rebranded the flu for a few years to commit genocide by inoculating billions of people globally. In fact, the flu disappeared for a few years. Nevertheless, the CDC fueled fear and trembling amongst the American public.

Perhaps so as to ramp up fortitude for the election season, the CDC backpedaled on this, as the scientists backpedaled on vaccine safety data, which we explored in an earlier chapter. This was a monumental "oopsies" by the media, but amounts to homicide for the patients and families with whom I've worked who not only lost loved ones to a "vaccine" they didn't need, but lost livelihood either via lockdowns or via lost time on the job due to grief from losing "vaccine-"injured family and friends.

The CDC admitted in late 2023 that COVID-19 is no worse than the seasonal flu. Really?! The media tried to play it off as if it wasn't a big deal with the headline in the Wall Street Journal that read, "It's Official: We Can Pretty Much Treat COVID Like The Flu Now. Here's A Guide."[126]

---

125. https://x.com/S_Pierucci/status/1849675169339519296

126. https://archive.is/ocovZ

HEALTH | WELLNESS | YOUR HEALTH

It's Official: We Can Pretty Much Treat Covid Like the Flu Now. Here's a Guide.

New guidelines from the CDC Friday bring Covid precautions in line with those of other respiratory viruses

 By *Sumathi Reddy*
Updated March 1, 2024 1:03 pm ET

Despite the cheeky headline that purports to have a "guide" to surviving the Wuhan Flu, WSJ perpetuated fear in their article and failed to apologize for years of aggressively promoting masks and "vaccines." The CDC continues to stand by its claim that COVID-19 is something other than the flu, even though there is no ascertainable difference between them. According to Ethan Huff for Natural News:

> *The latest data about Wuhan coronavirus (COVID-19) "vaccines" suggests that they only help one person for every one million people injected to avoid death by "COVID." The U.S. Centers for Disease Control and Prevention (CDC) now states in its newest datasets that "per million doses in 12-17-year-olds over 6 months, 0-1 deaths have been prevented."*

In other words, it is entirely likely that zero out of every one million people jabbed for the Fauci Flu skips death — but for the sake of arguing in favor of the shots doing anything other than killing people, we will go with one out of every one million, which is still dismal. [127] [128]

My estimation is that the 1,000 or more people who are dying weekly from "COVID" are actually suffering from "vaccine-"injuries. "Long" COVID is more likely a result of either "vaccine-"injury or shedding. Some even claim that the "vaccinated" are vulnerable to "5G activation" or other bioweapons to which they are more susceptible. I don't discount those claims, but I'm not going to dive too deep into them in this book.

Wall Street Journal perpetuates the false narrative that seniors need to be "up-to-date" on their COVID-19 shots, revealing in late 2023 that approximately sixty percent of seniors weren't keeping up with boosters.

Natali Morris from "Redacted" said it best on her podcast:

Well, a new study shows something that we already knew: that COVID deaths were over-reported during the pandemic, and the COVID "vaccine" did not seem to have much of a benefit of slowing or stopping the pandemic as we know it. Why has the pandemic stopped? Because governments decided that it could stop. That's what we know for sure. [129]

The study Natali is referencing is research from 125 countries and their "vaccination" rollout programs. They found that there was no systematically or statistically significant trend to corroborate the claim that campaigns in 2020 and 2021 reduced all-cause mortality, the study we referenced earlier by Denis Rancourt et al.

---

127. https://www.msn.com/en-us/health/other/cdc-confirms-COVID-19-vaccine-prevents-death-in-only-1-out-of-1-million/ar-AA1gKiHs

128. https://www.naturalnews.com/2023-09-18-COVID-vaccine-helps-one-in-a-million.html

129. https://rumble.com/v5afqkt-holy-sht-shocking-new-COVID-study-changes-everything-weve-been-told-redacte.html

Over Two Hundred Adverse Events?

According to Frank Bergman for Slay News, Japanese researchers are leading the charge in accusing the mRNA shots of "affecting every possible aspect of human pathology. " Bergman reports that Japan's leading scientists link the jabs to surges in 201 diseases, some deadly.

During a press conference, researchers link the COVID-19 "vaccines" to thousands of side effects following six months of investigations.[130] Professor Emeritus Masanori Fukushima of Kyoto University stated that "Thousands of papers have reported side effects after vaccination, affecting every possible aspect of human pathology, from ophthalmology to psychiatry."

These include an increase in the age-adjusted mortality rate for leukemia, breast cancer, ovarian cancer, diseases of the heart, kidney, thyroid, diabetes, liver, skin, eyes, blood, nerves, systemic diseases, brain, lungs, and so many brain-related adverse events that "researchers probably hadn't found all of them yet."[131]

Fukushima continued by stating, "Mental disorders, psychiatric symptoms, depression, mania, anxiety, came up in abundance, but it's endless."

Professor Yasufumi Murakami from the Tokyo University of Science says, "It's very clear what happens when you administer a toxic gene to a human. There are cases that occur within one or two weeks after injection, but there are also many cases that appear after one or two years…. with the current messenger-type [mRNA] vaccines, a significant amount of IgG4 is being induced."

Shockingly, in October of 2024, Fox News 45 Baltimore brought on Dr. Paul Marik to talk about turbo cancers, with Marik stating, "There seems to be an association between… vaccination, particularly the boosters, and the development of turbo cancer."[132]

---

130. https://embed.niCOVIDeo.jp/watch/sm43262153?autoplay=1

131. https://lionessofjudah.substack.com/p/safe-and-effective-japanese-researchers?utm_source=post-email-title&publication_id=581065&post_id=148561774&utm_campaign=email-post-title&isFreemail=true&r=tluyu&triedRedirect=true&utm_medium=email

132. https://www.foxbaltimore.com/news/nation-world/what-can-you-do-to-mitigate-risk-of-cancer-lifestyle-diagnosis-flccc-diet

This Is War

All this evidence (and this merely scratches the surface) of depopulation fanatics and a future "Children of Men" type scenario means one thing: it's time to fight. But as much as I love my 2A rights, this war will require you to take up your *spiritual arms*.

The Bible clearly states that different gifts are appointed to each devotee of the Lord. Holy Spirit bestows these gifts to empower believers for service and evangelism. The traditional seven gifts described in Isaiah include:

- **Wisdom:** the ability to discern and apply God's will
- **Understanding:** the capacity to comprehend spiritual truths
- **Counsel:** the gift of wise decision-making
- **Fortitude:** the strength to persevere in faith and witness
- **Knowledge:** the revelation of spiritual truths and understanding
- **Piety:** the devotion and reverence for God
- **Fear of the Lord:** the awe and reverence for God's majesty

Isaiah 11 in the New King James Version reads:

There shall come forth a Rod from the stem of Jesse,
And a Branch shall grow out of his roots.
The Spirit of the Lord shall rest upon Him,
The Spirit of Wisdom and understanding,
The Spirit of Counsel and might,
The Spirit of knowledge and of the fear of the Lord.

His delight is in the fear of the Lord,
And He shall not judge by the sight of His eyes,
Nor decide by the hearing of His ears;

But with righteousness, He shall judge the poor,
And decide with equity for the meek of the earth;
He shall strike the earth with the rod of His mouth,
And with the breath of His lips He shall slay the wicked.

Righteousness shall be the belt of His loins,
And faithfulness the belt of His waist.

In the New Testament, nine gifts of the Holy Spirit are identified in 1 Corinthians 12:4-11. The New King James Version reads:

And my speech and my preaching were not with persuasive words of human wisdom, but in demonstration of the Spirit and of power, that your faith should not be in the wisdom of men but in the power of God.

However, we speak wisdom among those who are mature, yet not the wisdom of this age, nor of the rulers of this age, who are coming to nothing. But we speak the wisdom of God in a mystery, the hidden wisdom which God ordained before the ages for our glory, which none of the rulers of this age knew; for had they known, they would not have crucified the Lord of glory.

But as it is written:

> *"Eye has not seen, nor ear heard,*
> *Nor have entered into the heart of man.*
> *The things which God has prepared for those who love Him."*

But God has revealed them to us through His Spirit. For the Spirit searches all things, yes, the deep things of God. For what man knows the things of a man except the spirit of the man which isin him? Even so, no one knows the things of God except the Spirit of God.

This passage in 1 Corinthians 12:4-11 lists nine gifts of the Holy Spirit, which include:

Wisdom: the ability to speak God's wisdom
Knowledge: the revelation of spiritual truths
Discerning of Spirits (also called discernment): the ability to distinguish between genuine and counterfeit spiritual experiences
Faith: the confidence to trust God's promises

Gifts of Healings: the power to heal physical and spiritual ailments
Working of Miracles: the ability to perform extraordinary signs and wonders
Prophecy: the gift of speaking God's message
Diverse Kinds of Tongues: the ability to speak in languages unknown to oneself
Interpretation of Tongues: the ability to interpret the messages spoken in unknown languages

I post on X.com and podcast constantly sharing the truth about what I've seen. I have fortitude; I have strength to persevere and bear witness to my Lord Jesus Christ. I am blessed to have wisdom and discernment, and I use those gifts to sound the alarm so that others will wake up themselves and their families, God willing. I also have fortitude: I move full-steam ahead every day to persevere in faith and witness.

What are your gifts and **how are you using them?**

Holy Spirit *will equip you* when you ask. I don't care if you have gifts of healing or you're that ballsy guy or gal who interprets tongues in the middle of a worship service. Maybe you're pious and your life sets and example for others. That's not me; not by a long shot. But I admire you and *your* gifts.

But here this. If you see what I've just described: the apparent genocide that we've witnessed in the past three years, and you're not doing anything about it... I wish God's mercy on your soul. That's all I can say. Here's your reminder, once again, to get off your ass and do or say something. Pray something. Show up in your community for someone. Get a grip on your God-given gifts and *let's fight back.*

Poem: Wildflowers

Its stem stands firm,
From bud to bloom,
On snow-capped peaks to the warmth of June.
Grows in days and nights of gloom,
Even in pots with little room.
Some stand alone beneath the moon.
They come and go, all too soon.
In every type of weather found,
Strong as ever, light as down.
A wildflower grows from seed God's sown,
In nature's vast, unending poem.

Chapter Twenty
The Real Bad Guys

My subtitle would be a misnomer if I didn't include a bit of my own fear porn, but not for the purpose of impressing anybody or, God forbid, perpetuating paralysis-inducing fear of the future, but so that you will know what darkness we're fighting before the dawn I trust is coming.

This chapter is going to detail some of the reasons I believe that the COVID-19 shots were not only "unsafe" and "ineffective," but a tool of genocide. History is full of murder. It's been happening en masse since the beginning of time. Evil people take out entire towns, cities, counties, or even ethnicities. All across the world Christians are being slaughtered in places like Nigeria, where the Boko Harem and its offshoot, the Islamic State West Africa Province (ESWAP) has attacked Christian communities. In the Middle Belt of Nigeria, conflict between Fulani herdsmen (primarily Muslim) and Christian farmers has resulted in significant casualties.

According to International Society for Civil Liberties & Rule of Law (Intersociety), a Christian rights advocacy group, between 2009 and 2023, around 50,250 Christians were killed in Nigeria, largely due to Islamist-related violence and the Fulani militia conflicts. The Christian Association of Nigeria (CAN) and other advocacy groups have also cited similar figures, reporting tens of thousands of Christians killed over the past two decades. Some estimates report that 100,000 Christians have been murdered in Nigeria, but other sources suggest it's many, many more.

In the case of Nigeria, tension primarily exists between Christians and Muslims. We'll see much more of this in the future as Muslims are having many,

many more children than Westerners and they clearly state that they want power and submission over the West. I hope my kids and grandkids aren't around when this happens; or that the Lord returns before we go into such a bloody battle.

But the murderers aren't always screaming "Allahu Akbar" and wielding hatchets or wearing sandals in the desert. Sometimes they're the whitest folks around. They're wearing $2,000 suits and standing on stages or at the heads of some of the world's major corporations. These people are eugenicists, and in this chapter I'll detail how they operate and how they might have to do with the COVID-19 shots.

Depopulation is a nice way of saying, "eugenicist," which is a nice way of saying "murderer." Eugenicists support eugenics, which is a set of beliefs and practices ostensibly aimed at improving the genetic quality of the human population by promoting the reproduction of people with desirable traits and discouraging or preventing those with undesirable traits from reproducing. The eugenics movement became well-known in 1883 when Francis Galton coined the term "eugenics" and suggested that selective breeding could improve human populations.

Fast forward to 2024: countless influential people promote a concept of depopulation with the claim that it's sustainable for the earth and that without the killing off of millions if not billions of people, we're going to be destroyed by climate change. When I broach this subject I'm often met with people who say, "that's ridiculous, Harry. It's a violation of human rights, which the modern civilized world cares so much about. Eugenics ended when we defeated the Nazis."

Um, no. No it didn't.

The Nazi's forced sterilization.

Ironically, the COVID-19 shot has caused miscarriages to skyrocket and fertility to decline.

The Nazis used discriminatory laws to enact their eugenics program.

Enter: COVID-19 mandates.

Nazi eugenics were a violation of human rights.

The plandemic was accompanied with mandates that included threats to livelihood (or, in some cases, prison) if some folks did not comply with the jabs or even masks.

The Nazis closed down the businesses, stole the farms, and locked up those who didn't' comply with their movement.

In a sneaky way through lockdowns, we did the same thing. Only people were so stupid this time around that we didn't need intimidating SS Soldiers to execute the orders.

Let's face the fact that there are people who want global depopulation… and the COVID-19 jabs were a great way to execute *that* perverted dream. In an interview with Audubon magazine in 1996, Ted Turner, founder of CNN, stated, "A total population of 250-300 million people, a 95% decline would be ideal."

To the UNESCO Courier, the late Jacques Cousteau said, "One America burdens the earth much more than twenty Bangladeshes. This is a terrible thing to say in order to stabilize the world population, we must eliminate 350,000 people per day. It is a horrible thing to say, but it's just as bad not to say it."

According to "Earthbound," a collection of essays on environmental ethics, William Aiken said: "Massive human diebacks would be good. It is our duty to cause them. It is our species' duty, relative to the whole, to eliminate 90% of our numbers."[133]

The late Prince Philip, Duke of Edinburgh and patron of the World Wildlife Fund said, "If I were reincarnated, I would wish to be returned to earth as a killer virus to lower human population levels."[134] [135]

Barack Obama's Science and Technology Advisor John P. Holdren co-authored a 1977 book called "Ecoscience" with Paul & Anne Ehrlich in which the authors advocated the formation of a "planetary regime" that would use a "global police force" to enforce totalitarian measures of population control. These included forced abortions, mass sterilization

133. https://www.investors.com/politics/commentary/liberal-world-view-sees-humans-as-a-plague-doom-inevitable/

134. https://www.independent.co.uk/news/people/prince-philip-quotes-jokes-gaffes-b1832059.html

135. http://zombietime.com/john_holdren/

programs conducted via the food and water supply, as well as mandatory bodily implants that would prevent couples from having children.[136]

What do these and so many other proponents of depopulation have in common? They use climate change to promote their murderous ideas. Holdren also promoted "Large-scale geoengineering projects designed to cool the Earth," such as "shooting pollution particles into the upper atmosphere to reflect the sun's rays," which, as Alex Jones pointed out, is already occurring via chemtrails.[137] Jones's movie "The End Game"[138] exhaustively details the plan to exterminate 80% of the population in order to create a one world government.

136. http://www.frontpagemag.com/readArticle.aspx?ARTID=34198

137. http://www.prisonplanet.com/obama-science-advisor-repeats-geoengineering-talking-point.html

138. http://www.endgamethemovie.com/

On page 944 of "Ecoscience," Holden and the authors state:

As of 1977, we are facing a global overpopulation catastrophe that must be resolved at all costs by the year 2000…Humanity cannot afford to muddle through the rest of the twentieth century; the risks are too great, and the stakes are too high. This may be the last opportunity to choose our own and our descendants' destiny. Failing to choose or making the wrong choices may lead to catastrophe. But it must never be forgotten that the right choices could lead to a much better world.

Other eugenicists include David Rockefeller and Bill Gates, who regularly mastermind with other "philanthropist" billionaires to discuss how they can leverage their wealth to reduce the world's population. According to the London Times, some of America's leading billionaires secretly met in 2009 at a summit convened by Gates to consider how their wealth could be used to slow the growth of the world's population.

Described as the Good Club by one insider it included David Rockefeller Jr, the patriarch of America's wealthiest dynasty, Warren Buffett and George Soros, the financiers, Michael Bloomberg, the mayor of New York, and the media moguls Ted Turner and Oprah Winfrey. These members, along with Gates, have given away more than £45 billion since 1996 to causes ranging from health programmes in developing countries to ghetto schools nearer to home.

Stacy Palmer, editor of the Chronicle of Philanthropy, said the summit was unprecedented. "We only learnt about it afterwards, by accident. Normally these people are happy to talk good causes, but this is different - maybe because they don't want to be seen as a global cabal," he said.

Another guest said there was "nothing as crude as a vote," but a consensus emerged that they would back a strategy in which population growth would be tackled as a potentially disastrous environmental, social, and industrial threat. 'This is something so nightmarish that everyone in this group agreed it needs big-brain answers…They need to be independent of government agencies, which are unable to head off the disaster we all see looming."[139]

But we defeated the Nazi's, right? Well, not entirely. Many of their sick ideals still live today. For example, David Rockefeller's father John D. Rockefeller was involved in promoting the ideology of the Nazi super race to the Third Reich. The allies protected Nazi eugenicists claiming they wanted to preserve their "expertise" in the post-war world.[140]

When former President Barack Obama's Science and Technology Advisor openly advocates mass sterilization of the public via the food and water supply through in his 944-page book, one that he never denounced at the time of this book's writing, we might still have some of these sickos from 1883, 1939, and other periods throughout history still roaming around in high places with their low moral standards.

Ninety miles northeast of Atlanta, Georgia sits a small town in Elbert County where "America's Stonehenge" stood for forty-two years from 1980 to 2022, at which time the "Georgia Guidestones" were partially bombed and eventually dismantled. The Georgia Guidestones were a large granite monument of six slabs, each weighing over twenty tones. They were inscribed with ten principles or guidelines in eight modern languages (English, Spanish, Swahili, Hindi, Hebrew, Arabic, Chinese, and Russian). The same message was also inscribed in four ancient languages on the capstone: Babylonian cuneiform, Classical Greek, Sanskrit, and Egyptian hieroglyphics.

The messages inscribed on the Guidestones were often seen as directives for humanity, especially in a post-apocalyptic or future context. They included:

1. Maintain humanity under 500,000,000 in perpetual balance with nature.
2. Guide reproduction wisely — improving fitness and diversity.
3. Unite humanity with a living new language.

139. https://www.thetimes.com/article/83b550ca-5e98-4eff-a078-a8daf399d58e
140. http://infowars-shop.stores.yahoo.net/endgamedvd.html

4. Rule passion — faith — tradition — and all things with tempered reason.
5. Protect people and nations with fair laws and just courts.
6. Let all nations rule internally, resolving external disputes in a world court.
7. Avoid petty laws and useless officials.
8. Balance personal rights with social duties.
9. Prize truth — beauty — love — seeking harmony with the infinite.
10. Be not a cancer on the Earth — Leave room for nature — Leave room for nature.

The identity of the person or group who commissioned the Guidestones remains unknown. In 1979, a man using the pseudonym R.C. Christian approached a local granite company with instructions to build the monument. He claimed to represent a small group of loyal Americans who believed in the principles inscribed on the stones.

Reduce the population to 500 million? Unite humanity with a "living new language?" Temper passion, faith and tradition with reason? Social duties? Be not a cancer on earth?

I've always thought the Georgia Guidestones resembled a One World Government decree slimily decorated with supposed environmental consciousness. I bring them up because they illustrate how clever the depopulation language has become over the decades. "Remain in harmony with nature," is coupled with "keep the population several billion less than it is today."

The same sneaky language is used in climate change rhetoric which Senator Frank Lasee calls "climate alarmism" to enact policies that will ultimately create energy poverty and destruction under the guise of ESG scores and "sustainability, as detailed in Senator Lasee's book "Climate and Energy Lies: Expensive, Dangerous, and Destructive."

Excess Mortality... Depopulation Manifests

Whether through a pandemic or the poisoning of our food and water supplies, we're seeing depopulation before our very eyes. In fact, since 2021, many life insurance companies have reported paying out more claims than expected. In 2021, life insurers paid out a record high of nearly $200 billion in claims, an 11% increase in claims compared to 2020, following a 15% increase from 2019 to 2020, the highest jump since the 1918 flu "pandemic."[141]

As a healthcare professional, I don't think the skyrocketing excess mortality has to do solely with the plandemic, but also due to toxic food, water, and environmental toxins or atmospheric harms from things like chemtrails or EMF exposure. That said, the plandemic sure did accelerate things. People who didn't die from the jabs might have neglected their health both physically and mentally in other ways due to lockdowns or fear of going to the hospital. As stories in previous chapters indicate, I saw people sit and choose death over going to hospitals during the lockdowns, and even thereafter. Fear kills.

That was the plan.

Most unsettling is the excess mortality in younger people.

Younger adult mortality rates are up more than 20% in 2023 according to the CDC, even as COVID-related causes declined in 2022. Causes of death that rose include stroke, diabetes, kidney and liver diseases, as well as suicide and complications from substance abuse.[142]

---

141. https://money.com/life-insurance-payouts-record-high/

142. https://insurancenewsnet.com/innarticle/excess-mortality-continuing-surge-causes-concerns

This appears driven by younger age deaths, particularly 15-45*

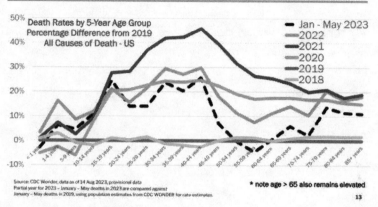

Gain of Function

Dr. Lawrence Tabak has been the Acting Director of the NIH since Dr. Francis Collins resigned in December of 2021. During a House Oversight Committee meeting on May 16, 2024, Tabak was asked, "Did NIH fund gain of function research at the Wuhan Institute of Virology through Eco Health?"

Tabak responded, "It depends on your definition of gain of function research. If you're speaking about the generic term, yes we did." When questioned by Rand Paul, Dr. Anthony Fauci had previously lied about NIH funding gain of function research.

The cover-ups don't stop with Fauci, though. Throughout congressional hearings, the origins of COVID-19 has been in the spotlight. Dr. Tabak admitted under oath that NIH was funding gain of function research, which confirms what "conspiracy realists" had learned years prior. Even more surprisingly, Dr. David Morens revealed that senior officials at NIG were using private emails and the use of in-person conversations in order to avoid FOIA requests. Although Eco Health Alliance and Peter Daszak have been stripped of funding from HHS, there remains the important question: why was this gain of function research being conducted in the first place?

I like pop culture influencers who call it out plainly for the common man or woman, like me. Joe Rogan stated, "... they were doing that to maximize profits because they wanted to keep selling these things, and a lot of people got extremely rich. Many billionaires were created because of the pandemic, because of the COVID vaccine. It's all very spooky to me because I think there's a long history in this country of people doing things for money, knowing that people are going to suffer because of it."

The rabbit trail gets weirder and deeper, though. David Hodges of "The Common Sense Show"[143] writes, "Fauci's gain of function research... all planned depopulation along with radical post-term abortion..."

Hodges goes on to describe the fact that FEMA had previously imported Hydrogen Cyanide from Brazil beginning in 2011, labeling the containers as materials other than what they were. Hydrogen Cyanide has been used in warfare, most notably to execute prisoners in Nazy concentration camps. Who is FEMA planning to use Hydrogen Cyanide upon? Who's going into FEMA camps?

I pondered this question over the past few years as I recalled mandates and threats by the World Health Organization officially stating that they would be going door-to-door to collect symptomatic people and taking them into camps. Canada, New Zealand, and Australia were particularly militant about locking up dissidents or quarantining citizens, and they still are. In early 2024, Canadian pastors responded to a new law warning that preaching Biblical sexual morality could carry a prison sentence. Bill C-4, which went into effect on January 8, 2024, describes hetero- and cisgender identity as myths. Fox News stated, "Counseling that does not align with such a worldview now carries a potential five-year jail sentence."[144]

From prosecuting Canadian Christians for believing biblical morality to threatening encampment for dissidents and even censoring people like me online, it feels like the signs of the "End Times" my grandmother warned me about are not only here, but they're slapping me in the face on a daily basis.

Leo Hohmann, investigative reporter on globalism, Christianity, Islam, Judaism, and where politics and religion intersect, has conducted

143. https://thecommonsenseshow.com/

144. https://www.foxnews.com/world/thousands-churches-raise-alarm-scope-new-canadian-conversion-therapy-ban

many deep dives into the concept of depopulation.[145] He states, "All of the globalist policies over the last three years are driving toward one thing: mass depopulation. Yes, they want to kill us. Until you understand that, you will never understand what's going on. You will never make sense of it… I know it's a hard pill to swallow… Many of those duped the first time lost their lives or ended up with life-long health issues. Some even offered their children to the military-biomedical-security complex."[146]

In 2014 there was an analysis done by The Deagel Corporation, whose founder was a military contractor with sources in the government swamp. Deagel collects data for high-level decision makers and prepares briefings for agencies such as the NSA, UN, and World Bank. They predicted in their "Deagel Forecast" that America's population would decline from 310 million in 2017 to just 99 million by the end of 2025,[147] indicating that Europe and North America would be the least safe places to live with Central and South America, China and Africa being the safest places to reside. Until COVID-19, these predictions left many people bewildered, but they're beginning to make sense as we see life expectancy plummet and cancer or heart disease skyrocket today, at the time of the writing of this book in late 2024.

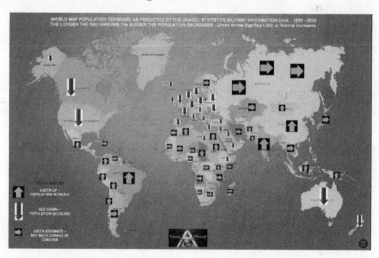

145. www.leohohmann.com

146. https://lionessofjudah.substack.com/p/deagel-population-forecast-of-nearly

147. https://nobulart.com/wordpress/wp-content/uploads/2021/08/Deagel-2025-Forecast-by-Country.pdf

Mahathir Mohamad served twice as Prime Minister of Malaysia, first from 1981 to 2003 and again from 2018 to 2020. As the longest-serving prime minister in Malaysia's history, Mahathir was instrumental in transforming Malaysia's economy from an agrarian base to a manufacturing and industrialized economy, focusing on infrastructure development and economic modernization. Unexpectedly, he blew the whistle about the depopulation agenda in 2015

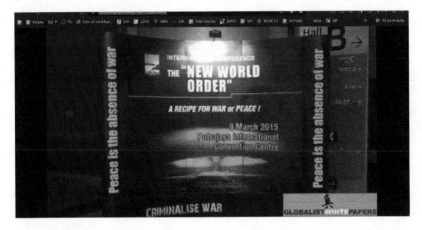

In 2015, at the International Conference of the New World Order, Mohamad stated:

> *Basically, it is about having a world government. We should abolish all states, all nations, and all borders. But instead of only one world government. And that world government is to be by certain people. Elites. People who are very rich, very intelligent, and very powerful in many ways. They are the ones who will govern the world. There was not much talk about democracy or the choice of leaders. Instead, there was to be a government by these elites who would impose their rules on everyone in this world. And for those who are unwilling to submit to them, there will be punishment. And the peace that we will get from this is the peace of the great era. Because the intention also is to reduce the number of people in this world at the time when the New World Order was enunciated, the population in this world was only three billion. The intention was to reduce it to one billion. Now the population of the world is seven billion. There will be a need to kill many billions*

of people or to starve them to death or to prevent them from giving birth in order to reduce the population of this world.[148]

In Malaysia, over 86% of the population received at least one COVID-19 jab.[149]

AI Thought Experiment

As a fun thought experiment, while I was thinking about genocide from the mRNA technology, I asked Microsoft, "What if a secret cult had control of mRNA? Explain the possibilities. Why would they use mRNA and testing for data collection? How could that plausibly be used for their ancient beliefs?"

Here is its answer:

Let's imagine a scenario where a secret cult has gained control over mRNA technology.

This cult, deeply rooted in ancient beliefs about the mystical properties of blood types, could leverage mRNA for several purposes:

Why Use mRNA?

1. *Precision and Control: mRNA technology allows for precise control over gene expression. This means the cult could potentially manipulate biological processes in ways that align with their rituals and beliefs.*
2. *Rapid Development: mRNA can be quickly designed and produced, making it an ideal tool for a group looking to implement their plans swiftly.*
3. *Data Collection: By using mRNA in various experiments, the cult could gather extensive data on how different blood types respond to specific genetic modifications.*

    a. *Testing and Data Collection*

---

148. https://rumble.com/embed/vrlb7f/?pub=rze3r

149. https://data.moh.gov.my/dashboard/COVID-vaccination

i. *Genetic Experiments: The cult could conduct experiments to see how different blood types react to specific mRNA sequences. This could involve testing for immune responses, physical changes, or even psychological effects.*

ii. *Personalized Rituals: By understanding the genetic makeup of their members, the cult could tailor rituals and ceremonies to enhance the perceived mystical properties of each blood type.*

iii. *Health and Longevity: They might explore ways to use mRNA to enhance the health and longevity of their members, believing that certain blood types have superior qualities that can be amplified.*

4. *Plausible Uses for Ancient Beliefs*

a. *Enhancing Mystical Powers: The cult could believe that mRNA technology can unlock or enhance the mystical powers associated with certain blood types. For example, they might think that those with RH-negative or O-positive blood can gain heightened abilities through specific genetic modifications.*

b. *Creating Superhumans: By combining ancient beliefs with modern technology, the cult could aim to create individuals with superior physical and mental capabilities, aligning with their mythological ideals.*

c. *Ritualistic Purposes: mRNA could be used in rituals to symbolize the merging of ancient wisdom with modern science, creating a new form of spiritual practice that honors their historical roots while embracing technological advancements.*

In response to my little experiment, a connection on X.com @jonileah85 asked Grok the same question. It answered:

If a secret cult were to gain control over mRNA technology, the implications would be profound, potentially blending modern biotechnology with ancient beliefs or practices in various sinister or manipulative ways. Here's how this scenario could unfold:

1. *Control and Manipulation of Genetic Information*

Genetic Modification for Compliance: *mRNA vaccines or therapies could theoretically be used to alter genetic expressions in ways that align with the cult's beliefs or goals, such as reducing aggression, enhancing obedience, or altering human traits to fit an ideal they hold.*

Targeted Mutations: *They might aim to introduce specific genetic mutations that could activate over generations, aligning human evolution with their prophecies or desired outcomes.*

2. *Surveillance and Data Collection*

Biometric Tracking: *mRNA technology could be modified to include mechanisms for tracking or identifying individuals through unique genetic markers. This could serve as a form of biometric surveillance, where individuals' genetic data is collected under the guise of health or vaccination programs.*

Behavioral Data: *By analyzing how individuals respond to mRNA-based treatments or vaccines, the cult could gather data on genetic predispositions to certain behaviors, mental states, or health conditions, which might be used to predict or influence future behaviors or societal trends.*

3. *Cultural and Ritualistic Integration*

Rituals and Symbols: *The cult might embed symbols or rituals into the distribution or administration of mRNA therapies, turning medical procedures into religious or mystical experiences, thereby deepening the psychological control over participants.*

Mythological Engineering: *They could claim that these treatments are part of an ancient prophecy or necessary for ascension, spiritual evolution, or survival against impending doom, as described in their lore.*

4. Population Control

Fertility and Birth Control: *mRNA could be used to control fertility rates, either by enhancing or reducing reproductive capabilities, aligning with their beliefs about population growth or specific genetic lineages.*

Selective Enhancement: *Offering genetic enhancements that only certain groups can access, based on criteria that align with cult beliefs (e.g., pure bloodlines, chosen ones).*

5. Psychological and Societal Influence

Mental Health and Behavior: *Alterations could aim at mental health, potentially reducing resistance to certain ideas or increasing susceptibility to hypnotic or persuasive techniques used by the cult.*

Social Hierarchy: *mRNA could be used to create or enhance physical or mental traits among followers that distinguish them from outsiders, reinforcing a caste system or hierarchy based on genetics.*

Why mRNA?

Versatility: *mRNA can be programmed to produce specific proteins, offering a direct way to manipulate biological processes without altering the DNA.*

Speed: *The technology allows for rapid development and deployment, which is crucial for a cult wanting to enact large-scale changes quickly.*

Invisibility: *Changes at the mRNA level might not immediately show up in standard genetic tests, providing a covert method of manipulation.*

Ancient Beliefs Integration

Fulfillment of Prophecy: *mRNA could be seen as a tool to fulfill ancient prophecies about changing human nature or ushering in a new era of humanity.*

Divine Intervention: *Positioning mRNA technology as a gift or tool from deities, aligning with myths about gods altering human form or consciousness.*

This scenario, while speculative, illustrates how a blend of high-tech bio-technology with ancient or mystical beliefs could be used for control, manipulation, or societal engineering by a secretive group. The ethical implications are vast, touching on consent, autonomy, and the nature of human identity itself.[150]

Microsoft and Grok AI fell short of using the word "genocide" in their description, but the mention of fertility rates and population control speaks for itself.

---

150. https://x.com/jonileah85/status/1851770129862001045

Poem: Sold For A Pound

Evil abounds, choosing lost over found.
Burying children deep underground.
Building the gallows, a chilling sound
In the heart of darkness, souls are sold for a pound.
The moon hides face, the stars turn away
Nightmares awaken; in the cold earth, they lay
soulless sneers echo in the void in which they stay
Few above now lament, most live in dismay.

Chapter Twenty-One
Removing YHWH

"I can't feel it anymore! I want to die!" A patient screamed as I arrived on the scene after a 911 call.

"Can't feel what anymore? Harming yourself isn't the answer. Please let me try to help you," I responded calmly.

The patient continued screaming, "I can't feel the presence of God. I can't feel my own soul. It's gone!"

"God will never leave you. How long have you felt this way?" The patient allowed me to secure them to my cot. Their vital signs were in the normal range, although their heart rate was slightly elevated.

"I've felt this ever since I took the vaccines! I can't feel me. I can't feel God. I don't even recognize my own family anymore!"

I asked the hysterically patient, "Do you still love your family? Do you still love God?"

"Yes," they answered pathetically, but from their head, not from their heart.

I attempted to work with that glimmer of hope. "Then recognize that love, hold on to that. If you can still feel love, then God has not abandoned you.

It didn't comfort the patient. They sobbed, "I want to die. I can't take this anymore."

I asked, "Would you like me to pray with you?"

"No!" They screamed.

I respected their wishes and continued to treat the patient while praying for them under my breath. It was one thing over the past few years to witness the staggering increase in psych calls, young heart attacks, strokes, and seizures. But I've also had patients describe a sudden "disconnect from God" or from their families.

There is death to the body. But there is no pain like death to the spirit.

Steph recently wrote a book about returning to Hebrew words to understand the Bible. By and large, I've always read from the New International Version because it's simple, I have an NIV Study Bible, and my grandmother Josie read it. Like so many things, I didn't question it until recently.

Although I've understood that there are dozens of translations, I have "assumed" that the good ol' theological doctors were giving me a prescription that would heal me, not keep my mind mushrooming and devoid of deep answers and passages that were written through Divine Inspiration so long ago by prophets and writers chosen by God.

I have learned that translations of Scriptures sometimes remove entire passages that verify the Divinity of Jesus Christ Yeshua, such as the NIV. Even the grandson of preachers, in all my years of Sunday School, I couldn't tell you the difference between the NIV and KJV a few years ago. I suppose I figured, "Well, the KJV is old-fashioned language. We needed a modern translation for our simple modern minds."

Most of my Christian friends read a New International Version of the Bible because it's read in most churches. None of us, myself included, spend a lot of time learning the intricacies in the various translations of the Bible. They've become like ice cream flavors; a matter of preference rather than matters of eternal importance to our souls.

To my particular dismay was the discovery of how much the modern evangelical church takes for granted how carefully the Word has been kept over the millennia and who has taken responsibility for guarding that Word, namely, the Jewish people. The more I learn and the more Jewish friends I make, the more I realize that not only are our translations watered down, but the entire evangelical culture is almost totally devoid of analysis. Again, we largely take our faith at face value. Going back into the Scriptures and cross-referencing the original meaning of the words is something left for seminary students, and even then, it's a temporary event. For the Jews, this is a way of life.

One of the first and most precious reveals was my realization that God has many names that all depict different characteristics of Him. Jireh is "God who provides." Jehovah means "the Lord is to be praised." Rapha means "God your healer," and Elohim means "the Creator." I rarely hear God referenced as anything other than, well, God.

But as I've grown in my understanding of God and the Word, I have begun referencing my Creator more as YHWH, the Hebrew name for God. YHWH is the name God uses for himself. In Exodus 3:14, Moses encounters God at the burning bush on Mount Sinai. Moses asks God for His name so that he can tell the Israelites who sent him, "And God said unto Moses 'I Am that I Am:' and He said, Thus shalt thou say unto the children of Israel, I Am hath sent me unto you." That phrase in the original Hebrew is translated as "הָיָה רֶשָׁא הָיָה" (ehyeh asher ehyeh). This statement signifies God's self-existence and timeless nature. The name YHWH is a four-letter Hebrew name of God associated with this declaration: I Am that I Am.

YHWH is the personal name of God, and it is recognized in Judaism, Christianity, and Islam. In Jewish tradition, this name is not pronounced, and even in books and writings, the name God is usually written as G-d. Often, when reading Hebrew Scriptures, the name YHWH is read as "Adonai," which means "Lord" out of reverence. The best description of how to pronounce YHWH that I have since seen comes from Pastor Greg Locke, who says that every baby's first breath is the name of God; once they're cleaned out, they inhale "YH," and as somebody passes away, their last breath is "WH" when they exhale. Even atheists, he points out, cannot escape saying God's name as YHWH is best pronounced as an inhale and exhale. Every breath gives glory to our God! I like this theory, and I love Pastor Greg's deep dive into the Scriptures here:

See Pastor Locke explain how he suggests we pronounce YHWH here:
https://www.instagram.com/reel/CwP_cClMHu8/?igshid=MzRlODBiNWFlZA==

In recent years, I have explored the possibility that corrupt actors have made a concerted effort to rewrite YHWH from our very DNA. I'm not alone, as many rabbis, neuroscientists, and scientists have been asking the same question. In 2020, we quickly saw videos going viral that portrayed Bill Gates stating proudly and eerily confidently that he would lead the charge in developing a "vaccine" for the COVID-19 virus, suspiciously within just months of the so-called pandemic. This, in particular his appearances with his now estranged wife Melinda wearing an upside-down cross around her neck, set off my internal alarm system that there may be spiritual forces at play with this supposed pandemic.

Understand that DNA tampering is not new. In fact, you can read about it in Genesis 6, where it is written: "And it came to pass, when men began to multiply on the face of the earth, and daughters were born unto them, That the sons of God saw the daughters of men that they were fair; and they took them wives of all which they chose." There is more evidence in the books of the Apocrypha, which, although not Scripture, still provide outstanding evidence of history.

What emerged from the still, small voices within many skeptics, Believers as well as unbelievers, was an underground and eventually magnificent voice of what have been called "anti-vaxxers." These anti-vaxxers had many reasons for their civil disobedience. Some of them were worried about an untested vaccine unleashed before clinical trials had been completed. Many of them told their doctors they wanted to wait to see what the results of the shot would be. To be clear, the COVID-19 injection is not a vaccine and doesn't meet the requirements of a vaccine. Therefore, for the purpose of this manuscript, we'll call it the COVID-19 gene therapy injection. This isn't just scientifically accurate, but it's downright terrifying.

You see, there are a myriad of additional reasons that a reported 25% of the US population rejected the much applauded media-propagandized COVID-19 gene therapy injection besides the fact that it was relatively untested and experimental. Namely, as Professor Philip Buckhaults, a doctor with a PhD in biochemistry and molecular biology, explains, "The Pfizer vaccine is contaminated with plasmid DNA; it's not just mRNA, it's got bits of DNA in it. This DNA is the DNA vector that was used as the template for the in vitro transcription reaction when they made the mRNA. I know this is true because I sequenced it in my own lab[151]." It's important to note that Dr. Buckhaults is a proponent of the modified-mRNA-LNP (lipid nanoparticle) platform because of his hope that it will serve to help ameliorate or cure cancer[152].

In the graph below, which was used during his Senate hearing, Dr. Buckhaults notes that pieces of DNA in the Pfizer vaccine batches he references are "small and are likely to damage the human genome by integrating and becoming permanent mutations (like shotgun pellets hitting a washboard). It's important to look at DNA taken from different body tissues of vaccinated people to see if this is happening and if it can be causing any adverse events now or if there is a future cancer risk down the road."

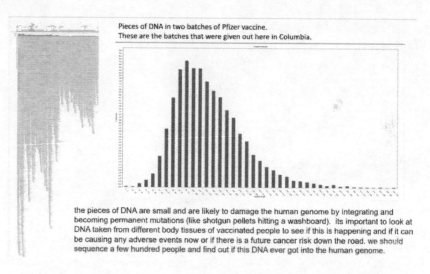

Pieces of DNA in two batches of Pfizer vaccine. These are the batches that were given out here in Columbia.

the pieces of DNA are small and are likely to damage the human genome by integrating and becoming permanent mutations (like shotgun pellets hitting a washboard). its important to look at DNA taken from different body tissues of vaccinated people to see if this is happening and if it can be causing any adverse events now or if there is a future cancer risk down the road. we should sequence a few hundred people and find out if this DNA ever got into the human genome.

A toxicologist with advanced degrees in molecular biology and biochemistry, Dr. Janci Lindsay suggests that modified mRNA may compel antibiotic

---

151. You can see Dr. Buckhaults speak before the South Carolina Senate about this subject here: https://www.youtube.com/watch?time_continue=4&v=IEWHhrHiiTY&embeds_referring_euri=https%3A%2F%2Ftwitter.com%2F&source_ve_path=MTY0OTksMjg2NjY&feature=emb_logo

152. https://jessicar.substack.com/p/south-carolina-senate-hearing-usc?nthPub=381

resistance genes, insertional mutagenesis, and risk of cancer in her own testimony in front of the South Carolina Senate. Lindsay bravely spoke in front of the United States Senate in 2022 about the risks from the parent inoculation being passed to children. In 2023, she stated that her original concern was reverse transcription from RNA before "we knew that there was DNA in the shots."

Lindsay stated, "I think that this is the most dangerous platform that has ever been released. That is very easy to see in the VAERS database where you have more deaths in just a couple of months after the rollout than you've had in the past thirty years for all the other vaccines combined."

This chart illustrates the magnitude of that statement.

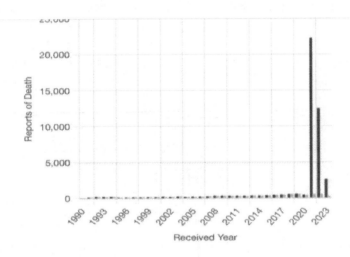

Stephanie has recently worked with an author who is suspicious that YHWH has been intentionally written out of Christian Scriptures and potentially out of our very bodies. Many teachers assert that our bodies are the "Third Temple," and it is through the mRNA shots that Satan seeks to destroy that Temple. Some go further to assert that the mRNA shots, commonly called vaccines, were the "mark of the beast" due to the genetic modification they are said to initiate. At this time, I do not ascribe to that belief, but I'm excited for the Lord to reveal this and so much more to me one day.

Our genes contain information that determines the size, shape, color, material, and other attributes of our bodies. DNA, or deoxyribonucleic acids, make up the gene chains that are part of chromosomes, which are components of cells. For those of you who enjoy true crime, this explains how your DNA can be acquired by just a small sample of cells, such as a blood sample or even a lock of hair.

The two bands you see in a "DNA strand" are held together with sulfide bonds. These bonds that appear as "bridges" occur after the tenth pair of nucleotides, after the fifth pair, after the sixth pair, and again five pairs later.

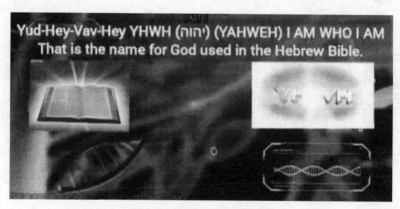

Image courtesy of the creator of this video at
https://www.bitchute.com/video/CrirtKcUgQtH/

Israeli scientist Sipos Richard confirms this on his blog at ErevShabbat.org. Richard writes,

Scientists have discovered that the deoxyribonucleic acids that make up our genes come together in such a way that a bridge forms after a certain amount of acids make up a row. These bridges are called base pairs. It is this process that allows the DNA chains to be linked together, thus creating that particular twisted ladder-like element that is part of the larger chromosome. This type of sequencing determines the information set of our genetics, which we pass on to our offspring. The rate of connection of deoxyribonucleic acids is as follows: 10-5-6-5. This means that between the acids Adenine-Guamine-Cytosine-Thymine, a bridge is formed after every ten acids, then every five acids, then every six acids, and every five acids. This connection process takes place constantly in each of our cells and in all living creatures[153].

Photo Courtesy of Getty Images

Here's where pastors, geneticists, scientists, and even simpletons like me are stunned. The Hebrew alphabet is associated with numbers, with the first letter of the Hebrew alphabet א being the number one and the second ב being the number 2, and so on.

Guess what you get when you put 5, 6, 5, and 10 next to one another? You might imagine it's the name YHWH.

| 5 = ה | 6 = ו | 5 = ה | 10 = י | | | יהוה |

153. https://erevshabbat.org/en/yhwh-is-genetically-coded-into-us/

Sipos Richard is among many scientists who marvel at the signature of God in our very DNA; his name, YHWH, is a signature in our very DNA. He continues,

Therefore, all genetic modifications are dangerous, mostly vaccines and especially those poisons containing RNA technologies, which are administered to the masses of misled and intimidated people through artificially generated pandemics and the fear resulting from them. Satan's objective is to interfere in this divine bioresonance to defile it with his own seal and possibly even with his own blasphemous name. These products are nothing more than foreshadows and preparations for the final seal of the beast. It's high time to start resisting[154].

So, 10-5-6-5 is God's signature on our innermost parts, and it's our responsibility to protect that signature as a product of his Creation. This argument gives a new meaning to the idea that we are fearfully and wonderfully made.

---

154. See Sipos Richard reveal his research here https://youtu.be/mWBpg5zsDhl

Poem: The Silent Dance

Baffled are the sheep,
The family starts to weep.
Silence cold as ice,
Sleeve rolled not once but twice.
In science placed your trust,
When research was a must.
The world licked lips of lust,
As coffins laid to dust.

Horrors now seem to last
nightmares present, future, and past.
lovers left lonely through the night,
Grief's embrace, a bitter bite.
Tears fall like autumn rain,
In the heart, an endless pain.
life fades with each passing breath,
In the silent.. dance... of death

Chapter Twenty-Two
Pandemic Nightmare

I have a lot of nightmares. In a recent one I opened a door to an old van and got into the driver's seat. Instead of turning on the ignition, I turned it off. I looked over my right shoulder to see if anyone was behind me so that I could drive in reverse. But the vehicle wouldn't go.

Suddenly I remembered that I turned it off. I turned the key and started the van again. Then, the van turned off again. It wouldn't start.

I looked back over my shoulder, and there was a baby in the back, lying inside an old car seat. The baby looked pale and lifeless. It had dark eyes. I got out of the van and went to the sliding back door. When I opened it, I saw a red bio back. My heart was pounding. I felt like there was an earthquake, but I knew that it was my heart beating hard enough to make me shake.

When I reached in to open the bio bag, I woke up.

I don't know why I repeatedly have this nightmare. I know at times that I have placed what we call "products of conception," which means dead babies, into bags.

But now I know that the powers that be and the mad scientists killed those children. They pushed women into taking a substance that caused them to miscarry in record numbers. This means that babies, dead ones, got put into bags.

I am a witness of this murder. I will carry those bags with me forever.

Sadness, pain, and rage are continually swirling in my mind, my chest, and my stomach. What I see at work makes me nauseous. When I see the faces of people watching their loved ones die before their time, I feel pain. And when I pull off my clothes at night and stand in a stream of hot water in the shower, I feel angry. I sometimes drop to my knees and weep. Sometimes, I kneel for a long time with the water running down my back and stare at the tiles in front of me until they blur into a white light as the steam envelops me. I try to sing a hymn. Sometimes, I can't think of any, even though there are a thousand of them etched in my memory that Grandma Josie used to sing to me.

So I just exhale Jesus. Jesus. Jesus. Sometimes, I inhale "Yah" with my chin in the air like a lion. I exhale "Weh" and push the pain out of my chest.

While the steam in the shower is circling around me and the white tiles are illuminated like the moon with the bright lights above me, I can forget about the body bags.

In my dream, I never started the ignition. I can't count how many times I've entered that van and sat in that driver's seat. The van won't go. I can't leave.

I think this book is the reason why.

I have to stay here and clean up the mess.

I Can't Drive Away

I know a lot of people with "avoidant" personality types. They're brutal, in my opinion. Sorry if you're one of them, but being in a serious relationship with you is something I cannot handle. I'm like the woman who throws a frying pan full of hot eggs at a man's face to get him to at least fight back: to show some emotion. I can't do avoidant. I'd rather a woman slap me in the face and scream her needs at me before I could handle the silent treatment. Nothing gets swept under the rug. My relationships are passionate, deep, and authentic. There's no small talk. We go to the deep end.

But then there's work. I have a job. I have four kids to feed and two ex-wives to support. I have to keep my lid sealed. Or do I?

The internet has been ablaze with people, even other healthcare workers, who want me to shut up about what I've seen. As I mentioned, this "sweeping things under the rug" thing doesn't work for me.

I was recently chatting with a physician's assistant (PA) about trivial things like the weather and football. NOT. I don't do small talk, remember?

Here's my best attempt at small talk, "so, the mRNA "vaccines" for COVID have killed a lot of people at this point. Injured many more, eh?"

As I said this, the PA was working to dispose of single-use gloves, syringes, and packaging we used to try and resuscitate a patient with cardiac arrest. The patient died. I wanted to cry. Instead, I made the "Harry Fisher" version of small talk with this poor, unsuspecting PA.

As she reached to grab a defibrillator pad, the PA responded without looking at me.

"There have been injuries and some deaths, but the mRNA technology is amazing."

"More than some deaths," I said, "I'd say millions."

"Nothing is going to stop the technology. They're about to make flu vaccines rabies vaccines, and all of these will be mRNA. I'm sure everything will be mRNA very soon, based on what I am hearing." The PA continues to look down, assessing the defibrillator pad and possibly lamenting the wastefulness of the single-use product.

For some reason, I was in the mood to keep pressing the woman. "Will you tell your patients that their vaccines are mRNA-based prior to giving it to them?"

I said this very matter-of-factly so as not to seem like I wanted a fight.

The PA responded, "I don't see why that's really important. If they're approved by the FDA, then there's no reason."

I tried to slow my exhale, although my first thought was, "Well, let's see. The FDA is captured by the pharmaceutical industry. Almost half of their funding comes from big pharma. Nothing could go wrong there."

After a long pause I stated, "I'll never take an mRNA technology. So I would like to know, if I was your patient. People deserve true consent. I'll never take another vaccine again, as it is. Much less an mRNA-based vaccine."

"You're going to have a hard time finding employment then," the PA stated.

"So be it," I said somewhat jovially, not wanting the conversation to end with an adversarial tone in case I need to see this PA again. In all likelihood, I'd be bringing in another dying patient to her table within an hour.

To my surprise, that PA and I ran into each other again since that conversation, and she told me that "since some of us are very passionate about not taking the new technology" that she would give appropriate consent after that conversation. She agreed that it's the right thing to do.

That van didn't start. But that's okay.

I have to stay right here in this nightmare.

This is the battlefield; this is where God wants me to be.

Poem: The Forgotten

Peeking through windows,
Locked away those you love.
Complied with tyrants, forgot God above.
A faithless place, we push, and we shove.
Neighbors, now strangers, we slaughtered our dove.
Rainbows conquered, though His promise was kept.
In heavens above, how he must have wept.
We gave over our families, this world all our trust.
Ashes to ashes, as dust falls to dust.

Chapter Twenty-Three
Suing The FDA

Dr. Mary Bowden was asked by Dennis Prager one time on a podcast, "The anger of many doctors at any of you who are not sheep told me that most doctors are sheep. I did not know this. Tell me if that is a harsh judgment?"

Dr. Mary responded, "That is entirely spot on. They were trained… you think about the typical person who gets into medical school is a complete rule follower. You have to make straight A's; you have to be very well-behaved; you have to be well-liked. You have to follow the rules, right? So, most people who can get into medical school are very much rule followers. And the biggest insult you could possibly call a doctor is a quack. Now I'm very used to it. …I imagine medical training is very much like military training. It's very rigid. You don't fall outside the rules. You take orders. It's 'yes sir, yes ma'am.' You don't question."

After becoming a mother, Dr. Mary Bowden wasn't interested in following rules but in saving lives. After having four sons in five years, she made the beautiful decision to take time off from her medical practice; she wasn't sure if she'd ever go back. However, as her boys grew older, she felt that she had an itch she needed to scratch; either that or God was beating down her door because He had an amazing calling for her.

Dr. Mary decided that she'd go back to practicing medicine, but on her terms. She hated interference from insurance companies and desired to practice independently, if possible. She wanted to work for her patients, third-party and government intervention-free as an ear, nose, throat and sleep specialist.

When COVID-19 hit, she thought, "Well, this isn't going to affect me, just the big medical centers and hospitals."

However, she had patients coming to her wanting to get tested. At that time, it was hard to get a test. She began using LabCorp, but they got slammed; it would take two weeks for results to come back.

She was using a PCR saliva test for COVID -19 that was non-invasive and delivered next-day results. In fact, she had the only practice in her town that was getting results back quickly without a swab in the nose.

At that time, telling people they tested positive was like handing out a death sentence. Although Dr. Mary would advise them to call a primary care doctor, their doctors would respond, "Do nothing until you can't breathe." With everything we've learned about hospital protocols handed down from the NIH and Remdesivir... this looks more ominous now than it did back then.

Dr. Mary wasn't giving up on her patients. Originally she used hydroxychloroquine but the Texas State Board of Pharmacies shut that option down; they prohibited doctors from prescribing it. To put it in perspective, hydroxychloroquine was used in President Trump's protocol to heal from COVID-19 and it's so safe that it's used in pregnant women safely, as was evidenced by Dr. Jim Thorp in an earlier chapter.

Dr. Mary went on to use steroids and antibiotics as well as monoclonal antibodies, for which she was able to get an unlimited supply, even reaching out to the manufacturer at times to get them the next-day. She didn't know who could or could not receive these treatments; even though she only charged $175, she could have gotten three times as much from Medicare due to the government taking over the distribution of monoclonal antibodies. Curious...

Unrelenting and deeply concerned for her patients, Bowden tried Ivermectin. She went to an FDA website and found an original study that a drug company used to get it approved. There's something called the LD50, which tells you what dosage would kill 50% of lab animals. The LD50 of Ivermectin is 50 -100x the dosage doctors used to treat COVID-19. Moreover, in a literature search looking for an overdose of Ivermectin, there was not a single study. Rather, Dr. Mary found that it kept people out of the hospital, where Remdesivir or ventilators might have killed them. Of the six thousand patients she treated, not a single person who did early treatment went to the hospital.

At that time Bowden had privileges with Houston Methodist Hospital. In April of 2021 they released the "vaccines," four months before the Biden administration. Bowden used the privileges at this hospital as a "just in case." While trying to understand demographics and logic behind the "vaccines," she reached out to Houston Methodist. They were working together on COVID-19 data research and publishing their findings.

The summer of 2021 carried with it the third and largest surge; she began seeing breakthrough cases. She tracked them by whether or not they were "vaccinated." What she noticed was that "vaccinated" patients were testing positive, and they were sicker by and large. Houston Methodist, with protocols that Dr. Mary wasn't adhering to (or even aware of) in her practice, dismissed Dr. Bowden. They claimed that there was a lower severity of symptoms, which was not in alignment with Bowden's findings. Like me, Mary had her "stand down or shout" moment. She chose to shout and began speaking out on what was "Twitter" at the time.

Dr. Mary conservatively pointed out that Ivermectin worked but also proposed that the "vaccine" mandates were wrong. This was the fall of 2021, and she was not aware of the "vaccine" injuries that would soon be on her radar. In fact, Dr. Mary waited in line for her own shot, but, getting impatient, she signed that she intended to get the jab but never got around to it.

Also, around this time, Dr. Mary, like me, witnessed many patients who were scared to go to the hospital. Hospitals were not letting loved ones in; those who went in with COVID-19 were being treated like prisoners. They were put on the protocols we discussed in an earlier chapter, being intubated way too early. They had extremely low oxygen saturations in the fifties and sixties. People would rather die than go into the hospitals, so Dr. Mary kept them alive with a high dose of IV steroids and a high dose of Vitamin C, and she'd bring them in every day to see her. She believes that some, if not all, of these patients would have died if they had gone to the hospital.

One woman reached out to Dr. Mary, whose husband died in the hospital; he'd been on the ventilator for a month. The woman begged the doctors to try Ivermectin and even hired two lawyers. Those two lawyers sued 189 hospitals at that time. Heroes.

For the record, Ivermectin is a drug that was initially used to treat parasitic diseases. It's among the WHO's "essential medicines list." In 2015, the medicine's developers won a Nobel Prize. It was found to be effective in animals after it had been tested on humans, and it has been credited with saving millions of lives. Only after it won the Nobel Prize did doctors learn that it could also be effective in animals, at which time it was reformulated for that use. The American Medical Association, American Pharmacists Association, and American Society of Health-System Pharmacists then issued a joint statement on September 1, 2021, opposing "the ordering, prescribing, or dispensing of Ivermectin to prevent or treat COVID-19 outside of a clinical trial."[155]

Curiously and potentially to the detriment of millions of lives, about one month prior, the FDA posted a tweet that stated, "You are not a horse. You are not a cow. Seriously, y'all. Stop it." This was a response to the doctors like Mary Bowden, who were effectively using Ivermectin to treat COVID patients. Doctors like Mary treated thousands of patients and kept them out of the hospitals where they would be euthanized on ventilators or by being administered Remdesivir. They nevertheless tweeted a message from FDA.gov showing a veterinarian with a horse and then a doctor on the opposite side, masked, of course, checking out the glands of a masked patient, pictured below. The message was clear: the FDA was denying the *science* of Ivermectin. Mary Bowden, however, wasn't buying it.

155. https://www.ama-assn.org/press-center/press-releases/ama-apha-ashp-statement-ending-use-Ivermectin-treat-COVID-19

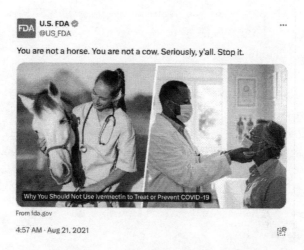

In the case of the woman whose husband was being denied Ivermectin in the hospital, the lawyers' strategy required them to find doctors who were willing to prescribe Ivermectin. That woman found Dr. Mary and wanted her to help the woman get Ivermectin to her husband. The lawyers needed an expert witness, so Dr. Mary complied and helped them win the lawsuit. The judge ordered the hospital to restore Dr. Mary's privileges, but then they put up many roadblocks; eventually, they said they wouldn't grant the privileges. The attorneys helped Dr. Mary and the woman appeal. The judge, once again, told Bowden to proceed. Now Bowden had to find a nurse who'd administer the Ivermectin to the patient. However, the hospital then claimed there was a stay on the order despite the attorneys advising otherwise. Then, the nurse showed up at the hospital, and the police were called. In late October, Dr. Mary learned that social media was ablaze with the story. One Friday in early November, three things happened in one day.

1. The hospital said they were going to deny Dr. Mary's privileges;
2. She was notified that she would have to receive a "vaccination" in order to serve in a surgery center at which she worked;
3. A patient with a history of bladder cancer called and was told she would have to find a new doctor and that she would have to get "vaccinated" to be seen.

That's when Dr. Mary sent out an email indicating that she would prioritize "UNVACCINATED" patients going forward and would no longer be seeing "vaccinated" ones. This wasn't a policy she upheld, but it served to prove a point. She sent a tweet that said, "Vaccine mandates are wrong" twenty-five times a day and got a lot of responses. She sent out a testimonial on those responses. One reporter called and asked if they could confirm that Dr. Bowden's privileges had been revoked at Houston Methodist. The hospital had gone to the Houston Chronicle and said that they were revoking Dr. Mary's privileges because she had "lied" about getting the jab. When they went on Twitter to say that Dr. Mary was a misinformation spreader, it went global. Their claim was that Bowden was "spreading dangerous misinformation which is not based in science."

Bowden talked to an attorney after the incident with the man and the Ivermectin; that hospital had turned Dr. Mary into the medical board. Houston Methodist, who has the Wall of Shame award for being the first hospital in the U.S. to mandate the COVID "vaccine," then said Bowden resigned while under investigation and they turned her in. Now several years later, Bowden is still fighting the medical board.

Since then, Bowden has sued the FDA alongside Dr. Paul Marik and Dr. Robert Apter. When Apter, Bowden, and Marik were successful, the FDA was forced to take that tweet off their website in March of 2024. To the credit of their attorneys at Boyden and Grey, PLLC, the FDA case was a pro bono gift to the three brave doctors and to the world.[156] "FDA can inform, but it has identified no authority allowing it to recommend consumers 'stop' taking medicine," wrote U.S. Circuit Judge Don Willett in the ruling.

When asked about why she keeps going, Bowden stated that she isn't trying to get back at the medical boards, but she is compelled to keep going out of anger at the injustice of the system. She sued Houston Methodist twice, once for defamation. As a non-profit, Houston Methodist is required to be transparent with its finances. Dr. Mary ended up giving up on that case; it was dismissed under several straining circumstances, including difficulty funding. Although they had filed an appeal, Bowden's attorney had a stroke

---

156. https://tn.childrenshealthdefense.org/disarm-pharma/Ivermectin-federal-court-ruled-fda-likely-abused-its-authority/

and made a grave error when filing the appeal paperwork, which meant that they were unable to file the appeal again.

Dr. Mary Bowden still practices in Houston in a "cash-only" practice and fights passionately with the "Americans For Health Freedom," a movement of over 17,000 physicians and scientists at the time of this writing who have called for the modified mRNA COVID shots to be pulled off the market. Included in this brave group of advocates are:

- 206 Elected Officials
- 62 Candidates
- 1 Surgeon General
- 1 State Republican Party
- 1 State Congressional District
- 17 Republican Party County Committees
- 7 Physician Organizations

They state:

> *America was founded on the idea 'that all men are created equal, that they are endowed by their creator with certain unalienable rights, that among these are life, liberty and the pursuit of happiness.' American liberty is a broad, yet priceless, concept that certainly extends to sovereignty over one's own self and the right of an individual to make medical and health decisions as that individual considers appropriate. ...We believe every person has the right to choose the healthcare options that align with their values, beliefs, and personal circumstances. In a free society, health freedom and bodily autonomy are absolute individual rights not to be infringed on by the whims of society or the decrees of ambitious politicians.*

A chart on the Americans For Health Freedom website shows that since November of 2023, the number of US Candidates and Elected Officials who have called for the COVID shots to be pulled off the market steadily increased from almost zero Elected Officials or Candidates to approximately 225 as of January 2025, with about half of those being Elected Officials and half being Candidates for Public Office. This is progress, but we need to make more.

Once we have pulled the COVID shots off the market, this will provide us with the "case law" to prevent other mRNA injections into things like livestock and our food supply, or prevent mRNA from being liberally applied to other shots for patients who do not require the mRNA.

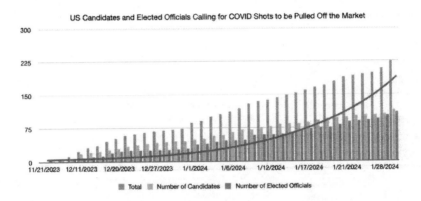

Chart Courtesy of AmericansForHealthFreedom.Org

Their mission includes:

— *Accessible, unbiased information for individuals to make informed decisions about their health;*
— *The right of individuals to make individual choices about their medical treatments, therapies, and interventions without coercion or undue influence;*
— *Public education, campaign awareness, and financial backing for local, state, and federal representatives;*
— *Healthcare transparency and access to information about various treatment options;*
— *Community engagement.[157]*

---

157. https://www.americansforhealthfreedom.org/about

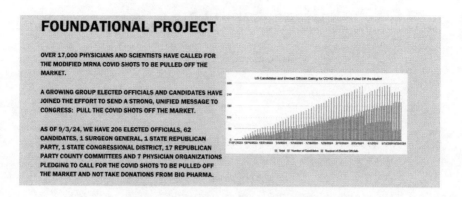

FOUNDATIONAL PROJECT

OVER 17,000 PHYSICIANS AND SCIENTISTS HAVE CALLED FOR THE MODIFIED MRNA COVID SHOTS TO BE PULLED OFF THE MARKET.

A GROWING GROUP ELECTED OFFICIALS AND CANDIDATES HAVE JOINED THE EFFORT TO SEND A STRONG, UNIFIED MESSAGE TO CONGRESS: PULL THE COVID SHOTS OFF THE MARKET.

AS OF 9/3/24, WE HAVE 206 ELECTED OFFICIALS, 62 CANDIDATES, 1 SURGEON GENERAL, 1 STATE REPUBLICAN PARTY, 1 STATE CONGRESSIONAL DISTRICT, 17 REPUBLICAN PARTY COUNTY COMMITTEES AND 7 PHYSICIAN ORGANIZATIONS PLEDGING TO CALL FOR THE COVID SHOTS TO BE PULLED OFF THE MARKET AND NOT TAKE DONATIONS FROM BIG PHARMA.

Photo Courtesy of Americans For Health Freedom[158]

Americans For Health Freedom is an organization that aligns with Bowden's laser focus to get the COVID jabs pulled off the market. She has recruited politicians who have pledged to state that COVID shots should be taken off the market, as well as calling for an end to big pharma financial meddling or bullying. For example, Dr. Mary was instrumental in recruiting Marjorie Taylor Greene, the Republican Parties of Arizona and Idaho, Florida Surgeon General Joseph Ladapo, and Senator Ron Johnson.

I asked Dr. Mary during a raw conversation one afternoon when I was feeling the weight of the threats to my life and my children if she felt safe. She said frankly, "I have four dogs and four boys at home; that helps me feel safe. And what's more, it's safer to be as vocal as possible because it won't go unnoticed if you disappear…"

Sober thoughts.

---

158. https://www.americansforhealthfreedom.org/

Postage Stamp Consensus

By David Icke

Look at a human life.
You come out of the womb, and you're immediately influenced in your perceptions
by your parents who've been through the process, you're about to go through.
Very soon, ludicrously soon, after entering this world,
you find yourself sitting at a desk with an authority figure now telling you what is,
what isn't, what's right, what's wrong, what's credible, what's not credible,
when you can go to the toilet when you can eat, when you can talk.
And this goes on through your formative years, where the system's version of everything,
what I call the "postage stamp consensus,"
because it's so narrow, it is downloaded to people.
And then they go off into the institutions.
They become journalists.
They become scientists.
They become doctors.
They become politicians.
They become CEO's or whatever.
And they take with them that core version of normal and
limitation of possibility that they have been downloading all their lives.
And then the people in these institutions then confirm to each other that this norm is normal.
So a journalist who's doing the story about, say,
a health organization won't go to an alternative practitioner
who may have had great success in it.
You'll go to a doctor who'll give him a "postage stamp normal."
David Icke

Chapter Twenty-Four
The World's "#1 Misinformation Super Spreader"

*"When you tear out a man's tongue, you are not proving him a liar;
you're only telling the world that you fear what he might say."*

-George R.R. Martin

"Harry, I have a question. Do you have a second?"

It's 9 p.m. on a Sunday night. I've had a couple of beers after a long shift… with my toddlers. They've just gone back to their mom's house, and I'm kicking back, scrolling X.com, trying to control myself from responding to trolls who are beginning to incense me. I'm actually pretty happy that Steve interrupted me before I roasted one of them tonight.

"Your timing is perfect," I state truthfully. The happiest will be my publisher, who is beginning to become increasingly interested in my "public relations."

"Harry, do you want to run that 'vaxxers are like swaddled babies, happy to lose their sovereignty' tweet past me tonight before you post it?" She asked me a few hours ago. I've been getting attacked more and more lately. Steve is one of the personalities who came to the rescue first when an actual quack doctor called for my termination, asking where I work. The trolls have even gone as far as to send pictures of my children. I'm not stoic. I'm angry. I'm bearing teeth. I want to fight back. It's definitely a good thing that Steve called me tonight.

"So Steve, what's your question?"

"Okay, so when you see these babies who are stillborn, do you notice anything odd?"

"Like a third arm or six toes?" I'm being a little sarcastic, but I'm actually surprised nobody has asked me this before, considering the hundreds of thousands of comments on my X.com tweets, some of them clearly carefully thought out and articulated.

"Anything abnormal," Steve replies. He's not one for hyperbole. He's a coder. He cares about data. All he cares about is data. And he cares a lot.

"Nothing abnormal. The babies look perfect. They don't have eyes where their belly buttons should be or reptile skin. They all look normal."

"Thanks, Harry."

Steve and I chatted for a few more minutes, and then we hung up.

Two nights later, he calls again.

"Harry, I just talked to your editor."

"Uh-oh. Should I be further along in the book before our interview on Thursday?"

"No, that doesn't matter to me. I want to know about your son, Harry, and his autism. I can't believe you never shared that with me before."

"I don't like to talk about it," I state bluntly. Steve and I have become good friends. He knows I'm not offended. I actually wonder why I haven't spoken about it with him, myself."

I continue, "I noticed almost immediately after his one-year well check. He had a fever and was uncomfortable. I approached my wife after the first 48 hours and again in 30 days when he presented as emotionally distant or detached. It took her an entire year to concede that our baby was autistic. He's five now. He's still non-verbal." I gave him some more sordid details that aren't fit for publishing, and he knows they're confidential. The man wants data. All the data he can get his hands on. So I released and, for the first time in four years, since my son was injured, I share every detail of my son's vaccine injury.

"How many vaccines did they give him at this well check? Which ones?" Steve wants more data.

"And about how many hours after the well check did you notice a problem?" Steve is being more gentle now. He offers consolation by speaking slowly and gently and choosing his words carefully, showing me that he respects this subject and how sensitive I might be to it.

I proceed to share every detail I know about my son's autism. About what I noticed. About what my wife didn't notice. About what strain that caused our relationship. I even threw in a few crude details about how it affected our relationship and how we fought. I stop short of blaming it on our divorce. But that's a question for both me and Steve.

Steve states again, "Harry, I didn't know this. This is the most shocking thing I've heard all week."

I sat with that later that evening. *The most shocking thing Steve frickin' Kirsch has heard all week?* The man who is known to start a conversation with anybody from fellow passengers on an airplane to guests at a dinner party with, "So how many of your relatives have had adverse events from the COVID-19 shot?" The man who digs into fascinating data for a *living?* Well, not for a living. Steve Kirsch doesn't get paid to do what he does, and the only time I asked him about that, he responded, "What else would I do? Something without meetings, like sitting on a beach drinking Mai Tais? What kind of life would that be? There is nothing I would rather do than this. We're all going to go some time. But this is something I can do to look back and say that my life had meaning. So, while you're alive, you can engage in self-fulfillment, but I don't think there's anything more fulfilling than what I'm doing. People come up to me all the time and say, "Thank you. Thank you for what you're doing." Is that more fulfilling than sipping Mai Tais on the beach in Hawaii? It depends on what's important to you. As for me, I'd rather be leading a life where I'm making a difference for people and saving lives."

These days, Steve isn't being recognized positively, but some time ago, he was. Steve was given an award for his philanthropy. He and his wife were honored in 2003 in Washington D.C. for his philanthropic work across a variety of environmental, medical, and planet-safety causes with the National Caring Award, presented to him by none other than then-Senator Hilary

Clinton. I've heard Steve mention this on podcasts before. Coincidentally, Wikipedia scrubbed that information from his profile page.

He's been called a "misinformation super spreader." He's a prolific tech entrepreneur who's started seven companies and is most well-known for one of the earliest search engines, "Infoseek," a company that is attributed to his sizable wealth. An inventor who is credited with, among other things, creating the "mouse." A brilliant executive who's led two companies that held billion-dollar market caps. I think he has an entire building named after him at MIT. And I still can't get over the fact that learning of my son's autism mattered to him. That my family matters to him. But maybe I'm being melodramatic. He may just want more data. But in his voice, I heard concern.

I still felt a bit rocked by that as I sat there that evening in my t-shirt, ignoring the sticky remnants of yogurt one of my sons spilled on me or the sidewalk chalk streaking my arms. I needed a shower, but I was tempted to go back to X.com to see what the trolls were doing after a recent post I shared about miscarriages got seen 11 million times, which means that somebody famous was out to get me. Steve and I have that in common if nothing else. Trolls, that is. He's stated that 95% of his and his wife's friends abandoned him. Fellow scientists call him crazy. I, for one, am grateful he's got time on his hands to commiserate with somebody like me. And patience, for that matter.

In this and all other interactions with Steve, I feel oddly seen, cared for, and recognized in a battle that's been very lonely, totally heartbreaking, and altogether isolating. When I talk to Steve, whether it's about miscarriages, pulmonary embolisms, or myocardial infarction, we speak of data, but I feel camaraderie. Kirsch is a man on a mission. He doesn't fill the space with flower language or accolades. But his presence, dedication, and curiosity over the years have illustrated to me that he is a man who will be forever known, although it's been scrubbed from Wikipedia for the time being, as a man who lives to care for others. When the world wakes up, if it ever does, I hope he'll be recognized again for his caring.

Kirsch was early to the COVID-19 response party with his "COVID-19 Early Treatment Fund." He felt satisfied investing time and money into searching for treatments before the shots rolled out. At that time, it was believed that vaccines would take years, and Steve must have known that it was not possible to roll out a true "safe and effective" vaccine without at least 6-8 years of testing. What's more, it's hard to create a vaccine for respiratory viruses because of how quickly they mutate.

The "COVID-19 Early Treatment Fund" (CETF) was launched with a million dollars of Kirsch's own money as well as some donations from Silicon Valley donors, including Marc Benioff and Elon Musk. At least $4.5 million was granted to researchers to test the use of drugs that were already FDA-approved in treating COVID-19 in the first 19 months after CETF's inception. Although the antidepressant fluvoxamine looked promising, Steve was hopeful that the vaccine would be a success and had two Moderna jabs himself. He tends to be positive about new technology, once even telling me that he isn't afraid of AI (unlike me) because he delights in using it to, yes, you guessed it, analyze more data about vaccines, adverse events, mortality, fertility, autism, and the like.

I quizzed him on this once.

"So Steve, you're not scared of AI? No terminator scenarios, then?"

"I think AI is a wonderful thing. I could not do what I do anywhere near as quickly without AI. I use AI to write code. I use AI to look up papers. I use AI to try to understand things that I don't understand. So use it all the time. Yeah, it's like that. It's like a friend who does everything."

Steve's a technologist and new technology isn't scary to him. Although he knew about early treatments, he got the shots for "extra protection" in March of 2021. Just a month later he heard of a friend who had three relatives die in a week after they were vaccinated. He believed the person because they were a friend (and they probably aren't anymore) but he was flabbergasted. "That's statistically impossible."

The friend stated, "Yeah. But they're dead."

A week later, Steve's carpet cleaner came in a mask. Steve teased him jovially, "You know, you don't have to wear a mask if you've had a vaccine!"

The carpet cleaner responded soberly, "Two minutes after the first shot, I had a heart attack and spent the night in the hospital." As Steve tells it, the man hasn't been the same since. The carpet cleaner's wife had symptoms, too. That was a wake-up call for Steve, who was already fascinated with the COVID-19 crisis from, of course, the perspective of a philanthropist who wanted people to get well, even to the point of obsession.

Obsession is what I see in Steve. It doesn't come in a volatile or emotional way. Steve is a father and husband who has the time and curiosity, not to mention the scientific know-how, to analyze every piece of data he can get his hands on. He began to see that the shots were causing adverse events, morbidity, and mortality that had never been seen before. He even told his wife that once he revealed his findings publicly, "this would be over in two weeks" because the data was so clear.

He found that this was the most dangerous "vaccine" of all time.

I asked him once what he thought about mRNA technology and he stated flatly, "Color me skeptical." That spoke volumes coming from a man who's excited about new technology.

Steve expounded for me. "First, the mRNA goes everywhere, and to make a vaccine this way, it's just a lousy delivery vehicle if you're trying to deliver a vaccine." I make a mental note to throw this back at one of my trolls who noticed Steve sharing my X.com posts and tried to make a claim that he's "controlled opposition," probably "benefiting financially from the vaccines in secret." People love to find a way to fight, even sometimes within our own "medical freedom" community.

As for that community, I, for one, am relieved to have a guy like Steve in "our" corner, although I'm sad to hear of the blowback he's received. Kirsch didn't know that his deep dive down the rabbit hole would dismantle his reputation as a technologist and philanthropist and place him starkly in the category of "thought criminal." Among Steve's most shocking first discoveries was the fact that the COVID-19 jab triggered 770 safety signals in VAERS. To put it in perspective, a normal vaccine would trigger NO safety signals in VAERS. Among these safety signals included myocarditis, pulmonary embolism, and even suicidal ideation. Because I'm generally the first healthcare professional people see in an emergency, he enjoys quizzing me on what I see. He finds a nugget of information and follows that rabbit trail, looking for the data to explain what I'm seeing on the ground.

Kirsch is famous for once asking a woman how much money she would take to remove her mask in the first-class cabin on a plane or by challenging the CDC or HHS to simply query data from VAERS, Medicare, or Medicaid databases to see what results they get… and to share those results transparently with the public. Ninety-five percent of Steve's friends won't talk to him, but the ballsy way he calls out corrupt organizations like the CDC has gained him, as he's referenced, a million new friends in the form of an engaged social media following, especially for his epic Substack[159] which is probably the best Substack, and frankly one of the only Substacks, that I enjoy reading.

The hill Steve appears to be prepared to die on doesn't have to do with COVID-19, although details about adverse events and mortality intrigue him, and he writes about them daily. Rather, the drum he beats most passionately has to do with kids. This makes sense to me, as a father myself, no less a father with a vaccine-injured five-year-old. Kirsch has stated,

> *It's not just the COVID-19 vaccines; it's every single one of them. There has never ever been a study comparing fully vaccinated kids who follow the CDC schedule versus kids who have not been vaccinated at all, who did not get a Vitamin K shot, which is not a Vitamin, and whose mothers did not get vaccinated. If you compare the results of kids whose moms didn't get vaccinated, no K shot, and no vaccines, and if you compare the outcomes of those kids versus kids who got the CDC schedule, there is a dramatic difference. It is an unbelievable difference. It is a difference that nobody wants to talk about. There are no studies, zero, that show the opposite.*[160]

CETF put Steve on the map as a player in the conversation about COVID-19, but he's even more well known in the medical freedom community for the "Vaccine Safety Research Fund," or VSRF, an organization whose mission is to keep the conversation of the COVID-19 shot in the public consciousness

---

159. https://kirschsubstack.com/?utm_source=substack&utm_medium=email

160. https://www.bitchute.com/video/NpTl5ZVei8PM

by contributing through scientific research, public education and advocacy, and support to the vaccine-injured.

"People need to know about the risks. People need to know that there are *no* safe vaccines. Parents need to know that their children do not need *any* vaccines. The point of VSRF is to spread that awareness," Steve says. "There are no safe vaccines. None."

In a world full of snake oil and even "snake venom" salesmen, Steve is refreshing in his commitment not to theory but to data. Even as I write this passage, my notifications are buzzing with news about H1N5 MonkeyPox or Bird Flu being the next pandemic. "By fall, schools will be locked down, we'll be in masks again, businesses will be shut down again, oh yeah, they're trying to find another way to kill us off. They want to depopulate us?"

I tend to side more with the theories that the COVID-19 injections were designed to do precisely that: depopulate the earth. I tend to think that we haven't even begun to see the destruction that will ravage our communities, much less our population. But Steve isn't so sure.

"You're fed this story in peer-reviewed literature about "safe and effective," and then when you look at the reality in your own family with turbo cancers, heart disease, and death, you can't believe that stuff."

"But do you think there's a "they" that wants to harm the population?"

"No," Steve responds flatly and with assurance. "There are easier ways to depopulate people. I don't think this was engineered in a lab. I don't think it was a bioweapon. I think *they* all thought this was going to save people. I don't think the governments are deliberately trying to kill people."

Steve must know I disagree, so I say lamely, "Yeah, that's good."

And then I had another thought, "Steve if there isn't a concerted effort to harm people, why all the censorship?"

"Defense mechanism. People don't like to be shown that they're wrong. People shouldn't get any vaccines at all for anything. People should even research every supplement that they take and look at the upsides and the downsides. There are upsides and downsides to everything, and people just need to understand the risks and how they apply to them. But for the vaccines, it's pretty obvious. For supplements, it's less obvious, and it depends on your particular situation. You really should carefully research anything that goes into your body, whether it's a vaccine or a supplement. Look at the upsides and downsides, and make sure you're not just relying on peer-reviewed literature for that. Talk to other people. Get their perspectives. The most trusted stuff is not the stuff you're going to read in literature. The most trusted stuff is the stuff you see with your own eyes."

Steve came quickly to my rescue recently when a doctor on X.com called for a witch hunt against me, claiming my tweets violate the legal scope of practice & basic ethics. Kirsch responded, "Hey, @ryanmarino. I know Harry very well and we talk to each other every day. He'd be happy to have a live X discussion with you for all to hear. If you want to accept, please respond do the DM that I just sent you and I'll set it up."

Marino hasn't responded yet. When I saw Steve's tweet, I laughed. He loves challenging people to a proper intellectual duel, a discussion of data about which he's profoundly confident. I saved a screenshot of Steve's response to the aggressor. I know he won't respond. I wouldn't want to be on the opposite side of the table against Steve, myself.

All of us are lucky to have him on our team.

Safe And Effective, For Profit

Not only is Steve a good friend, but his enormous brain has never let our conversations end at mere communion; he's been tracing, tracking, and analyzing the data I present and recently made the results of his analysis public in an article on his Substack entitled, "It's Ridiculously Easy To Calculate A Lower Bound Estimate On The Number of Americans Killed By The COVID Vaccine: 500k" on September 19, 2024.[161]

In short, Kirsch surmised that based on the stories I provided him in relation to the number of paramedics in practice, he estimates that at least 500,000 Americans were killed by the COVID-19 "vaccines." This was based on twenty texts I sent him after seeing a death I was certain to be a result of the COVID jabs, not to mention over 100 serious "vaccine" injuries.

This estimate relies on the estimation that there are over 172,000 paramedics employed in the United States. Kirsch then assumed that seeing 20 deaths was high and that I was a statistical outlier. For this data, Kirsch used "The Poisson Distribution," a probability distribution used to model the number of events occurring within a fixed interval of time or space when these events happen independently. The Poisson distribution results indicate that six events were more likely than twenty. Using that math, Kirsch estimated that paramedics only witnessed six "vaccine" deaths so far. Using this logic, 172,000 paramedics seeing six deaths each works out to slightly over a million dead Americans.

Five doctors interviewed by Kirsch reported seeing an average of five deaths per thousand "vaccinated," However, these doctors were two standard deviations from the mean. Using that logic, two "vaccine" deaths in a patient practice of 1,000 gave Steve reason to estimate that 540,000 Americans were murdered by the jab.

Kirsch wrote:

If I'm wrong, why aren't we seeing the correct estimates from any mainstream epidemiologists anywhere in the world? Any decent scientist would want to do estimates using various statistics to make sure they got the right answer. But nowadays, nobody is showing

161. https://kirschsubstack.com/p/its-ridiculously-easy-to-calculate?r=o7iqo&utm_campaign=post&utm_medium=web&triedRedirect=true

292

us their work. I've been doing this for over 3 years now, and all the estimates I get (from various methods) are in the same ballpark, including this one. My numbers agree with those of others who have been doing the same thing using a variety of methods (VAERS, large family member surveys, etc.).

I'm finalizing this chapter on the morning after Donald J. Trump was declared the winner of the Presidential Election of 2024. As I read through my story, I can't help but feel optimistic that with Trump giving authority to Robert F. Kennedy Jr. to clean house and hold three-letter agencies accountable, especially the NIH and FDA, we will, one day, know how many innocent people have been genocided by this shot, and I'm even more hopeful that one day, their families and fellow Americans will get justice.

This Is My Lane

This is my lane.
This is where I belong.
It's the government entities that are in the wrong lane.
They're trying to throw us into a corner.
But they messed up by throwing us into a corner.
Here, we've made friends. We've made connections.
Our stones of truth will come together, and the Goliath will go down.
Without legal action, these monsters will never be brought to justice.
Parents who've lost children are stepping up.
Nurses, EMTs, paramedics, doctors, and even Elon Musk are creating a platform for us to finally have a voice.
Your voice is your weapon.
Sharpen your sword by speaking even louder.

Chapter Twenty-Fiv

Regrets

"I believe we are stronger than they want us to believe."

Harry Fisher

I spend a lot of time on contracts in Alaska. It's damn cold, but I choose to hike as much as possible for as late into the fall season as I can. Getting around the remote places where I work requires helicopters, four-wheelers, and lots of dodging bears during most of the months I'm there. Although that sounds like a lot of action, it's typically a remarkably quiet life peppered with mortal emergencies. The hours in between emergencies are long.

Among the many calls I take regularly includes renal failure or liver failure in young people, even those who don't drink alcohol. Two men we lost were forced to be jabbed for their job. They were told their pay would be cut in half if they didn't comply, like most that are now injured or dead. It's truly tragic.

Periodically, the weather doesn't permit the transport of these patients to hospitals in larger towns. During those times, I turned a pup tent into an ICU for days at a time while we waited for the weather to clear. I keep people alive in this remote temporary camp for other contract workers like myself, mostly men, all trying to feed their families and accepting frigid, uncomfortable, and dark days to do it.

There is no runway for a plane in the place I'm most often contracted, where I'm fondly called "doc" by the community. Helicopters, as terrifying as they are in winter storms, are our only mode of transportation to and from the area unless you want one hell of a rough backpacking trip, one you'd never survive.

I was hiking recently with a man whose uncle died after the shot. He, too, was bullied into getting jabbed, and now he's terrified for himself and his staff. He received an eight-figure sum to run this camp, where I contract from time to time. Thankfully, he didn't let his kids get the shots.

"Do you think I'll end up okay?" He asked me one morning, breathless, as we summited a hill on one of our many walks and talks. He had just ordered four more Automatic External Defibrillators for the camp.

I paused as I shared this story with Stephanie one afternoon when we were discussing the contract and the two tragic deaths I mentioned above.

"What did you say?" She asked.

She continued, "The immune systems in the jabbed are getting weaker and weaker. How do you tell him the truth? It doesn't look good."

"Nah, I didn't perpetuate more fear; that would weaken his immune system even more. Sometimes, you have to sell hope. There's a lot to be said for the placebo effect. But personally, I don't believe any of these spike protein protocols are going to extend your life."

"Dark." She replied. And then she, too, was silent.

One of the hardest parts of writing this book has been Steph's monthly check-ins and her own optimistic prying because she is scared for her "vaccinated" family members, too.

The unfortunate reality is that I don't see a lot of hope for those who complied. However, I do have hope that this culling will create a higher vibrational world; those who survive won't bend over and let such atrocities continue.

On September 18th, 2024, Hunter Fielding reported that scientists have the results of laboratory testing that suggest that the mRNA shots accelerate cancer in all who were jabbed. U.S. Republican Senator Ron Johnson from Wisconsin held a round table shortly after the findings were published entitled, "Federal Health Agencies and the COVID Cartel: What Are They Hiding."[162]

---

162. https://www.ronjohnson.senate.gov/2024/2/icymi-sen-johnson-leads-roundtable-discussion-federal-health-agencies-and-the-COVID-cartel-what-are-they-hiding

Internal Medicine Specialist Sabine Hazan, a medical doctor who conducts and supervises clinical trials for medical research, was present at the discussion. She calls out big pharma corruption and points out that what makes up 90% of our biological capacity for immunity is killed off by spike proteins from the COVID jabs. Those spike proteins travel to the gut, which is why cancer, IBS, autism, dementia, and even becoming reinfected with single-strand RNA viruses like Bird Flu, Monkeypox, or COVID variants increase among the jabbed.

It is for this reason that I propose that if there is any hope for the jabbed, the first place I'd begin would be by strengthening the gut microbiome. Her research paper "The Lost Microbes of COVID-19" is one of the most powerful illustrations of the clever way sickos have committed genocide by having the population take an experimental gene therapy treatment for the flu that destroys their guts, arguably the most important environment to keep strong for immunity.[163] In her paper, she posits that the loss of bifidobacteria causes humans to contract and suffer from a myriad of diseases that could be prevented by simply boosting good gut bacteria with probiotics, eating clean, organic whole foods, and avoiding any more jabs by all means necessary.[164]

The second thing I'd recommend to all people, both jabbed and unjabbed, is to stock up on the medications listed in the Zelenko protocol. Before he passed away in May of 2022, Dr. Vladimir Zelenko recorded his "final message to humanity." He told Stephanie a week before on the phone that it would be the simple key to beheading the snake or, as he said, "decapitating the serpent," which was the subtitle of his book co-authored with Brent Hamachek and mentioned earlier, "Zelenko: How To Decapitate The Serpent."

Near the time of his death, Dr. Zelenko was busy gathering all available research, often into the wee hours of the morning, to test a theory of his that all single-strand RNA viruses are treatable with a combination of medications that are fairly easy to obtain.

163. https://pubmed.ncbi.nlm.nih.gov/35483736/

164. https://newsaddicts.com/scientists-sound-alarm-COVID-shots-accelerate-cancer/

Very simply stated, Zelenko claimed that one might need, critically, zinc plus a zinc ionophore, such as Ivermectin or Hydroxychloroquine (which are prescription-based) or Quercetin or EGCG (which are in every pharmacy in America.) The image below shows other steps included in the "Zelenko Protocol" that have been used by legions of Americans and members of the global community for years now.

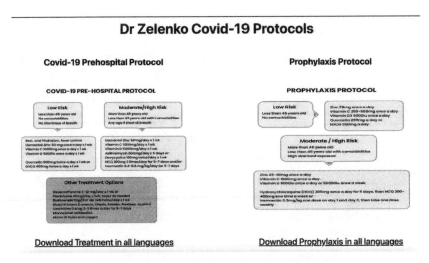

Treatment Protocols Courtesy of ZStack[165]

As my friend, the CEO of a corporation on a contract in Alaska, and I both returned to work after our hike the morning mentioned above, I felt compelled to bring up this immune system theory with him.

The next morning we bundled up and as we stepped slowly up the hill and I listened to his breath shorten on the ascent I stated, "you look strong, sir. And you're getting your daily dose of Vitamin D way up here. You're doing great. But take care of your gut."

"What do you mean 'take care of my gut?'" He asked; matters of health were not a regular conversation topic, despite my being the paramedic at his camp.

---

165. https://vladimirzelenkomd.com/

"You know, your gut microbiome is critical to keeping you healthy. Probiotics are an example of one way to keep a healthy gut. Functional medicine doctors often specialize in gut health."

As we hiked, he told me about his increasingly diligent regimen in fitness and nutrition. Then he piped up with pride and stated, "One thing I'm never doing again is drinking."

I laughed. "I wish I could say that. I quit for a long time. Just started up again a few weeks ago. Not while I'm working, of course. But during the tough weeks in between…"

At that time in September, I didn't know that I would soon be forced to hop on the sobriety bandwagon; my life depended on it.

Just a few days after that hike in Alaska with my friend, I boarded a plane to Oklahoma, where I got bullied by a family member in a bad way. That on top of the death and horrors I see regularly at work, I went over the edge.

My life was the embodiment of a country western song. My patients were dying. My girlfriend was playing games. One of my kids was estranged, and two were critically ill. And to boot, I am regularly attacked and threatened both by doctors, medical boards and organizations, and trolls who threaten the lives of me and my children.

Although I'd been sober for a long time, I drank.

And I don't drink to party; I drink to forget. But this night is one I'll never forget.

The night didn't start at dark. By nine in the morning, I had already had several beers. I went to a gazebo by a pool at the hotel where I was staying with a friend. He had rented the gazebo, and it was stocked with all the food or drinks you could want. We had a server who kept us satisfied, first with Bloody Marys. I accepted the drinks as I was determined to transition from dark Alaska and depressing Oklahoma from the week prior to a week in the sunshine in Mexico.

I sat down after I had the Bloody Mary at around 11 a.m., and my heart rate skyrocketed. It was irregular, which I could ascertain in part because I'm a paramedic. I knew I was in "AFIB RVR," which is really fast AFIB, meaning "atrial fibrillation rapid ventricular response."

Then I got diaphoretic, meaning sweaty. I thought I was going to pass out.

As a paramedic, I knew I was "symptomatic." People live in AFIB but not AFIB RVR, which means that my heart rate was in the 200s. A lot of times, if I have a patient like this in my care, I have to shock them. I couldn't believe the pulse I felt underneath my own fingertips.

I stood up, worried I would pass out, and made it to my room on the fifth floor. I kept praying and thinking, "I'm going to die in a Mexico hotel."

I looked at myself in the mirror, struggling to stand up. I pondered calling the hotel so that a paramedic like me could apply electricity.

I decided to lie down and close my eyes. My last thought was, "Okay, God. You're either going to take me or fix me."

When I woke up, the first person I called was Dr. Peter McCullough. "Dr. Peter, it's me, Harry."

"Harry, it's good to hear from you. What's happening? You sound panicked."

"My heart rate was insane this morning. I thought I was dying."

"What happened Harry?"

"I'm in the middle of Mexico. I'm here to get some sun with a good friend, but I drank some alcohol."

"Harry, this is a sign from God. You don't need alcohol anymore."

Dr. Peter knew that I didn't need medical advice. He's a good friend; he's been a good friend throughout my journey to sound the alarm on this genocide. At that moment, he knew that I knew what was happening. And took advantage of the situation to tell me courageously, like a brother, that I didn't have a heart problem to deal with going forward. This was a moral problem. And to heal my heart, I need to make the decision to never drink again.

My friends, my children, and the world deserve that.

In 2022, when I left the bottle, I focused on social media action and storytelling, sharing my experiences first on TikTok before I got banned. I grew closer to God than I'd been since I was a kid. I worked harder at home, on the job, and in my advocacy online in order to battle this attack on humanity, this genocide.

When I cast aside the bottle and sought solace in faith, I found strength. God became an anchor amidst the tempest of despair. I channeled my energies into a fervent crusade. My voice once drowned in spirits, resounded across the digital expanse.

Then, the ugly happened. Legions of trolls began attacking me for sport. I first took it as a sign that I was above the target and welcomed the haters. In time, however, as pictures of my children were sent to me with threats by anonymous sources, I became convinced that my life would be very, very short. This is a particularly dark thought to have while I'm covered in blood and tears on the daily from patients suffering from adverse events from their jabs. There is no describing hell like this: it is the absence of hope.

After two years sober, the spirits called me again, and I satisfied their taunts and pleas. I wanted all of them to shut up. But instead of using my power to rebuke the darkness and calm the storm, I took the easy way out. I drank in the in-between periods when I wasn't on the job, sometimes for a couple of weeks at a time while I was in between contracts.

Though I was drinking while off duty, my diligence at work was still unwavering. Thankfully, I never allowed my demons to bleed over into my work environment. Each attempt to save a life was still fueled with the sense that if I could save those who were meant to die by a genocidal three-headed monster of Big Pharma, Insurance, and Government, then this could be a form of protest.

Excellence was my rebellion, my stand against the shadows of darkness. My chance to fight, heal, and hopefully inspire a revolution of the human spirit.

But for a few weeks, I relapsed; I surrendered to fear.

Sometimes, when we're in trauma, our logical minds go offline. This was the case with me for this brief relapse into drinking. Rather than reason that drinking wasn't good for me and that I was so much happier sober (which I am,) I got caught in my monkey mind. It was irrational; it was foolhardy, and it was almost the end of my life.

The Bible states 365 times that we should have no fear. This is, coincidentally, the number of calendar days in the year. When we're in fear, we go into a "fight or flight" state. Rather than operating from our logical mind, we operate from a more animalistic mind. For some people, the fight or flight state includes "fawn." This is the place from which many codependent individuals operate or those who lack enough self-identity or self-realization to stand up to bad guys. They "fawn" by bending over for bullies. They kiss ass instead of kick ass. They surrender their power because they are scared to fight back.

In this chapter I discussed the Zelenko Protocol as well as the importance of your gut microbiome for creating a healthier immune system. My final desperate plea is that you remove fear from your consciousness any way you can. Don't be an idiot like me and relapse back into a place of fear; at the end of that gulp is a wave of self-destructive behaviors.

Poem: Cowards

Consent removed, experiments approved, people languish as evil improves.
Your loved one's torment now is yesterday's news.
Sit down and shut up; you have too much to lose.

Chapter Twenty-Six
Stand Down… or Shout?

You watched "The Hunger Games," and you sided with the resistance.
You watched "Star Wars," and you sided with the resistance.
You watched "The Matrix;" you understood and sided with the resistance.
You watched the movie "Divergent," and you sided with the resistance.
You watched "V for Vendetta," and you cheered on and sided with the resistance.
You read about history and sided with the resistance.
When it's fiction, you understand oppression. Why do you refuse to see it when it's reality?
When it's happening to you in real life right now, in the news, in the world, right now;
You refuse to see it. When it's the reality that you are living in. You're afraid to resist in real life.[166]

I had a hard time when my editor, Stephanie, was bothering me for screenshots of all the threats I've received since going on Alex Jones.

"The thing is," I explained, "it's not all that remarkable. I deleted them, but I'll have more coming in every day, mark my words. You're not missing anything. The threats have been going on for years, and they aren't stopping until I stand down. But I won't be doing that anytime soon."

---

166. https://www.instagram.com/reel/C9F8jNeu_-D/?igsh=MTd2NHBwZ2h6NG5ieQ==

Calls to my cell phone, some with voicemail messages. My X.com inbox is riddled every other day with death threats. I mute the threats online and delete texts while blocking senders for threats that come into my personal cell phone. After the Alex Jones show Stephanie said, "I'm trying to find the threatening online posts, can you post them in the manuscript so we have a visual."

"The thing is, I mute the evil people," I responded. It's not fun reading the threats. When I mute them, they go away forever.

"Aren't you scared?" She asked.

"Acts 6, Stephanie."

That's our code now.

On June 2, 2024, Stephanie's pastor preached a sermon at Cornerstone Christian Center[167] in the small town of Basalt, Colorado, that has become a reminder for us that we have no reason to fear death and that, in fact, great signs and wonders are often preceded and succeeded by it. The sermon, titled "The Roots of Our Faith,"[168] first detailed the history of the disciples multiplying with the tension between Hellenists and Hebrews. Stephen, the faith's first martyr, was among seven put in charge. Stephen was full of faith & Holy Spirit, Hebrew Ruach Ha-Kodesh,[169] which in Judaism refers to the divine force, quality, and influence of God over the universe.

In Acts 6, we read that the Hellenists were Jews who celebrated Greek culture. The Hebrews, of course, celebrated Jewish culture. As people accepted the Messiah, they sold possessions to support and sustain the new church. The Scriptures state that Stephen was doing great signs and wonders. Men from the "synagogue of the freedmen" (Cyrenians, Alexandria, and those from Cilicia and Asia) began arguing with Stephen, who was taking to the Sanhedrin.

167https://www.cccbasalt.com/

168. https://www.cccbasalt.com/sermons/sunday-service-6-2-24

169. https://en.wikipedia.org/wiki/Holy_Spirit_in_Judaism

Acts 6:13-15, NKJV

They also set up false witnesses who said, "This man does not cease to speak [c] blasphemous words against this holy place and the law; for we have heard him say that this Jesus of Nazareth will destroy this place and change the customs which Moses delivered to us." And all who sat in the council, looking steadfastly at him, saw his face as the face of an angel.

The first three hundred years of Christianity were full of unspeakable horrors. Nevertheless, Christianity still grew to be adopted by ten percent of the world's population, notwithstanding the threats those adherents were under. Stephen was the first of many, many martyrs for the faith.

In his final moments, Acts 7 states that Stephen's persecutors "gnashed their teeth" and were "cut to the heart," much like the violent trolls who threaten me for speaking the truth against the unsafe and ineffective death jabs.

In Acts 7:55-56 it reads in the New King James Version:

But he, being full of the Holy Spirit, gazed into heaven and saw the glory of God, and Jesus standing at the right hand of God, 56 and said, "Look! I see the heavens opened and the Son of Man standing at the right hand of God!

And in verses 58-60:

Then they cried out with a loud voice, stopped their ears, and ran at him with one accord, and they cast him out of the city and stoned him. And the witnesses laid down their clothes at the feet of a young man named Saul. And they stoned Stephen as he was calling on God and saying, "Lord Jesus, receive my spirit." Then he knelt down and cried out with a loud voice, "Lord, do not charge them with this sin." And when he had said this, he fell asleep.

Shortly after completing my book trailer, I got another call from my editor. "Are you sure you want us to put this out there, all over the internet, shared by scores or even hundreds of influencers?"

"Yes."

In the face of death, just before he was martyred, Stephen's face was like an angel.

"Stephanie, I've seen thousands of people die in my life," I said.

"But the saints transition before they feel pain."

I believe that His Grace is sufficient for me. I have asked the Lord to receive my spirit, as did Stephen, as he was being stoned. For in Matthew 10:28, we learn that they can kill the body, but not the soul.

And so, for now, and forever, I hereby choose to shout, not to stand down. Just like my Grandma Josie, if there are people in the church, I'm gonna kick off my shoes and set myself behind the podium until they turn off my lights.

Lord, do not hold this sin against them.

There will be in the next generation or so a pharmacological method of making people love their servitude and producing dictatorship without tears, so to speak, producing a kind of painless concentration camp for entire societies so that people will in fact have their liberties taken away from them but will rather enjoy it. Medical science has made such tremendous progress that there is hardly a healthy human left.

Aldous Huxley
From a live speech at Berkeley in 1962

Poem: Ravenous World

*The valley of death shadows over us all; hold tight to love, and don't
dwell on the fall.
Each branch we climb, life's tree so tall.
Listen close to Father's call.
Loud the roar from the lion's
den, rotten fruit, a world of sin.
Hide your head or carry your cross; what is now found will not be lost.
Stand firm on your ground,
and keep the sword in sheath.
Fear not the lion or its teeth.*

Chapter Twenty-Seven
Your Mission

You keep shooting bad guys until we run out of ammo.
And then when the barrels are hot, you poke 'em in the eyeballs.

Victor Marx

It doesn't matter who is in the White House. We have work to do to clean up this mess. While wrapping up this book, I had a seven hour layover and twenty-four hour travel day to get back to Oklahoma from the remote camp I was contracted to serve in Alaska over the past few weeks. I pondered what my final message would be since the first word I wrote on a Google Doc.

I squarely believe that there are few things more important than following, promoting, and donating to causes you believe in. Stephanie actively promotes Preborn and her local church community, among others. She periodically donates charitably to publishing dissident voices, a sacrifice of both time and financial resources.[170] She has been active in a legal battle to protect her son from the COVID-19 jab with the hopes of helping create case law for parents to protect their children against the will of a shared custodial parent. At one point, her legal bills were so high over the course of two years (and she was never successful in her case being taken pro bono in either her District Court or Appeals cases) that she and her son were homeless when he was six in 2022. Do you know what that did? It brought out the mama bear, and she was fearless.

---

170. https://preborn.com/

I have friends who work to train others in self-defense and firearms. We have many friends who work door-knocking in their communities, educating people about Propositions or votes in the community, county, or state elections. We have friends who literally never, ever miss school board meetings in their towns.

If you're sitting around sharing podcasts and memes all day without getting involved in your local community, you're pretty worthless. That said, I spend the majority of my time on the road. My voice and mission are online, reporting the true events I witness as a paramedic. But tweeting all day isn't necessarily your calling. It works for me and my mission. But for Steph, somebody who stays behind the scenes and has no social media presence, that's a worthless task, a waste of time. She doesn't mind it; she prefers to see, touch, and embrace the people she ministers to in her Aspen Valley, where a revival of both truth and faith will trickle into the entire country; lots of influential people there, and forty billionaires in her town of Aspen.

If you're unsure of your mission and school board meetings or church activities aren't calling you, get involved with helping get the shots off the market. There is no greater threat to humanity outside of nuclear war, in my estimation than these jabs. Follow, share, and support doctors and attorneys who are on the front lines of this fight, such as one of the many organizations mentioned in this book, from Americans for Health Freedom to Children's Health Defense. The more money you can donate to these organizations, the more empowered their legal teams will be in fighting for justice. If you don't have money, stand up in your school board meetings or local elections to support candidates who believe in sovereignty or protecting children. **Grassroots work DOES make an impact;** it can be the difference we need to win the war, whether that's against big pharma, insurance companies, three-letter agencies, or the deep state.

One of the most impactful former "nobody's" in America, and possibly the world, is Scott Presler. Presler was a twenty-four year old dog walker who felt ashamed when Barack Obama was elected president in 2012, citing that he wished he had helped campaign for Republicans.

In 2016, Presler made his voice known. He worked with the advocacy group ACT for America in 2016 and, in 2020, was a vocal participant in the

"Stop The Steal" protests when Democrats committed electoral fraud to prohibit Donald Trump's second term. Presler was shaken after the 2017 "Pulse" gay nightclub shooting in Orlando, Florida, which took the lives of forty-nine people. At the time of this tragedy, Presler had already worked to knock on doors and register voters for the first Trump Presidential campaign. An openly gay man, Presler has worked passionately to defend 2A rights and a "March Against Sharia" event organized by ACT For America when volunteering for them in June 2017. Obviously, any intelligent gay man does not want Muslim extremism on our soil; he would be dead, stating, "I one hundred percent believe in the notion that armed gays don't get bashed. It is our right to feel safe."[171]

In January of 2023, Scott Presler founded the "Early Vote Action (EVA)," a nationwide group of grassroots activists who labor to register Republican voters and get them committed to vote by any means necessary. The EVA team focused their efforts on the key swing states of Arizona, Michigan, Nevada, Nevada, Pennsylvania, and Wisconsin, although their network spans 50 states and many U.S. territories, as well. In Pennsylvania alone, EVA had 74 full-time staff members during this election. Some political commentators say that it was because of Scott's work that Trump won the swing state of Pennsylvania and, ultimately, the 2024 Presidential election. EVA workers or volunteers canvas the country, contacting voters with handwritten postcards and letters, texts, phone calls, and door-knocking to connect with unregistered voters.

They report, "Our grassroots network has proven time and time again that, no matter where they live in these great United States, any motivated conservative American can join in the fight to save our country."[172]

Scott Presler is an incredible example of a young man who saw a problem (Obama winning the presidency in 2012) and knew that he couldn't wait around for somebody else to fix it. If my readers take nothing else away from this book, I hope they will be inspired to make a difference in-person, not just by spewing entertainment online and calling themselves "awake."

171.https://meaww.com/who-scott-presler-ronald-reagan-award-cpac-2021-gay-republican-activist-anti-muslim-baltimore

172. https://earlyvoteaction.com/

You aren't awake if you're sitting on the sidelines watching. You're awake when you take action.

Share Your Story

Three years ago, I prayed that God would turn me into a lion and let these words travel far and wide. He answered that prayer in a big way. One of my first videos about the adverse events I was witnessing accumulated millions of views in just twenty-four hours. Since then, I have been targeted by the Government to be silenced and de-platformed. My accounts reached millions of people per month, and when Biden called us out on national television, those accounts got deleted.

What I have witnessed among the people in this chapter, whom I call brothers and sisters, is something truly Biblical; it's a spiritual war of good versus evil: truth versus censorship. These are men and women willing to face a big war and fight without reprieve. Often, they receive no gratitude nor thank yous as well. Yet they wake up, put on their boots, and get ready for battle every day. The "anti-vax" community is a special breed of heroes.

If you have lost a loved one due to the jabs or if you have an injury yourself, we need you to speak up. We are building an army, and we'll need numbers. Here are a few "vax-" injured heroes to inspire you. Find them on X.com or use my footnotes to check out other podcasts they've done so that you can have inspiration about how to share your story.

A woman I deeply respect is Lyndsay House, RN, a "vaccine-"injured nurse who received "Dose 3" of her Pfizer jab on 12/29/2023 and filed a VAERS report on January 14th of the following year due to experiencing over forty symptoms, with the following adverse events summary:

> *Eight hours post-injection symptoms of fatigue, body aches, muscle and joint pain, dizziness, nausea, hot and cold flashes, injection site pain, near syncope, malaise, tiredness, and fever occurred. Two weeks after that and still going on all new onset: ADHD, depression, anxiety, PTSD, POTS, dysautonomia, MCAS, dizziness, syncope, shob on exertion, shingles, tremors, i Apter, Dr. Robert nternal vibrations, paresthesia, neuropathy of hands and feet, zaps and shocks of hands, brain fog, decreased concentration and mental dexterity, insomnia, hair*

loss, cellulitis, tinnitus, hot flashes, hypertension, tachycardia, muscle mass weight loss, decreased appetite, speech difficulty, gi issues, difficulty swallowing, dry eyes and mouth.[173]

The same report can be seen by MedAlerts.org below. Since her injury, Lyndsey decided to turn her injuries into advocacy. Besides appearing on dozens of podcasts,[174] House works c to have the shots investigated and banned.[175] [176] She shares her story on X.com boldly [177]

COVID19: COVID19 (COVID19 (PFIZER-BIONTECH)) / PFIZER/BIONTECH	FH8027 / 3	RA / IM

Administered by: Private   **Purchased by:** ??
Symptoms: Alopecia, Anxiety, Arthralgia, Autonomic nervous system imbalance, Cellulitis, Depression, Disturbance in attention, Dizziness, Dry eye, Dry mouth, Dysphagia, Dyspnoea exertional, Electric shock sensation, Fatigue, Feeling abnormal, Flushing, Gastrointestinal disorder, Herpes zoster, Hypertension, Injection site pain, Insomnia, Malaise, Muscle atrophy, Myalgia, Nausea, Neuropathy peripheral, Pain, Paraesthesia, Post-traumatic stress disorder, Presyncope, Pyrexia, Speech disorder, Syncope, Tachycardia, Tinnitus, Tremor, Weight decreased, Hot flush, Decreased appetite, Feeling of body temperature change, Postural orthostatic tachycardia syndrome, Vibratory sense increased, Mast cell activation syndrome, Fine motor skill dysfunction, Attention deficit hyperactivity disorder
Life Threatening? No
Birth Defect? No
Died? No
Permanent Disability? Yes
Recovered? No
Office Visit (V2.0)? Yes
ER or Office Visit (V1.0)? No
ER or ED Visit (V2.0)? Yes
Hospitalized? No
Previous Vaccinations:
Other Medications: Claritin
Current Illness: None
Preexisting Conditions: Pollen allergy
Allergies: None
Diagnostic Lab Data:
CDC 'Split Type':
Write-up: 8 hours post injection symptoms of fatigue, body aches, muscle and joint pain, dizziness, nausea, hot and cold flashes, injection site pain, near syncope, malaise, tiredness, and fever occurred. Two weeks after that and still going on all new onset : ADHD, depression, anxiety, PTSD, POTS, dysautonomia, MCAS, dizziness, syncope, shob on exertion, shingles, tremors, internal vibrations, paresthesia, neuropathy of hands and feet, zaps and shocks of hands, brain fog, decreased concentration and mental dexterity, insomnia, hair loss, cellulitis, tinnitus, hot flashes, hypertension, tachycardia, muscle mass weight loss, decreased appetite, speech difficulty, gi issues, difficulty swallowing, dry eyes and mouth.

---

173. https://ugc.production.linktr.ee/77a60584-aa34-4f74-91e9-86042ed980c3_Vaers-report--2560047.pdf

174. https://linktr.ee/lyndseyhouseRN

175. https://www.change.org/p/demand-immediate-ban-and-investigation-of-mr-na-COVID-19-vaccines/psf/share?source_location=petition_page&psf_variant=combo&-from_guest_psf=1&short_display_name=Stephanie&allow_actions=true&cbd_s=eyJle-HBlcmltZW50TmFtZSI6InBzZl9jb21iby0zNzk2NzY3MSIsInZhcmlhbnQiOnsidmFyaWFu-dE5hbWUiOiJhNSIsImRhdGEiOnsiYW1vdW50IjoxMSwiYW1vdW50X2lkIjoiYTUifSwicH-VsbHMiOjgxMSwicmV3YXJkcyI6NzExMTV9LCJ2YXJpYW50TmFtZSI6ImE1IiwiY29tYm9CY-W5kaXRBbW91bnQiOjExLCJhbW91bnRJZCI6ImE1In0%3D&share_intent=1

176. https://chng.it/78nDZrqCst

177. https://x.com/HouseLyndseyRN

The image above courtesy of MedAlerts.org[178]

You've seen other superheroes who speak out with risk of losing their livelihood, such as a few featured in this book, including Dr. Kelly Victor, Dr. Mary Bowden, Dr. Jim Thorp, Steve Kirsch and Dr. Peter McCullough.

Another hero I would be remiss not to include in this book is my friend Dr. David Cartland. Cartland has been holding the line in the U.K., where they need courageous doctors as much or even more than in the United States; censorship and threats to speech are even more atrocious across the pond.

Dr. Cartland worked as a general practitioner (GP) in Cornwall, England, during the pandemic. He began bringing papers into the break room to warn other doctors of what he was seeing, such as the myocarditis signals early on from the jabs. He says that there weren't a lot of formal meetings going on during that time, and the lunchroom was about the only place he could discuss his concerns with other doctors and nurses. At that time, he also observed that certain colleagues who stated that they weren't going to get the shots nor allow their children to receive them would then inject other children on that same day. Until 2023, a doctor in Cornwall, according to Carland, would receive about 15 quid per jab, increasing the revenue of the practice by at least 180,000 pounds on average or increasing the doctors' salaries by about 10-15% based on his estimations of the average patient volume of a practice.[179]

It was seeing these children being jabbed by doctors who wouldn't administer the shots to their own families that triggered his public resignation in 2021. Even more horrifyingly, he witnessed dangerous administration of the shots in jab clinics, similar to mine, where individuals would be qualified to administer vaccines with as little as a thirty-minute online module to train them. He saw shots going into the biceps and triceps, even close

178. https://www.medalerts.org/vaersdb/findfield.
php?IDNUMBER=2560047&WAYBACKHISTORY=ON&utm_medium=social&utm_
source=linktree&utm_campaign=%7C+my+medalerts+vaers+report+%7C+%232560047

179. https://rumble.com/v42r0pe-11223-dr-david-cartland-doc-malik.html?e9s=src_
v1_ucp

to a corroded artery, in one instance. He noted that many of the folks administering the jabs weren't even aspirating during these intramuscular injections, which could be in and of itself dangerous. Aspiration during an injection involves pulling back the syringe plunger after needle insertion but before administering the medication. This technique checks for blood return, indicating whether the needle has inadvertently entered a blood vessel. Where were the medical professionals? According to Cartland, the nurses and doctors at these clinics worked at the front door, processing the patients and handing out stopwatches. The local florist, the local football team, and the local firemen were administering the shots.

Dr. Ahmad Malik is a doctor and orthopedic surgeon who found that his medical training fell short when it came to the importance of a healthy lifestyle. "I believe that experts aren't always to be trusted, and I want to give a voice to those who are often overlooked," he writes about his podcast mission on the "DocMalikPodcast."[180]

Malik found me on X.com and reached out to me in the summer of 2024. I learned that he has been a tireless supporter and voice for both dissident healthcare workers and the "vaccine-" injured. He interviews a variety of guests, from famous public figures to yet-unheard of people with fascinating stories, and is a champion of free speech and medical ethics, claiming that "the healthiest version of yourself is the ultimate expression of freedom."[181]

One of my favorite Doc Malik moments comes from a podcast he did with my good friend Dr. David Cartland, which I've long since dreamed of immortalizing in a book. Malik stated:

There was no informed consent being given.

No one who's had a shot has had proper informed consent.

No one has been told what the real absolute risk reduction was, given a relative risk reduction from a faulty study.

---

180. https://x.com/DocMalikPodcast

181. https://docmalik.com/

No one was told how long the spike protein would last in their body and how much spike protein would be made.

No one was told it was gene therapy. No one was told that it was experimental. No one was told what effect it would have on their fertility whether it would go to other organs in their body.

Remember when they used to say it would just stay in the arm for a couple of weeks?

No one was told that you would need multiple boosters and it might affect your immune system.

No one was told jack shit.

No one was told there was DNA contamination in it.

No one's had informed consent. And I can tell you right now is the recipient of one shot, under duress and coercion and mental torture, and I regret that decision so much; and I'm always someone who said, 'never regret, never regret...' but I do regret this. I lined up, and I went there, and I went there to get some questions answered first, and literally the guy was like, 'Roll up your arm,' and I was in short sleeves, and I was like, 'I have a question,' and bang, it was in my arm.

And I was like, 'I haven't finished asking the question.'

'What is it you want to know?'

'I want to know what was in that.'

'Oh, it's just mRNA.'

I was like, 'yeah, but was there anything else?'

'I don't know.'

And I was like, 'You didn't even answer my question; I was just in the middle of a question.'

And he went, 'Well, I'm sorry. You're here, so I thought that was your consent to having the injection.'

And I was like, 'my presence here and sitting down doesn't mean that I was ready to consent. I wanted to know a little bit more.'

I went into my car in the car park and cried for a little bit. I felt so violated. And having given consent to other patients for twenty years plus twenty-five years, it was just the most shocking thing ever. And I can tell you right now, I don't think anyone in this country or in the world has had proper informed consent.[182]

Among the many fights we have ahead of us is protecting our patients by ensuring that with future vaccines, especially among minors, informed consent becomes sacred again.

Glimmers of Hope

Idaho Health Board

Over the course of this book, you've been fed glimmers of hope and prayers so that although you're getting a report of horrific events on an almost unimaginable scale, you will stay in the fight with me and the heroes I've mentioned.

My hope in toggling between my stories and the references to major medical journals isn't to bore you with scientific research but to celebrate the attention that this genocide is receiving: the truth cannot be silenced. At least, not forever.

In October of 2024 the Idaho Health Board removed the COVID-19 "vaccines" from their clinics, stating, "these products are unsafe, we do not promote them."

Laura Demarah, Southwest Idaho nurse, told Children's Health Defense that Idaho's Southwest District Health, who pulled the jabs from thirty locations where it provides healthcare services in a 4-to-3 vote, has become "the first health agency in America to do that."

---

182. https://rumble.com/v42r0pe-11223-dr-david-cartland-doc-malik.html?e9s=src_v1_ucp

The board of Southwest District Health heard presentations from doctors such as pathologist Ryan Cole, obstetrician and gynecologist Dr. James Thorp, pediatrician Dr. Renata Moon, and cardiologist Dr. Peter McCullough.

Dr. John Tribble, the board's only physician, said: "This experiment with mRNA gene therapy during COVID-19 will be shown to be one of the most egregious examples of democide in world history."[183]

I read the article and smiled, but what made my heart leap a bit was the report that there were over 300 souls involved in the public comment before this decision was made.

BCBS Lawsuit

In November 2024, a federal jury in Detroit awarded approximately $12.7 million to Lisa Domski, a former employee of Blue Cross Blue Shield of Michigan (BCBSM), in a religious discrimination lawsuit. Domski, a devout Catholic, was terminated in January 2022 after refusing to comply with the company's COVID-19 "vaccine" mandate, citing her religious beliefs.[184]

Domski had been employed by BCBSM for nearly 40 years as an IT specialist. In October 2021, BCBSM implemented a policy requiring all employees to be fully "vaccinated" against COVID-19 or else obtain a religious or medical accommodation.

Domski requested a religious exemption, stating that her Catholic faith opposed the use of vaccines developed or tested using fetal cell lines derived from abortions. Despite providing a written statement and contact information for her priest, her request was denied.

After her exemption was denied, Domski was placed on unpaid leave and subsequently terminated on January 5, 2022. At the time, she was working remotely and had limited in-person interactions. Domski filed a lawsuit alleging that BCBSM violated federal and state laws by failing to accommodate her sincerely held religious beliefs. The jury awarded Domski

---

183. https://childrenshealthdefense.org/defender/idaho-health-board-defy-cdc-fda-COVID-vaccines-clinics/

184. https://nypost.com/2024/11/13/us-news/michigan-catholic-lisa-domski-awarded-12-million-in-discrimination-suit-after-blue-cross-blue-shield-fired-her-during-pandemic/

$10 million in punitive damages, approximately $1.7 million for lost wages, and $1 million in noneconomic damages, totaling nearly $12.7 million.

Shelley Luther

Shelley Luther, a former salon owner from Dallas, Texas, gained national attention in 2020 when she defied lockdown orders by reopening her business, Salon à la Mode, ahead of state guidelines. Her actions led to a seven-day jail sentence and a $7,000 fine for civil and criminal contempt of court.[185]

In November 2024, Luther transitioned from business owner to politician by winning a seat in the Texas House of Representatives for District 62. Running as a Republican, she secured approximately 77.7% of the vote, defeating Democratic opponent Tiffany Drake.[186] Her campaign focused on themes of individual rights and government accountability, resonating with voters who were critical of the government's handling of the pandemic. Luther's experience as a small business owner who faced legal consequences for defying lockdown orders positioned her as a symbol of resistance against government overreach.[187]

Are you one of those souls who's going to stand up and shout? Or are you just sitting on X sharing things without taking action? After reading this book, for the love of God, please don't be the latter.

A final note on standing up and shouting is the subject of apologizing.

Few things have gone more viral on social media than a doctor who previously promoted the jabs showing remorse. Both Dr. Robert Malone and Steve Kirsch admitted that they had taken the shots but now regret it. In addition, Dr. Suneel Dhand wrote on X.com:

> *I would sincerely like to apologize to the thousands of patients I interacted with in the few years after I graduated and repeated establishment nonsense like "The CDC recommends this/that" or "The latest study in this journal showed X/Y/Z." I was not awake. And unaware 80 percent+ of everything coming*

---

185. https://www.fox4news.com/election/shelley-luther-wins-texas-house-seat

186. https://en.wikipedia.org/wiki/Shelley_Luther

187. https://www.econotimes.com/Shelley-Luther-Triumphs-Salon-Owner-Who-Defied-COVID-Lockdown-Wins-Texas-State-House-Seat-in-Stunning-Victory-1693727

from medical authorities is riddled with conflicts of interest, and basically a fraud. I'll always do better for the rest of my career.[188]

If you've been jabbed and regret it, or if you've administered or promoted the shot but haven't publicly apologized, now is the time. You're going to need the public's grace when the truth comes to light.

Join me on the right side of history because one day, there will be a revolt. I pray that for those who publicly apologize for their compliance in crimes against humanity, that we will show you grace.

---

188. https://x.com/DrSuneelDhand/status/1837251463996919915

So the people shouted when the priests blew the trumpets. And it happened when the people heard the sound of the trumpet, and the people shouted with a great shout, that the wall fell down flat. Then the people went up into the city, every man straight before him, and they took the city.

Joshua 6:20, NKJV

Conclusion

They skinned Matthew alive.
Crucified Peter upside down
Boiled John in oil.
Hung Luke from an olive tree
Dragged Mark through the streets by his neck til he died.
Beheaded Paul.
All these men, they could have saved themselves,
All they had to do was say it wasn't true.
Say what they wrote, what they preached, and what they saw with
their own eyes was a lie.
The Romans would have let them go.
But they couldn't deny God.
They knew it was the truth.
They watched their families fed to lions.
Burned alive in the cColosseumTheir wives, children, and friends all
murdered because of what they were saying.
If it wasn't the truth, they wouldn't have done it. Period.
These men didn't die for a lie.
Jesus is real. He's the only truth.

The truth I'm revealing in this book is, to me, worth dying for. Exposing the genocide and depopulation agenda doesn't help victims much, but it fuels a larger purpose, especially for Americans, to fight for freedom. Through financial and psychological manipulation, we are living in a land that is increasingly outnumbered by slaves, not free men. Historically, it is the Gospel of Jesus Christ that brought freedom to slaves in Western civilization.

The United States has a special history with regards to freedom from slavery. The country was founded on the concept that the Creator endows us with rights, not our government. That means the government can't take them away from us; and if they do, we must fight.

I have one final story to share before we close this book, and I've left it for the end because it's the most important one. It started with King Nimrod thousands of years ago. According to Jewish, Christian, and Islamic traditions, King Nimrod was a powerful and rebellious ruler who wanted to challenge God. You may know him as the king who ordered the construction of the Tower of Babel.

The story of the Tower of Babel is found in Genesis 11:1-9. After the Great Flood, humanity spoke a single language and settled in the land of Shinar, often thought to be ancient Mesopotamia. They decided to build a great city with a tower that would reach the heavens, symbolizing their unity, ambition, and desire for fame. However, God saw this as an act of pride and defiance, so He intervened, confusing their language and scattering the people across the earth, which led to the origin of different languages and nations.

The teacher William Federer once shared with Stephanie that the story of King Nimrod and the Tower of Babel is an apt example of the dangers of a globalized or "one-world government" agenda, as the narrative highlights themes of centralized control, human ambition, and the rejection of divine authority. Nimrod demanded a centralization of power under one powerful, authoritarian ruler who sought to unite people under a single purpose and language. Similarly, concerns around a "one-world government" often center on fears of excessive power becoming centralized in the hands of a few.

The Tower of Babel also represents a loss of individual and national identity. An example of this is wearing masks, an ineffective form of prevention for viruses that was most likely employed as a tool to erase individuality, but also potentially used as a form of humiliation (people look ridiculous in masks) as well as, even more frighteningly, to mimic Satanic rituals of wearing masks and, of course, keeping six-foot distance between one another. Eroding cultural, national, and individual identities pushes everybody towards a global standard; stifling diversity of human thought and expression is a way of creating slavery. It is no coincidence that churches closed while liquor stores stayed open: free religious expression is inherently anti-globalist.

The Tower of Babel also represents a rejection of limitations and divine order, challenging the idea that humanity should stay within the limits of a higher structure, such as moral, religious, or traditional authority. The overreach of Nimrod represents the overreach of our world governments; they seek to homogenize and control rather than allow individual freedom and sovereignty to flourish. In the Bible, it is revealed to us that there will be a push for a one-world religion from which the antichrist will emerge as the "savior."

No man is or ever will be your savior, especially not Donald Trump nor Elon Musk, despite their ostensible desire to protect freedom. It is our sacred duty to always remain on guard against anything or persons who obtain power. It is our duty to rise above propaganda by both the left and the right, conservatives or progressives and everything in between, by remaining always skeptical.

Happily, those who are in power are outnumbered. Although they have sequestered money and public office, they have not gained what matters most: they will never own the human spirit.

In the seventeenth century, between 1630 and 1640, twenty thousand Puritans moved from Europe to the "new world." New England was founded by pastors. Prior to this network of cities governed by the consent of the people, nothing like this had ever been done in the history of the world. It is what makes the United States so special and what we must fight to protect as we keep moving toward the globalist camp. Prior to the "new world," which later became the United States, power was designed for subjects (the people) to submit to a king. What's unique about the U.S. is that we created the first-ever republic wherein citizens are the king and authority is by consent of the people.

Where did the republic "go wrong?" It began when, in the 1700s, a group referred to as pietists believed that one should withdraw from the government because it was worldly. That was the ultimate deception that put our republic at risk. Pietism emphasized a relationship with Jesus but ignored their duty to participate in government. Conversely, the Puritans involved themselves in church *and* state. The entire concept of "separating church and state" is anti-American to its core. The country was founded by pastors, and the people were empowered and free precisely because their rights were perceived to be a divine, immutable gift from God. If we take God out of the equation, we lose that protection. We must bring God into the governance of our country to protect citizens from returning to a monarchy or, worse, a one-world government.

As a final message in this book, I implore you to remember every day that you mustn't fear the globalists because **they fear you.** That is why we are censored. You are powerful by wielding truth and threatening to expose the criminals with that truth. The globalists need our compliance to survive, and so it is, therefore, your duty to resist anything that homogenizes culture, religion, tradition, or the sovereign human spirit.

The globalists fear men who will not bend a knee to earthly masters nor cower to any threat. One man with courage is a majority, as you've seen through the impact of the warriors highlighted in this book. In fact, God calls us not to conform to this world but to be bold and courageous; He knew that the pressure to conform would be among the many temptations we face in our human experience. Rather than conform, courageously act in truth, regardless of what others are doing or saying.

If your church is not talking about protecting freedoms through political action, they are failing.

One of my favorite historical studies is what is referred to as the "100th monkey" phenomenon. In this 1970's era experiment, Western scientists uncovered the presence of something now referred to as "group consciousness." It illustrates how our consciousness may elevate the world around us. In fact, Dr. David Hawkins wrote extensively about how high consciousness vibrations are so powerful that the elevated consciousness of just a handful of people can literally stop wars, as you can read about in his book "Power vs. Force."

The highest levels of consciousness include courage (just above the level of survival or "low consciousness"), neutrality, willingness, acceptance, reason, love, joy, peace, and, at the highest level, enlightenment.[189]

Map of Consciousness
Developed By David R. Hawkins

	Name of Level	Energetic Log	Predominant Emotional State	View of Life	God-view	Process
Spiritual Paradigm	Enlightenment	700-1000	Ineffable	Is	Self	Pure Consciousness
	Peace	600	Bliss	Perfect	All-Being	Illumination
	Joy	540	Serenity	Complete	One	Transfiguration
	Love	500	Reverence	Benign	Loving	Revelation
Reason & Integrity	Reason	400	Understanding	Meaningful	Wise	Abstraction
	Acceptance	350	Forgiveness	Harmonious	Merciful	Transcendence
	Willingness	310	Optimism	Hopeful	Inspiring	Intention
	Neutrality	250	Trust	Satisfactory	Enabling	Release
	Courage	200	Affirmation	Feasible	Permitting	Empowerment
Survival Paradigm	Pride	175	Scorn	Demanding	Indifferent	Inflation
	Anger	150	Hate	Antagonistic	Vengeful	Aggression
	Desire	125	Craving	Disappointing	Denying	Enslavement
	Fear	100	Anxiety	Frightening	Punitive	Withdrawal
	Grief	75	Regret	Tragic	Disdainful	Despondency
	Apathy	50	Despair	Hopeless	Condemning	Abdication
	Guilt	30	Blame	Evil	Vindictive	Destruction
	Shame	20	Humiliation	Miserable	Despising	Elimination

Photo courtesy of Live-longlearner.com[190]

The 100th monkey phenomenon is particularly fascinating because there is, to this day, no real scientific explanation for what was witnessed by monkeys on the Japanese island of Kōjima. Scientists would provide sweet potatoes for the monkeys, which was a favorite treat. However, the monkeys didn't appreciate the sand that would stick to the sweet potatoes they were provided.

One day, an 18-month-old monkey took her potato to the water to wash the sand off, a behavior that had not been observed before in the

189. https://www.amazon.com/dp/1401945074/ref=cm_sw_r_as_gl_api_gl_i_1HGZRH7QR5A6Q8EF50Q9?linkCode=ml2&tag=stephaniehirs-20

190. https://life-longlearner.com/how-to-measure-consciousness-using-the-map-of-consciousness-3-of-7/

thirty years of the scientists' experiment. In time, the practice of washing potatoes with sand became common among the other monkeys on the island. Washing food soon became the new norm for monkeys all over this island. But what happened next is stunning.

Across the ocean, on another island that was completely secluded from the original monkeys, the practice of washing potatoes became common among a totally separate and otherwise isolated group of monkeys. In time, the behavior was observed in five other colonies of monkeys from different islands in that area, including on the Japanese mainland. Although the concept of group consciousness is still considered esoteric, some have tried to explain the science of group consciousness by saying that, in this case, the monkeys were communicating with each other through sound waves.

In the 1970s, several books were published that included the story of the monkeys, but the phenomenon became popularized by Ken Keyes Jr.'s book "The Hundredth Monkey" in 1984. Keyes writes about the ravaging effects of nuclear war on the planet but uses the "hundredth monkey" story as a parable to illustrate the concept of effecting positive change through vibration.[191]

Another study that illustrates how our own positive energy may affect the world around us comes from Dr. Masaru Emoto's "Water Experiment," a classic illustration of how powerful your words are. Dr Emoto is best known for his claims that human consciousness affects the molecular structure of water. Emoto claimed that positive words, prayers, or even songs could positively affect water. Water covers 80% of our planet, and our bodies are 80% water, too. This has led many to claim that if positive human consciousness affects the molecular structure of water, then it also affects human consciousness. Your high consciousness vibrations can positively affect the molecular structure of the bodies around you, so to speak.

Whether through Dr. David Hawkin's studies in kinesiology and consciousness, Dr. Emoto's water studies, or the group consciousness concepts from the "hundredth monkey" study, and although I'm downright pissed about the genocide we're experiencing, I am continually anchored to

191. https://youtu.be/3j5ckEK_D6Y?si=t-Hg8sPefPzsgrJ_

positive vibrations by the freedom community around us; which includes you, the reader.

We have been playing defense against corrupt legislation long enough to know bad things can and will happen when corruption is left unchecked. Thankfully in America we have a constitution that is incorruptible as long as good men and women stand for what's right.

That said, I'd like to offer a thought experiment. Let's call it "Tomorrow." Tomorrow we wake up and all the tv stations announce massive lockdowns due to a virus. The media is screaming fear and telling you to stay home.

Most people stay home. Some choose to venture out. But businesses are predominantly closed and most complying. Within weeks the TV shows that those who don't comply are being arrested. The "bad guys" are making examples of the non-compliant.

Then, out of nowhere, an mRNA vaccine is said to be a miracle cure-all. This time, FEMA, WHO, WEF and all other heads of state are demanding compliance. They are going to go house to house and vaccinate everyone who refuses to show up to their designated vaccine location. Those who don't take it will be subject to fines and home isolation. Those speaking out against it will be deemed terrorists who reject the greater good. Threatened with prison or worse.

How could we as a people that believe in bodily autonomy and freedom come together currently to offensively rebuke any possible action prior to it ever occurring?

Would signing a declaration of war against such treatment be strong enough to deter future tyrants? Would it require a more bold approach? Maybe constitutional watchdogs who consistently prepare for such a time?

Whether your left wing or right wing, we are all living with the possibility of tyrannical times ahead. History, as we know, repeats itself. I, for one, don't want to experience this, and I don't think you do, either.

Over the past couple of years, I've been labeled a conspiracy theorist, a shill, a grifter, and worse. I've had pictures of my children sent to me and more death threats on X, TikTok, email, and even to my cell phone than I could ever find time to count.

At the end of the day, as the images and cries haunt me on my pillow, based on what I've seen that day or in the decades that I've worked as an EMT or paramedic, there is only one place I can go. It's to God. If I didn't go to him, I'd surely go to the bottle, as described in this book.

But when I come to God and ask for peace, love, reason, joy, and even enlightenment, I find the strength to remain noncompliant for the greater good of humanity and for the continually elevated state of my own consciousness.

In sports, a great coach puts his best players last. God made sure his hardest hitters and fastest runners were unleashed for this very moment in time: the End. Throwing up your hands and saying the problem is too big or there's no use in fighting is not exactly why you were born at this moment.

You were born to roar.

You were born for the last leg of the race.

You were born to finish strong.

Above all, remember this: *silence is consent.*

INDEX

Symbols

A

B

Book iv, v, vi, vii, viii, xi, 15, 16, 19, 20, 21, 30, 31, 35, 37, 38, 39, 40, 41, 54, 56,
    62, 68, 70, 72, 73, 77, 78, 79, 82, 83, 91, 93, 96, 97, 98, 112, 122, 126, 132,
    137, 142, 144, 151, 152, 153, 158, 159, 168, 169, 177, 194, 200, 202, 207,
    224, 225, 230, 233, 241, 244, 245, 249, 258, 268, 284, 296, 297, 307, 311,
    312, 313, 316, 317, 319, 321, 325, 326, 328, 330, 332
Buell, Shane 19
Buckhaults, Philip 260
Bowden, Dr. Mary 126, 273, 279, 316
Boyden and Grey, PLLC 278

C

California 83, 87, 88, 110
Cancer 20, 26, 27, 41, 122, 136, 143, 163, 164, 165, 181, 234, 245, 249, 261, 262,
    277, 296, 297
Cardiac Arrest 48, 83, 111, 113, 210, 269
Cardiologist 112, 124, 158, 320
Cardiopulmonary Arrest 211
Cartland, Dr. David 316, 317
CDC/ Centers For Disease Control) 55, 84, 99, 112, 113, 125, 128, 129, 134, 145,
    154, 207, 214, 231, 232, 246, 289, 321
Coulson, Foster 82
Censored/Censorship 22, 36, 94, 97, 99, 151, 157, 164, 169, 175, 178, 190, 191,
    194, 219, 290, 314, 316, 328
Children 54, 58, 68, 76, 138, 231, 235, 312, 319
Children's Health Defense 76, 231, 312, 319
China 48, 49, 85, 249
Christian Association of Nigeria, The 239
Church 17, 26, 94, 171, 182, 200, 258, 306, 308, 311, 312, 328
CIA 96, 97, 98, 121, 223
Cognitive Dissonance 19, 20, 84, 91, 183
Cold War 98
Coleman, Vernon 150, 151, 168, 187, 208, 230
Compliance 20, 22, 91, 93, 94, 129, 137, 138, 143, 219, 322, 328, 331
Concentration Camps 248
Controlled Opposition 112, 200, 201, 202, 288
Corroded Artery 317
Counce, Dr. Diane Ryder 156
Counterintelligence 202
COVID-19 vi, 36, 43, 55, 59, 60, 62, 65, 67, 68, 69, 70, 71, 72, 73, 74, 76, 81, 85,
    86, 87, 89, 90, 91, 94, 95, 98, 99, 109, 111, 112, 113, 114, 116, 117, 118,
    121, 122, 124, 126, 127, 129, 130, 136, 145, 147, 150, 152, 153, 154, 155,
    156, 157, 163, 189, 191, 192, 207, 208, 209, 211, 215, 217, 218, 224, 230,
    231, 232, 233, 234, 239, 240, 241, 247, 249, 251, 260, 274, 275, 276, 285,
    286, 287, 288, 289, 290, 292, 297, 311, 315, 319, 320
CPR 29, 48, 56, 65, 66, 103, 163, 174, 175

D

Death 21, 25, 28, 31, 32, 37, 40, 41, 48, 50, 56, 57, 60, 64, 65, 66, 67, 70, 71, 74, 83, 86, 100, 101, 105, 110, 113, 115, 118, 138, 143, 144, 147, 150, 166, 168, 171, 173, 176, 177, 179, 183, 190, 194, 195, 196, 198, 208, 209, 213, 216, 217, 219, 232, 233, 246, 251, 258, 266, 274, 290, 292, 297, 299, 306, 307, 308, 310, 331
Daszak, Peter 74, 247
Deep State 312
Defender In-Depth, The (Children's Health Defense) 68
Democrat 36
Derwin, Traci 19
Desmet, Mattias 18
Diabetes 26, 182, 193
Disability 166, 207
Dizziness 314
Dowd, Ed 83, 99, 205, 207
DNA 164, 254, 260, 261, 262, 263, 265, 318
DNR (do not resuscitate) 53, 61
Doctor 42, 66, 67, 83, 87, 91, 99, 110, 115, 121, 123, 125, 126, 127, 130, 132, 144, 154, 157, 206, 260, 273, 274, 276, 277, 282, 283, 291, 297, 316, 317, 321
Domski, Lisa 320
Dulles, Allen 98
Dystopian 22, 59, 62, 68

E

Early Vote Action (EVA) 313
EGCG 298
Elledge, Kevin 129
Emergency Response 56, 87
EMT 29, 30, 36, 40, 41, 115, 159, 188, 230, 332
Epoch Times 144, 154, 155
Epstein-Barr virus 159
ER (Emergency Room) 48, 57, 66, 67, 69, 82, 101, 103, 134, 172, 173, 188, 189, 206
Erectile Dysfunction 158
Eugenicists 223, 240, 243, 244
Evil 22, 25, 30, 35, 36, 38, 39, 40, 41, 43, 94, 100, 119, 122, 136, 137, 177, 184, 197, 198, 303, 306, 314
Excess Deaths 207, 208, 218

F

Facebook 35, 50, 65, 151
Father/Dad 15, 25, 26, 29, 42, 62, 63, 105, 119, 126, 179, 191, 192, 193, 223, 244, 288, 289

Fauci, Dr. Anthony 57, 72, 74, 130, 247

Fatigue 314

FDA/Food and Drug Administration xiv, 73, 76, 112, 113, 114, 134, 154, 225, 226, 227, 228, 269, 273, 274, 276, 278, 287, 293

Fear 18, 20, 28, 35, 49, 51, 53, 54, 55, 56, 57, 60, 85, 88, 100, 101, 112, 179, 181, 190, 198, 199, 212, 231, 232, 235, 239, 246, 265, 283, 296, 301, 302, 306, 328, 331

Fisher, Josie (Grandma) 26, 184, 268, 308

Foreman's Gangrene 191

G

Gaslighting 83, 84, 145, 174

Georgia Guidestones 244, 245

Gates, Bill 223, 243, 260

Gates, Melinda 260

Gates Sr., William H. 223

Gilead Sciences 72

GMB Union 60

God 15, 16, 27, 36, 37, 38, 39, 40, 44, 45, 62, 63, 104, 119, 121, 130, 131, 134, 138, 142, 144, 159, 163, 174, 182, 183, 184, 193, 196, 197, 206, 235, 236, 237, 238, 239, 257, 258, 259, 260, 265, 270, 271, 273, 300, 301, 306, 307, 314, 321, 325, 326, 328, 332

Good vi, 20, 28, 30, 40, 57, 63, 70, 82, 86, 87, 88, 91, 110, 118, 122, 129, 130, 131, 138, 148, 149, 163, 166, 168, 169, 171, 172, 174, 177, 182, 184, 194, 197, 198, 199, 200, 241, 243, 258, 283, 284, 290, 292, 296, 297, 300, 301, 314, 317, 331, 332

Grandpa/Grandfather 25, 62, 102

Grandma/Grandmother 15, 21, 22, 26, 27, 28, 29, 31, 58, 62, 184, 248, 258, 268, 308

Greene, Marjorie Taylor 281

Gut (Microbiome) 159, 297, 299, 302

H

H5N1 99

"Hand of Hope, The" (Photograph) 123

Happy Hypoxia 49, 50, 51, 67, 212

Harvard 124, 150

Hazan, Dr. Sabine 297

Hawkins, Dr. David 328

Hazmat 49

Heart 15, 25, 27, 39, 40, 43, 48, 52, 53, 70, 83, 84, 87, 94, 102, 113, 122, 136, 142, 143, 152, 172, 189, 191, 193, 203, 210, 225, 234, 236, 249, 256, 257, 266, 267, 287, 290, 299, 300, 307, 320

Minister 41, 250
Miscarriage 30, 103, 110, 113
Misinformation 81, 112, 126, 278, 286
MKUltra 97, 98, 99
Mob 176, 199
Moderna 110, 111, 287
Monoclonal Antibodies 274
Mother/Mom iv, x, 25, 28, 42, 62, 63, 111, 121, 123, 143, 179, 193, 196, 273
mRNA vii, 70, 88, 90, 99, 105, 144, 150, 154, 156, 157, 158, 163, 164, 206, 218, 224, 225, 228, 234, 251, 252, 253, 254, 260, 261, 262, 269, 279, 280, 288, 296, 318, 320, 331
Mohamad, Mahathir 250
Morris, Natali 233
mRNA Vaccine Toxicity vii, 70, 88, 90, 99, 105, 144, 150, 154, 156, 157, 158, 163, 164, 206, 218, 224, 225, 228, 234, 251, 252, 253, 254, 260, 261, 262, 269, 279, 280, 288, 296, 318, 320, 331
Murder 21, 68, 74, 94, 157, 172, 175, 177, 184, 194, 219, 224, 225, 239, 267

N

NASA 96
Nattokinase 158
Nazi 96, 165, 202, 240, 244
NEJM, New England Journal of Medicine 195
Neuroinflammation 147, 158
Nevradakis, Dr. Michael 68
New International Version (NIV) 258
New York 42, 49, 56, 57, 67, 69, 101, 102, 243
New Zealand 218, 219, 220, 248
NIH (National Institutes for Health) 69, 70, 72, 76, 99, 155, 157, 174, 175, 229, 247, 274, 293
Nuremberg Code, The 165, 167
Nurse 54, 56, 65, 66, 67, 83, 102, 154, 176, 189, 277, 314, 319

O

Obama, Barack 130, 241, 244, 312
OBGYN 109, 125
O'Brien, Cathy 97
Obstetrics 110, 127
Office of Strategic Services (OSS) 96
Oklahoma 22, 25, 30, 42, 43, 49, 56, 57, 65, 136, 171, 172, 299, 311
Oncology 90
OSS (Office of Strategic Services) 96

P

Q

R

S

T

EMERGENCY MEDICAL KITS NOW AVAILABLE

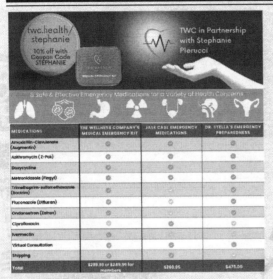

GOVERNMENT THREATENING TO BLOCK SALES OF LIFE-SAVING TREATMENTS...

The best way to avoid the hospital during an emergency is to have life-saving medications on hand. That's why The Wellness Company is now providing Emergency Medical Kits so that you and your family will have 8 Safe & Effective Emergency Medications on hand for a variety of health concerns. But the government doesn't want the public to have these 8...

**MORE INFORMATION AT
WWW.TWC.HEALTH/STEPHANIE**

Made in the USA
Monee, IL
08 January 2025

a5d81cad-65ba-4742-9c64-1e54dc0a1fb1R01